CHANGING PATTERNS OF INDUSTRIAL CONFLICT

CHANGING PATTERNS

One of a series of books from the research program of the Institute of Industrial Relations, University of California

OF INDUSTRIAL CONFLICT

ARTHUR M. ROSS
and
PAUL T. HARTMAN

Institute of Industrial Relations
University of California, Berkeley

JOHN WILEY & SONS, INC., NEW YORK · LONDON

To Jane N. Ross and Shirley J. Hartman

Preface

The year 1959 was a banner year for industrial conflict in the United States. There have been more man-days of idleness because of strikes than in any previous year in our recorded history, with the exception of 1946. Although the steel strike is chiefly responsible, large and prolonged stoppages have also occurred in the longshore, rubber, and meat-packing industries, as well as in more localized activities such as newspapers and trucking.

The 1959 experience has been encountered at the end of a twelve-year period during which strains on the collective bargaining system have been moderate, emergency disputes have been infrequent, and strike activity has been diminishing. Has there been an important reversal in the trend, or does the eruption of industrial conflict in 1959 merely reflect the concurrence of various circumstances which have temporarily impeded collective bargaining?

Certainly it is too early to offer any confident reply. We may gain some perspective, however, by examining the drift of industrial disputes in this country over a longer period of about six decades. A description of the union policies, employer practices, and government programs which influence the volume of strike activity in the United States may also be instructive.

In this volume we analyze national trends and international differences in strike activity in fifteen countries of North America, Europe, Asia,

Africa, and Australia. We endeavor to explain the "withering away of the strike" in most of the countries of Northern Europe. We show the relation between national patterns of industrial conflict and certain principal features of the industrial relations systems. Although we do not undertake to project the future of industrial conflict, except for a few observations in the final chapter, we believe the analysis might be used as a starting point for informed predictions.

We are glad to acknowledge our indebtedness to Professor Mason Haire, Professor George H. Hildebrand, Dr. Margaret S. Gordon, and Professor Lloyd Ulman of the Institute of Industrial Relations, who read our manuscript and offered valuable suggestions. Professor Adolf Sturmthal of Roosevelt University also reviewed the manuscript and gave us the benefit of his comprehensive knowledge of foreign labor movements and bargaining systems. Correspondence with Professor J. E. Isaac of the University of Melbourne, Professor Kenneth F. Walker of the University of Western Australia, and Professor Mark Perlman of Johns Hopkins University was most helpful in coming to an understanding of strike activity in Australia.

ARTHUR M. ROSS
PAUL T. HARTMAN

Berkeley, California
February 1960

Contents

		Page
1.	**Introduction**	1
2.	**Measures of Strike Activity**	8
3.	**International Comparisons of Strikes**	15
4.	**Problems of Analyzing Industrial Conflict**	34
5.	**The Withering Away of the Strike**	42
6.	**Influences on Relative Strike Activity**	62
7.	**North European Pattern—First Variant**	82
	Denmark	82
	The Netherlands	85
	The United Kingdom	89
	Germany	95
8.	**North European Pattern—Second Variant**	103
	Norway	103
	Sweden	107

Page

9. Mediterranean-Asian Pattern   **115**

    France   115
    Italy   120
    Japan   126
    India   131

10. Special Cases and Mixed Situations   **141**

    Australia   141
    Finland   151
    South Africa   156

11. North American Pattern: United States and Canada   **161**

12. Conclusion   **172**

Appendix   **183**

    Tables

    A-1   Number of Industrial Disputes, Fifteen Countries, 1900–1956   194

    A-2   Workers Involved in Industrial Disputes, Fifteen Countries, 1900–1956   196

    A-3   Working Days Lost in Industrial Disputes, Fifteen Countries, 1900–1956   198

    A-4   Union Membership, Fifteen Countries, 1900–1956   200

    A-5   Estimated Number of Non-agricultural Employees, Fifteen Countries, 1927–1956   202

    A-6   Union Membership as a Percentage of Non-agricultural Employment, Fifteen Countries, 1927–1956   203

    A-7   Membership Involvement Ratio   204

    A-8   Employee Involvement Ratio   206

    A-9   Employee-Loss Ratio   207

    A-10   Duration of Strikes   208

    A-11   Membership-Loss Ratio   210

Index   **213**

CHAPTER 1

Introduction

The strike[1] has been a classic feature of industrial relations since the early days of the labor movement. Just as political history is chiefly built around wars, a large part of labor history is a recounting of major strikes. Picket-line struggles have a proud and prominent place in the lore and symbols of unionism. The lay observer's awareness of union-management relations, like the traveler's view of the iceberg, has been a limited one, mainly confined to irritation and apprehension over strikes and threats of strikes. Press, parliament, and pulpit have preoccupied themselves with this aspect of the labor problem.

Like many other institutions, however, the strike is going through evolutionary changes, taking on new forms, and assuming new meanings. The time has come, particularly for us in the United States, to review our assumptions about this phenomenon and take cognizance of what has been happening to it in other parts of the world.

Examining the existing literature on strikes, we find it narrowly based on American experience and deficient in historical perspective. Most writers do not profess to offer a general theory of industrial conflict, it is true. Nevertheless the conventional analysis does create several impressions that are incomplete and potentially misleading.

The first of these impressions is that the strike is an integral and inevitable aspect of free unionism. Knowledgeable authors have insisted that the economic losses are moderate; they have pointed out the bene-

1

fits arising from overt expression and explicit resolution of conflict; they have held that stoppages can be minimized by adopting proper techniques, eliminating underlying causes, reconstructing attitudes, and so on.[2] But in the end they have concluded that a substantial amount of conflict was part of the game.

Thus, few would disagree with Dr. George W. Taylor's statement that "economic force is prime motive power for agreements in free collective bargaining . . . the risks and the costs that go with a stoppage of production are vital parts of a collective bargaining system." [3] In a similar vein a labor spokesman holds that "the strike is the union's major sanction in bargaining with employers. Approximate bargaining equality can be achieved only if the union is in a position to exercise an effective choice between working or not working, and the strike is the collective act of refusing to work." [4] And a report to the U. S. Senate makes the same point:

> Under collective bargaining, disagreements of the parties which appear to be final are tested by work stoppages before the parties are willing to make further compromises and adjustments in order to settle the dispute. . . . This is a price paid for the function of the joint determination of the terms and conditions of employment by the parties most at interest. . . . That there could be such stoppage of production is the risk of every effort at collective bargaining.[5]

To be sure, we must distinguish between the right to strike and the exercise of that right. Most authorities would insist, however, not only that the right to strike is *sine qua non* of free collective bargaining, but also that substantial use and even abuse of it must be expected. In Dr. Taylor's words:

> Some abuses of the rights to strike and to lockout, and some intelligent uses of these powers, are inevitable. They are part of the cost of keeping industrial relations in private hands. . . . Only by counting up alternate costs of the usual proposals for strikeless systems does it become clear that some labor policies can have consequences far worse than strikes.[6]

The second impression is that the strike is generally an incident of the collective bargaining process. To be sure, various types and species have been distinguished, such as organizing strikes, economic strikes, grievance strikes, wildcat strikes, hit-and-run strikes, sympathy strikes, and jurisdictional strikes; but with the exception of political strikes, all have been regarded as aspects of the union-management relationship.

> It is common in the press to characterize a strike as a breakdown in collective bargaining. However, on closer analysis it will be found to be a continuation of collective bargaining.[7]

Finally, the strike is typically defined as a trial of economic strength, or a contest of staying power, initiated to bring pressure to bear on the opposing party in the employment relationship in order to secure more favorable terms of employment. (It is often looked upon as "labor's weapon," in contrast to the lockout, because labor begins the stoppage. In fact, there are two parties to every dispute, in equal disagreement with each other. The union must take the initiative because the employer offers terms that are agreeable to him and the union must decide whether to accept them. Therefore the strike is really a bilateral suspension of work, although it is generally described as a unilateral act. The reader should also keep in mind that we are using the term *strike* to designate all work stoppages, including lockouts initiated by employers.)

The concept of the strike as a trial of economic strength is embraced in popular and professional usage. Thus the dictionary defines "strike" as "act of quitting work; specif., such an act done by mutual understanding by a body of workmen as a means of enforcing compliance with demands made on their employer;"[8] or "a concerted cessation of work on the part of a body of workers, for the purpose of obtaining some concession from the employer or employers."[9] Scholarly definitions are in accord. Back in the nineteenth century the pioneer social scientist William Graham Sumner observed that:

> Strikes . . . are costly, but they test the market. . . . It is for the health of the industrial organization that they should do so. The other social interests are in the constant habit of testing the market, in order to get all they can out of it. A strike, rationally begun and rationally conducted, only does the same thing for the wage-earning interests.[10]

This traditional concept is admirably expressed in an influential new textbook in labor economics:

> Collective bargaining is a process of voluntary agreement, but agreement comes when the terms proposed by one of the parties appear more disadvantageous to the other than disagreement on those terms. Agreement thus depends on making disagreement more costly. It is here that the strike—whether initiated by the union in support of demands which it makes on management or in rejection of demands which management makes on it—demonstrates its function. A stoppage of work is the chief means by which parties make disagreement costly to the other.[11]

Looking around the world today, however, we find compelling evidence that the conventional treatment of the strike lacks historical and international perspective. The strike has been changing over time, and is a different phenomenon in different parts of the world.

We find a pronounced decline in strike activity throughout the world.

Man-days of idleness in the late 1950's are fewer than in the late 1940's or the late 1930's, despite the increases in population and union membership. Let it be noted that we are speaking of countries with a free labor movement. The Communist nations, where strikes seldom occur and are not recorded, have been excluded from the present study.

The decline is most dramatic when described in comparative terms. One significant measure of industrial conflict is the number of strikers in relation to the number of union members. This proportion has fallen off sharply in most of the countries we have studied. Throughout Northern Europe, for example, the ratio between strikers and union members during the past decade has been only *one-third to one-seventieth* of what it was during the first three decades of the present century. In the United States the ratio has been cut in half.

Secondly, those strikes that do occur have been growing much shorter. In this book we measure the duration of strikes by a ratio between man-days of idleness and the number of strikers. This ratio has fallen greatly in every nation we have studied. In a number of countries, the average strike has been lasting *only one-fifth to one-seventh* as long as in the 1900–29 period. In fact, during recent years the average duration of strikes has been *less than five days* in about half the countries.

As a result of these developments, the loss of working time in relation to union membership is generally only a small fraction of what it was a few decades ago. During the 1900–29 period, there were from two to nine days of idleness, during the average year, for each union member in every country studied. Since 1947, however, the annual loss of time per union member has been as much as two days only in the United States, India, and Finland.

National patterns of industrial conflict have been changing radically. We find a number of countries, particularly in Northern Europe, where strike activity has become nominal during the past two or three decades. Stoppages occur so infrequently, and are typically so brief, that the strike no longer plays a significant role in the conduct of industrial relations.

There are other countries in which strikes are long enough to constitute sustained trials of economic strength, but they are almost never called. Management and labor have outlived this instrument just as the European Socialist movement has largely outlived the issue of public ownership. The right to strike survives and is accorded its customary veneration but is seldom utilized in practice.

Then there are several nations with exactly the opposite pattern of industrial conflict. Workers frequently go on strike, but generally only for one, two, or a few days at a time. Australia furnishes a notable example: more than 60 per cent of the strikes have lasted no more than a day in recent years, and more than 90 per cent have been terminated in less than a week. These brief stoppages may serve as political demonstrations, spontaneous protests against unfavorable working conditions, gestures of dissent directed at conservative union leaders, or as expressions of discontent over compulsory arbitration awards. They do not constitute true economic warfare, in the sense of real trials of staying power between employers and workers. Thus, it is clear that the strike is not a homogeneous phenomenon but has different meanings in different parts of the world.

A number of countries, including Poland, Czechoslovakia, and China, were the scene of substantial strike activity prior to World War II, but have since passed into the Communist orbit. Other nations, such as India, Israel, and Egypt, have initiated programs of economic development during the same period, and have brought together a sizable industrial labor force. It might be thought that such nations would pass through the cycle of labor-management conflict that has been characteristic of older industrial societies. History does not always repeat itself, however. Labor unrest is inevitable, it is true; as Kerr and others have stated, "One universal response to industrialization . . . is protest on the part of the labour force as it is fitted into the new social structure." [12] But protest can manifest itself in a variety of forms and can be handled in a variety of ways. As we shall note, protest is being manifested in different forms and handled in different ways in the "underdeveloped countries."

The fact is that the textbook or dictionary definition of the strike is fully applicable only in the United States and Canada. Only in these two countries—which really comprise a single system of industrial relations—is the strike still sufficiently frequent to constitute a significant method of determining conditions of employment, and at the same time sufficiently long to test the staying power of workers and employers. (Strike statistics in India and Finland have some resemblance to those in the United States, but the explanations are quite different.) The changes in union program, employer organization, bargaining structure, and government policy which have held the strike weapon in abeyance in many countries have not been so prominent in the United States and Canada. As Richard A. Lester has shown, however, unionism and collective bargaining in the United States are moving in a continuous process of evolution. He warns of "the shortcomings of attempts to interpret American unionism by means of a static or mechanistic type of thinking." He stresses "the importance of institutional development over time," and insists that "a theoretical construct designed for the early phases of unionism, when it is in the crusading and conquest period, may need to be significantly modified for later, more mature stages of evolution." [13]

As subsequent chapters of this book are read, it should become apparent that we must enlarge our view of the strike. We must recognize that American experience is not representative of industrialized countries as a whole. We must also understand that industrial conflict, like so many other institutions, is passing through an evolutionary process. Otherwise we will not be in a position to apprehend two highly significant developments. One is the withering away of the strike, the virtual disappearance of industrial conflict in numerous countries where collective bargaining is still practiced. The other is the transformation of the strike, which in many countries is no longer a sustained test of economic strength but a brief demonstration of protest.

The purpose of our book is to supply perspective on these matters. To prevent misunderstanding, we should like to enter some disclaimers at this point. We have made a factual investigation and have attempted to interpret the facts, but we have not undertaken to pass judgment on them. When we point out, for example, that labor parties and labor governments have the effect of dampening industrial conflict, we are not recommending that an American Labor Party be established. To prove that highly centralized bargaining structures are conducive to industrial peace is not to advocate economy-wide bargaining. To show a decline in strike activity is not to praise such a decline. Many questions would have to be answered before judgments of this kind could be made. Maybe more strikes, not fewer, would be a good thing. Whether a particular medicine is better or worse than a particular disease depends on how bad the medicine tastes and how much the disease hurts. On this matter we do not undertake to express an opinion.

NOTES TO CHAPTER 1

1. Throughout this book we frequently employ the term *strike* to designate work stoppages in general, including both strikes and lockouts in their technical meanings. There are several reasons for this usage: (*a*) The term *work stoppage* becomes awkward and tedious upon frequent repetition; (*b*) other possible alternatives, such as *labor-management dispute, industrial conflict,* and *industrial unrest,* are not sufficiently specific, except in a particular context; (*c*) most work stoppages take the form of strikes; and (*d*) we have not found it necessary to develop a separate analysis for strikes and lockouts.

2. See Arthur Kornhauser, Robert Dubin, and Arthur M. Ross (eds.), *Industrial Conflict* (New York: McGraw-Hill Book Co., 1954), *passim.*

3. George W. Taylor, *Government Regulation of Industrial Relations* (Englewood Cliffs, N. J.: Prentice-Hall, 1948), pp. 18–20.

4. Jack Barbash, *Labor Unions in Action* (New York: Harper and Brothers, 1948), p. 124.

5. *Emergency Dispute Settlement: Staff Report to the Subcommittee on Labor and Labor-Management Relations,* Committee on Labor and Public Welfare, U. S. Senate, 82nd Congress, 2nd Session (Washington, 1952), p. 3.

6. Taylor, *op. cit.,* p. 19.

7. Robert Dubin, *Working Union-Management Relations* (Englewood Cliffs, N. J.: Prentice-Hall, 1958), p. 208.

8. *Webster's Collegiate Dictionary,* fifth edition, (Springfield, Mass.: G. and C. Merriam Co., 1948), p. 986.

9. *The Oxford Universal Dictionary,* p. 2042.

10. Quoted in Maurice R. Davie, *Summer Today* (New Haven: Yale University Press, 1940), p. 63.

11. Neil W. Chamberlain, *Labor* (New York: McGraw-Hill Book Co., 1958), p. 301.

12. Clark Kerr, Frederick H. Harbison, John T. Dunlop, and Charles A. Myers, "The Labour Problem in Economic Development," *International Labour Review,* 72 (March 1955), pp. 13–14.

13. Richard A. Lester, *As Unions Mature* (Princeton: Princeton University Press, 1958), pp. 128–29.

CHAPTER 2

Measures

of Strike Activity

In this volume we attempt to establish and explain the general trend of strike activity in the non-Communist world; and to explore differences in trend, and in the meaning of strikes, between one country and another.

There have been previous international comparisons of industrial conflict. K. Forchheimer and Robert Morse Woodbury published some interesting articles in the late 1940's, but did not perceive any particular direction of change or develop any distinctive classification of countries.[1] Clark Kerr and Abraham Siegel have made an international comparison of "propensity to strike" in specific industries, dealing with different issues from those discussed in this volume.[2]

The present study is a sequel to an article called "Strike Experience in Five Countries," written by Arthur M. Ross and Donald Irwin in 1951. In that article, which covered the period 1927–47, the following conclusions were reached:

(a) Labor unions have been growing in size and strength. (b) An increasing percentage of the employed labor force has been drawn into strikes. (c) Over the years such strikes have been growing shorter. (d) Consequently, despite higher rates of participation, the loss of working time per wage and salary earner has been diminishing.

8

It was stated that "what was hoped by the syndicalists of the nineteenth century and what is feared by the conservatives of the twentieth century—the destruction of capitalism by strikes—is not coming to pass." But with respect to the contrary theory—that unions outgrow the need to strike after the organizing conflicts and power struggles have come to an end, this observation was made:

> The fact is, however, that in three out of the five countries studied (the United States, Canada and Australia) the strike has *not* been withering away. Strikes have been growing shorter, it is true, but union members have been called on strike more frequently. Only in Great Britain and Sweden has there been any tendency for strikes to disappear.[3]

We decided to restudy the problem for two reasons. The first is that a survey limited to five countries was obviously incomplete. The present study has the advantage of much better coverage, fifteen countries rather than five being systematically compared. These fifteen include all the countries of any substantial size for which adequate statistics on strike activity, union membership, and non-agricultural employment were available, or reasonably good estimates could be developed. We think that inclusion of some of the Mediterranean and Asian countries has been particularly helpful in leading us to certain insights which did not emerge in the earlier research. The second reason is that "Strike Experience in Five Countries" was written in the shadow of the postwar strike wave and covered a period of only thirty years. There was every reason to believe that firmer conclusions could be established if the analysis were carried back to 1900 and carried forward to 1956.

The raw material for this study consists of annual data on workers involved in industrial disputes, man-days lost in disputes, union membership and non-agricultural employment, for each of the fifteen countries studied. These are set forth in Appendix Tables A-2 through A-5, along with data on the number of strikes, which have been included for the sake of completeness although they have not been used in the analysis. The strike statistics are gathered and published by the governments of the various countries. Since 1927, they have been compiled and published also by the International Labor Office. The union-membership and employment figures have been pulled together from numerous sources and supplemented with projections and interpolations. We cannot state that these figures are precise in every instance, but we do believe that they are accurate enough for the purpose and that reasonable methods have been used in putting them together. Fortunately, the margin of error would have to be rather wide before our conclusions and interpretations could be affected. In fairness to the reader, however, sources of data and methods of making estimates are explained fully in the Appendix.[4]

We have attempted to compile statistics on union membership and strike activity from 1900 through 1956, although there are numerous gaps in the record. It was not practical to make estimates of non-agricultural employment prior to 1927.

A word should now be said concerning our comparative measures of strike activity. For many years strike statistics have been collected in all nations where industrial disputes are of common occurrence and facilities for obtaining the information are sufficiently developed. Universally three measures are employed. The first, showing the number of strikes, is not particularly informative in itself. The second, measuring the number of workers involved, tells whether the strikes are large or small. The third indicates also whether they are long or short, by showing man-days of idleness within the establishments directly concerned.

International comparisons of strike activity have seldom been attempted because raw statistics on the number of strikes, workers involved, and man-days of idleness are not comparable between countries. It proves little that in 1956 some 4,136,700 man-days were lost in Italy and only 1,246,000 in Canada. Differences in population and size of the labor force obviously must be taken into account. Neither is it particularly significant in itself that between 1936 and 1946 the number of strikers doubled in Great Britain and sextupled in the United States. Differences in the rate of industrial development and union growth must be considered. If we wish to learn whether workers in one country are more prone to strike than those in another, some common denominators must be employed.

What are the most appropriate common denominators for comparing industrial disputes in various countries? Strike activity could easily be related to population; ratios of workers involved as a percentage of the population and man-days lost per capita could be developed. But inasmuch as there are great variations in occupational composition and industrial structure, such ratios would have little value. To compare strike activity among coal miners and peasants would make little sense. It is primarily among the "workers"—wage and salary earners in non-agricultural employment—that strikes are likely to occur. Therefore the number of wage and salary earners provides a more satisfactory basis for comparison.

There are two rather heterogeneous groups among the wage and salary earners, however. These are the organized and the unorganized. Although strikes were not invented by unions[5] and are not restricted to organized workers, it remains true that most modern strikes are conducted by unions and that organized workers are in a better position to strike than are the unorganized workers. For this reason an increasing participation of wage and salary earners in strikes may reflect merely a greater intensity of organization. Whereas employment is a satisfactory basis for showing the relative impact of strikes on the economy, union membership is a more valid common denominator for indicating relative inclination to strike.

Two other comparative measures are desirable, one appraising the average duration of strikes in the various countries and the other showing differences in the extent to which wage earners have been enrolled in the unions.

Accordingly, we are using six comparative measures in this study. We have given each of these measures an arbitrary nickname for convenience in discussing it throughout the text. They are as follows:

1. *Intensity of organization,* 1927–56. The first measure does not relate directly to strike activity but is useful in analyzing it. This measure shows union membership as a percentage of non-agricultural employment. Although agricultural workers belong to unions in some parts of the world, in general, they are only a small fraction of total membership. The ratio between union members and non-agricultural wage and salary earners is the best available index of intensity of organization.

2. *Membership involvement ratio,* 1900–56. This shows the number of workers involved in strikes as a percentage of union membership. We use it as roughly equivalent to the percentage of union members who go on strike, although it overstates the latter percentage insofar as some workers may strike more than once in a year and some non-unionists may participate in strikes. More precisely, the membership involvement ratio is the sum of all workers involved in all strikes during the year, divided by the average number of union members during that year. Workers are counted once for each strike in which they participate. This measure, as well as the four remaining ones, is affected by the definitions and procedures used by the various national governments in collecting strike data. (See the Appendix.) It also reflects differences in union tactics. For example, several brief protest strikes in an industry would multiply the number of workers involved compared with a single longer strike, although man-days of idleness might be the same

in both cases. These tactical differences are incorporated into our analysis of strike behavior.

3. *Employee involvement ratio, 1927–56.* We use this designation for the ratio between the number of workers involved in strikes and the number of non-agricultural employees. The ratio is equivalent to the percentage of wage and salary earners going on strike, except that strikes of agricultural workers are not unknown and, as mentioned previously, some people may strike more than once a year.

4. *Duration of strikes, 1900–56.* This ratio is constructed by dividing the number of workers involved into the number of working days lost for the particular year. In other words, it shows time lost per striker. There are other possible measures of average duration, but this one is probably the most significant. It is equivalent to the average duration of the individual strikes, each strike weighted in accordance with its size as measured by the number of workers involved.

5. *Membership loss ratio, 1900–56.* This is the ratio between the number of union members (in hundreds) and the number of working days lost. With some slight inaccuracy it can be described as showing the average loss of time per hundred union members.

6. *Employee loss ratio, 1927–56.* Similarly, this ratio can be described as showing the average loss of time per hundred non-agricultural wage and salary earners.

All of these measures are set forth in the Appendix for each of fifteen countries and for each year between 1900 and 1956 (or between 1927 and 1956 where employment estimates are involved), to the extent that information is available. To make the statistics manageable, we have computed three-year averages, which are found in Tables 1 through 6 in the following chapter.

Each measure will serve different purposes. For example, the employee involvement ratio (percentage of wage and salary earners going on strike) and the employee loss ratio (working days lost per hundred wage and salary earners) come closest to showing the relative impact of strikes on the economy. We have found, however, that distinctive patterns of industrial conflict can be described most intelligently in terms of the membership involvement ratio (percentage of union members going on strike) and the duration of strikes (days lost per striker). Accordingly, these two measures will receive primary emphasis in the latter chapters of the book. The membership loss ratio (working days lost per hundred union members) is helpful in showing the combined effect of changes in the degree of participation and the duration of strikes.

TECHNICAL NOTE

Some readers may be interested in symbolic representations of our comparative measures of industrial conflict. These help to indicate the relationship between one measure and another.

We begin with four basic variables:

U Union membership.
N Non-agricultural employment.
W Workers involved in disputes.
L Working days lost.

We then construct six ratios:

$i = U/N$ Intensity of organization.
$m = W/U$ Membership involvement ratio.
$e = W/N$ Employee involvement ratio.
$d = L/W$ Duration of strikes.
$f = L/U$ Membership loss ratio.
$g = L/N$ Employee loss ratio.

Various relationships which follow from these definitions might be indicated. For example,

$$g = d \cdot e = f \cdot i = d \cdot m \cdot i$$

That is, the employee loss ratio is the product of the employee involvement ratio and the duration of strikes. It is also equal to the product of the membership loss ratio and the intensity of organization. Likewise, it is the product of duration, membership involvement, and intensity of organization.

In analyzing strike activity we have found the membership involvement ratio and the duration of strikes to be the most fruitful measures. All the comparative measures are on the same level of abstraction or synthesis, however. Each is a ratio between two of the basic variables. Each can be stated as a product or quotient of the other measures. For example, membership involvement is the quotient of the membership loss ratio and the duration of strikes. Duration is the quotient of the employee loss ratio and the employee involvement ratio. And so on. We have emphasized membership involvement and duration because they appear to reflect most sensitively the institutional and historical forces at work.

We are indebted to Professor Mark Leiserson for suggesting this type of analysis.

NOTES TO CHAPTER 2

1. K. Forchheimer, "Some International Aspects of the Strike Movement," *Bulletin of the Oxford Institute of Statistics,* 10 (January 1948), pp. 9–18, and 10 (September 1948), pp. 294–304; Robert Morse Woodbury, "The Incidence of Industrial Disputes: Rates of Time-Loss, 1927–47," *International Labour Review,* 60 (November 1949), pp. 451–66. See also an unsigned article entitled "Industrial Disputes, 1937–54," in *International Labour Review,* 72 (July 1955),

pp. 78–91; and John A. Fitch, "Strikes and Lockouts," *Encyclopedia of Social Sciences,* (New York: MacMillan Company, 1934), Vol. 14, pp. 419–25.

2. Clark Kerr and Abraham Siegel, "The Inter-Industry Propensity to Strike: An International Comparison," in A. Kornhauser, R. Dubin, and A. M. Ross, (eds.), *Industrial Conflict* (New York: McGraw-Hill Book Co., 1954), pp. 189–212.

3. A. M. Ross and D. Irwin, "Strike Experience in Five Countries," *Industrial and Labor Relations Review,* 4 (April 1951), p. 335. With Dr. Irwin's permission a few passages from this article have been incorporated in this volume without much change.

4. Some of the estimates of non-agricultural employment differ from those used in "Strike Experience in Five Countries." The new estimates are felt to be more accurate.

The *International Labour Review* articles mentioned in Note 1 present ratios of working days lost per 1,000 employees in mining, manufacturing, construction, and transport. These ratios are useful for some purposes but are not fully satisfactory. The statistical base is deficient, since many employees outside these industries go on strike. Moreover, when the ratios are turned inside out and reconverted to employment estimates, using published data on working days lost, improbable year-to-year fluctuations are shown in certain countries, and the resultant estimates are often inconsistent with published employment figures. For these reasons, we decided to develop our own measures of strike activity, using non-agricultural employment as the base.

5. See Arthur M. Ross, "The Natural History of the Strike," in Kornhauser, Dubin, and Ross, *op. cit.,* pp. 23–36.

CHAPTER 3

International

Comparisons

of Strikes

In examining the changing patterns of industrial conflict throughout the world, we can use the situation in 1947 as a convenient point of departure. "Strike Experience in Five Countries" was based on a rather limited sample, but did reveal that several significant developments were under way. Expansion of union membership, in proportion to the number of wage and salary earners, appeared to be leveling off after World War II, although the time was too short to draw any confident conclusions. Strike participation among union members had remained approximately stable after 1932, except for an increase at the very end of the period reflecting the postwar strike wave. The average duration of strikes had declined steadily [1] from about twenty-nine days in 1927–29 to approximately seventeen days in 1945–47. Loss of working time per union member had declined markedly in Great Britain and Sweden, had evened out in the United States, and failed to show any particular trend in Australia and Canada. It was felt that loss of time per wage and salary earner was diminishing, although on reviewing the statistics, we must say that the evidence on this point was rather inconclusive. Finally, it was noted that "to whatever extent strikes are a problem, they have been a greater problem in the United States than elsewhere." [2] For 1927–47 as a whole, the average annual loss per union member in the United States had been approximately twice that in Sweden and Canada, three times that in Australia, and four times that in Great Britain.

As previously noted, we now have the advantage of covering more countries over a much longer span of time. In this chapter we shall describe the main trends in strike activity, with particular reference to the period after 1947, and shall indicate in a preliminary way some of the differences between one country and another. The discussion will be based primarily on Tables 1 through 6, although occasionally we shall draw on the Appendix tables in the interest of greater clarity.

Intensity of Organization

It is well known to American readers that the labor movement in this country has barely kept up with expansion of non-agricultural employment during the past decade. It is not so widely understood that this is true generally of industrialized nations. The average intensity of organization rose steadily and gradually from 22.7 per cent in 1927–29 to 43.5 per cent in 1945–47. Expansion had tapered off in most countries by the end of World War II, but during the immediate postwar period there was a feverish growth or regrowth of unionism in Germany, France, Italy, and Japan.

Subsequently the relative strength of the labor movement has declined significantly in three of these countries—France, Italy and Japan—and also in Finland. There were modest increases in a few countries, including Australia, Sweden, Norway, and Canada, but the average intensity of organization for all fifteen countries was actually lower in 1956 than in 1947.

The reasons for this attenuation of union growth are beyond the scope of the present study, but the fact of attenuation is pertinent. Periods of rapid organization are often marked with industrial conflict; the case of the United States in the 1930's and 1940's will serve as an example. It also appears that periods of membership loss are associated with a high propensity to strike, as in France, Italy, and Japan during recent years. We are not prepared to say whether unions call strikes because they are losing members, or members quit because of unfavorable reaction to strikes, but the association is clear. Where union membership has become stabilized, on the other hand, strike activity has generally declined.

TABLE 1. Intensity of Organization

Union Membership as a Percentage of Non-agricultural Employment, 1927–1956, Annual Averages for Three-Year Periods

	1927–1929	1930–1932	1933–1935	1936–1938	1939–1941	1942–1944	1945–1947	1948–1950	1951–1953	1954–1956
Denmark	—	44.6	43.3	42.1	44.9	48.7	56.2	56.0	56.9	57.3
Netherlands	29.9	41.0	50.4	43.8	43.0	—	41.6	42.5	42.8	40.4
United Kingdom	29.3	30.0	28.2	31.3	34.6	42.4	46.3	48.1	47.8	46.8
Germany	—	—	—	—	—	—	—	41.5	45.0	41.3
Norway	—	21.2	32.7	43.4	42.2	36.2	53.5	55.4	57.5	57.5
Sweden	32.3	40.3	44.8	46.9	52.9	54.8	55.4	57.7	61.0	62.7
France	—	16.9	18.8	49.3	43.2	—	85.3	55.4	36.8	26.5
Italy	—	—	—	—	—	—	—	90.1	80.3	74.5
Japan	2.8	3.5	3.2	2.8	—	—	50.3	52.8	42.0	40.9
India	—	—	—	—	—	—	12.0	15.3	15.8	16.5
United States	11.6	12.6	13.5	20.0	24.9	27.0	31.9	32.1	33.2	33.9
Canada	13.4	15.1	15.4	17.8	17.5	22.8	27.1	30.3	30.2	32.9
Australia	55.6	60.4	52.1	45.9	53.9	62.9	60.6	61.8	64.4	—
Finland	18.6	5.1	6.1	10.5	12.8	17.1	44.7	30.7	26.3	27.7
South Africa	11.2	8.5	8.6	11.3	12.6	15.2	16.6	15.3	15.0	—

Source: Computed from Appendix.

Membership Involvement

One of the most revealing measures of industrial conflict is the percentage of union members becoming involved. It is affected by the number of strikes as well as their average size, so that a given percentage might reflect either many small stoppages or a lesser number of larger ones. In either case it shows the frequency with which union members are called out on strike. Table 2 shows the three-year averages of propensity to strike.

The first point to be noted is the gradual decline in the proportion of union members going on strike. Compare the 1900–29 averages with those from 1930–47 and 1948–56, reproduced in the following tabulation:

	1900–29	1930–47	1948–56
	%	%	%
Denmark	6.3	2.4	1.4
Netherlands	7.0	2.6	1.3
United Kingdom	16.1	6.4	5.9
Germany	14.2	3.7	2.6
Norway	27.0	6.8	1.2
Sweden	22.7	3.0	0.3
France	27.1	29.0	62.4
Japan	30.3	39.0	21.5
India	...	102.2	37.2
United States	33.2	20.3	15.4
Canada	14.7	13.3	6.3
Australia	18.2	14.8	25.2
Finland	24.5	9.0	13.9
South Africa	24.4	3.9	1.4

Participation by union members has declined in each of these countries with the exception of France and Australia. In some cases the reduction has been dramatic indeed—from 14.2 to 2.6 per cent in Germany, from 27.0 to 1.2 per cent in Norway, and from 22.7 to 0.3 per cent in Sweden.

Notwithstanding this general decline, there are still some crucial differences between one country and another. On the basis of the 1948–56 averages, we may classify the countries into three groups having nominal, moderate, and high ratios between the number of strikers and the number of union members.

We have defined as "nominal" a ratio averaging less than 3 per cent annually subsequent to 1947. Using this test, we can say that the strike no longer plays any significant role in the union programs of Denmark, the Netherlands, Germany, Norway, Sweden, and South Africa. The *right* to strike may remain precious and inviolable, in most of these countries at least; the *possibility* of a strike may lurk in the shadows when labor contracts are negotiated; but actual *recourse* to strikes has been largely eliminated.

The distinction between the ability to strike and the need to strike must be strongly emphasized. We are not suggesting that Swedish or Norwegian unions, for example, are unable to strike or that they have disowned the principle of the strike. On the contrary, resort to strikes may be least necessary where threats are most effective. Furthermore, tacit or implied threats are no less effective than those that are made explicit.

At the other extreme are five countries where participation in strikes has been extremely high, in relation to union membership, in recent years. These are France, Italy, Japan, India, and Australia. The number of strikers has averaged from 22 to 62 per cent of union membership each year since 1947.

In the middle are four nations with a "moderate" degree of participation—5.9 per cent in the United Kingdom, 6.3 per cent in Canada, 13.9 per cent in Finland, and 15.4 per cent in the United States. (In the United Kingdom the duration of stoppages has been so brief that we are justified in saying that strikes have been largely eliminated in that country.)

During the first three decades of the century, union members in the United States were more prone to strike than those anywhere else. On the average, about one-third of all unionists went on strike each year. Since the end of World War II there has been a sharp and steady decline, however. The ratio has dropped from 26 per cent in 1945–47 to about 10 per cent in 1954–56. Thus the comment in "Strike Experience in Five Countries" concerning the unusually high propensity to strike of American unionists no longer applies.

It is not the purpose of this chapter to explain the trends and differences in strike activity, but we can take note of a few matters in a preliminary way. Among the countries with nominal membership involvement, only one (Sweden) experienced any sizable change in degree of organization after 1944. Collective bargaining structure has become highly centralized; there are strong labor parties and frequent labor governments. But in the countries where strikes are most frequent, labor

TABLE 2. Membership Involvement Ratio

Workers Involved in Strikes as a Percentage of Union Membership, 1900–1956, Annual Averages for Three-Year Periods

	1900–1902	1903–1905	1906–1908	1909–1911	1912–1914	1915–1917	1918–1920	1921–1923	1924–1926	1927–1929	1930–1932
Denmark	5.0	3.6	5.9	8.8	3.8	4.3	6.4	10.5	12.1	0.3	1.4
Netherlands	—	—	—	—	9.4	6.9	10.4	8.0	4.7	3.3	3.4
United Kingdom	—	—	—	30.3	23.2	10.7	24.3	14.8	13.7	5.3	8.5
Germany	10.6	17.6	11.3	10.9	9.3	19.1	20.9	18.6	15.8	9.5	3.7
Norway	—	21.4	21.0	33.5	13.0	16.4	15.5	64.2	45.9	11.7	16.2
Sweden	—	25.2	13.2	75.3	8.5	11.2	25.6	19.8	18.8	6.6	6.2
France	32.9	26.6	28.3	23.0	20.8	—	83.3	33.9	19.6	13.3	15.5
Italy	—	—	—	—	—	—	—	—	—	—	—
Japan	—	—	—	—	—	—	—	38.5	34.6	17.8	18.3
India	—	—	—	—	—	—	—	—	—	398.9	76.0
United States	55.3	28.0	—	—	—	48.9	55.2	28.0	13.4	8.9	8.6
Canada	—	—	—	22.6	17.7	14.4	26.1	11.3	10.3	5.9	5.3
Australia	—	—	—	—	11.9	25.8	19.2	17.0	18.8	14.7	5.2
Finland	—	—	—	29.2	32.4	87.0	22.5	16.4	9.6	17.1	4.5
South Africa	—	—	—	4.3	184.0	8.7	34.1	14.9	1.5	3.3	4.7

TABLE 2 (Continued)

	1933–1935	1936–1938	1939–1941	1942–1944	1945–1947	1948–1950	1951–1953	1954–1956	1900–1929	1930–1947	1948–1956
Denmark	1.0	7.4	0.1	1.0	3.7	0.4	0.2	3.6	6.3	2.4	1.4
Netherlands	1.4	1.0	0.6	—	7.6	1.5	0.6	1.6	7.0	2.6	1.3
United Kingdom	3.9	6.9	5.0	7.6	6.5	4.2	7.6	5.8	16.1	6.4	5.9
Germany	—	—	—	—	—	1.3	1.6	5.5	14.2	3.7	2.6
Norway	3.1	7.3	4.5	—	1.4	1.4	1.0	1.2	27.0	6.8	1.2
Sweden	3.2	2.5	0.3	0.5	5.6	0.3	1.1	0.3	22.7	3.0	0.3
France	7.6	68.1	—	—	22.8	83.9	48.8	50.5	27.1	29.0	62.4
Italy	—	—	—	—	—	42.7	38.3	27.1	—	—	35.2
Japan	11.6	8.3	189.0	—	7.2	21.1	23.9	15.5	30.3	39.0	21.5
India	71.9	13.9	82.6	93.9	149.8	46.2	33.1	22.6	—	102.2	37.2
United States	36.8	19.4	16.5	14.4	26.0	17.4	16.9	10.1	33.2	20.3	15.4
Canada	12.5	11.6	15.7	21.0	13.9	4.8	8.4	4.8	14.7	13.3	6.3
Australia	5.6	11.6	20.0	20.5	26.1	22.2	28.2	—	18.2	14.8	25.2
Finland	11.7	7.4	4.1	—	17.4	24.3	4.9	11.7	24.5	9.0	13.9
South Africa	1.7	1.7	1.5	3.1	10.6	1.2	1.8	—	24.4	3.9	1.4

Source: Computed from Appendix.

movements were either newly organized or reorganized after World War II, except for Australia. None of these countries (again excepting Australia) relies primarily on collective bargaining to establish terms of employment; so that the strike, as practiced there, cannot be viewed as a phase in the process of contract negotiation.

The United States is similar to the Northern European countries in having a well-developed collective bargaining system, but is unlike these countries in other respects. Employers have resisted collective bargaining more strongly, unions have pushed their demands more vigorously, the bargaining structure is decentralized, there is no labor party, and there has never been a labor government.

Employee Involvement

The ratio between strikers and employees is affected by intensity of organization as well as membership involvement and varies directly with each.

The proportion of wage and salary earners going on strike has fallen since the prewar period in Denmark, the Netherlands, Norway, Sweden, India, and South Africa. In each case the trend is explained by a declining membership involvement rate.

On the other hand, the degree of participation has risen greatly in France, Japan, Australia, and Finland. More intensive organization of workers as well as greater proneness to strike is responsible.

There has been a more moderate increase in the United States, and a level trend in the United Kingdom and Canada. In these countries, workers have become more intensively organized but union members are not so likely to strike as formerly.

During the most recent decade an unusual combination of circumstances has occurred in France, Italy, and Japan. Although membership involvement in these countries has been among the highest, the unions have suffered large membership losses. In consequence, the ratio between workers involved in strikes and non-agricultural employment has fallen off rapidly.

Employee Involvement

(per cent)

	1948–50	1951–53	1954–56
France	48.9	17.8	12.6
Italy	36.1	30.8	19.8
Japan	11.3	10.0	6.5
Average	31.8	19.5	13.0

TABLE 3. Employee Involvement Ratio

Workers Involved in Disputes as a Percentage of Non-agricultural Employment, 1927–1956.
Annual Averages for Three-Year Periods

	1927–1929	1930–1932	1933–1935	1936–1938	1939–1941	1942–1944	1945–1947	1948–1950	1951–1953	1954–1956	1927–1947	1948–1956
Denmark	—	0.6	0.5	3.0	0.03	0.5	2.0	0.2	0.1	0.6	1.1	0.3
Netherlands	1.2	1.4	0.7	0.5	0.3	—	3.2	0.6	0.3	0.7	1.1	0.5
United Kingdom	3.2	2.5	1.1	2.2	1.7	3.2	3.0	2.0	3.6	2.6	2.3	2.7
Germany	—	—	—	—	—	—	—	0.6	0.7	1.5	—	1.0
Norway	0.8	0.7	0.5	3.2	2.1	—	0.7	0.8	0.6	2.4	1.7	1.3
Sweden	—	2.5	1.5	1.2	0.1	0.3	3.2	0.2	0.7	0.2	1.4	0.4
France	—	2.7	1.4	18.2	—	—	19.5	48.9	17.8	12.6	9.6	26.4
Italy	—	—	—	—	—	—	—	36.1	30.8	19.8	—	28.0
Japan	0.5	0.6	0.4	0.2	—	—	1.9	11.3	10.0	6.5	0.5	9.3
India	—	—	—	—	—	—	16.5	7.0	5.2	3.9	16.5	5.5
United States	1.0	1.1	5.0	3.7	4.1	4.0	8.3	5.6	5.6	4.1	3.9	5.1
Canada	0.8	0.8	1.9	2.1	2.7	4.7	3.8	2.8	2.5	1.6	2.4	2.4
Australia	6.4	3.1	2.9	4.3	10.8	12.9	15.8	13.7	18.1	15.2	8.3	15.7
Finland	3.4	0.2	0.7	0.8	0.5	—	7.7	7.0	1.3	17.6	2.2	8.6
South Africa	0.3	0.4	0.1	0.2	0.2	0.5	1.8	0.2	0.2	0.3	0.5	0.2

Source: Computed from Appendix.

Duration of Strikes

We have already observed that the duration of strikes is one of the most significant measures of industrial conflict from a behavioristic as well as an economic standpoint. Certainly the diversity in the meaning of the strike from one country to another, or from one period of time to another, shows up most dramatically in variations of length.

The average striker in Norway remained off the job about *eighty* working days during 1930–32, for example. Compare this with about *two* days in Australia, France, Italy, Japan, and South Africa during 1954–56.

Really it is misleading to use the same word for such different phenomena. It stands to reason that a "strike" of eighty days and a "strike" of two days do not have the same causes, nor the same consequences, and cannot be explained by the same theory. To consider all strikes as homogeneous occurrences stands in the way of enlightenment.

Before exploring such differences, however, we should note the remarkable abbreviation of strikes as a whole during the twentieth century. This trend has operated almost everywhere.

Average Duration of Strikes

	1900–29 (days)	1948–56 (days)	1948–56 as per cent of 1900–29
Denmark	28.7	4.3	15
Netherlands	32.7	7.5	23
United Kingdom	23.0	4.3	19
Germany	15.6	9.9	63
Norway	33.6	15.2	45
Sweden	37.1	22.6	61
France	14.4	2.9	20
India	26.6	8.8	33
Canada	27.1	19.3	71
Australia	14.2	3.2	23
Finland	36.0	15.8	44
South Africa	15.8	2.6	16

Statistics covering earlier years are unavailable for Italy, Japan, and the United States.

The decline has not come about quickly or spasmodically, but steadily and gradually. In the majority of countries the average duration of strikes in the 1930–47 period was less than in 1900–29 and greater than

in 1948–56. Only in Finland and Canada did strikes grow longer after
World War II, and in both countries the postwar strikes have remained
much shorter than those that occurred in the early years of the century.

Two reasons for the general trend will be emphasized in later chapters.
First, the modern strike is less frequently a trial of economic strength,
and more often a demonstration of protest, than the strike of previous
decades. Second, even the classical collective-bargaining strike is settled
more rapidly than it previously was.

Turning now to differences in length of strikes, we have classified the
countries into three groups according to average duration in the 1948–56
period. The "low" category (less than five days) includes Denmark, the
United Kingdom, France, Italy, Japan, Australia, and South Africa. At
the other extreme are Norway, Sweden, Finland, the United States, and
Canada, with an average duration exceeding fourteen days. The Netherlands, Germany, and India fall into an intermediate group with an average duration of more than seven but less than ten days.

The relationship between membership involvement and duration of
strikes is an interesting one, and serves to define several distinctive patterns of industrial conflict. We have chosen to call these the North
European Pattern—First Variant; North European Pattern—Second
Variant; Mediterranean-Asian Pattern, and North American Pattern.

The North European Pattern—First Variant is characterized by
nominal membership involvement and a low or moderate duration of
strikes. Denmark, the Netherlands, and Germany are clearly included.
The United Kingdom is on the borderline, union members being more
prone to strike than in the other countries, but can be admitted without
stretching the definition very much.

The North European Pattern—Second Variant is defined by nominal involvement and a high duration of strikes. In other words, there
are very few stoppages, but those that do occur are long ones. Norway
and Sweden are in this category.

Exactly the opposite situation is found where the Mediterranean-
Asian Pattern applies. Strikes are very frequent, as measured by the
proportion of union members participating, and, at the same time, very
brief. France, Italy, and Japan undoubtedly belong in this classification.
India, with a somewhat longer duration of strikes, has much in common
with countries in this group.

The North American Pattern of strike activity, found in the United
States and Canada, denotes a high or medium propensity to strike, during recent years, as well as an unusually long duration of strikes.

TABLE 4. Duration of Strikes

Working Days Lost per Striker, 1900–1956, Annual Averages for Three-Year Periods

	1900–1902	1903–1905	1906–1908	1909–1911	1912–1914	1915–1917	1918–1920	1921–1923	1924–1926	1927–1929	1930–1932
Denmark	33.5	43.8	20.0	23.7	22.7	18.3	35.0	28.2	27.1	34.7	36.2
Netherlands	—	—	—	—	24.6	13.8	22.3	40.9	58.4	33.7	36.9
United Kingdom	17.5	17.2	18.1	10.7	21.6	7.3	10.8	36.7	53.1	12.5	15.2
Germany	—	—	—	20.9	16.4	2.8	10.9	13.4	20.2	19.1	12.5
Norway	—	18.9	32.4	39.2	28.5	27.3	29.3	32.2	44.8	49.2	80.1
Sweden	—	43.5	31.0	25.7	34.6	21.0	38.7	52.0	33.4	54.1	58.4
France	18.5	16.6	19.1	18.7	10.8	5.5	12.2	14.5	11.3	17.0	20.4
Italy	—	—	—	—	—	—	—	—	—	—	—
Japan	—	—	—	—	—	—	—	—	—	15.1	13.3
India	—	—	—	—	—	—	—	12.5	37.2	33.5	12.8
United States	16.2	18.0	19.6	50.7	36.4	15.0	18.8	37.8	44.8	46.1	23.6
Canada	—	—	—	—	—	—	—	—	—	10.5	12.2
Australia	—	—	—	—	13.9	14.5	19.4	9.4	8.0	19.8	13.6
Finland	—	—	33.5	51.2	40.3	10.7	22.5	26.4	31.1	54.6	5.3
South Africa	—	—	48.5	22.1	5.9	3.2	14.2	23.8	3.2	1.8	5.2

TABLE 4 (Continued)

	1933–1935	1936–1938	1939–1941	1942–1944	1945–1947	1948–1950	1951–1953	1954–1956	1900–1929	1930–1947	1948–1956
Denmark	22.1	23.2	26.2	6.2	31.9	2.7	3.1	6.9	28.7	24.3	4.3
Netherlands	24.9	12.9	16.4	—	5.2	12.3	5.2	5.1	32.7	21.3	7.5
United Kingdom	7.4	5.5	3.4	3.7	4.5	4.5	3.5	5.1	23.0	6.6	4.3
Germany	—	—	—	—	—	4.7	14.6	8.5	15.6	12.5	9.9
Norway	47.5	28.2	53.7	—	12.6	12.3	12.0	21.3	33.6	43.0	15.2
Sweden	69.7	65.8	47.2	29.0	26.0	20.8	31.6	15.5	37.1	51.0	22.6
France	16.1	—	—	—	4.9	3.8	3.0	1.8	14.4	14.9	2.9
Italy	—	—	—	—	—	3.4	1.9	2.9	—	—	2.7
Japan	8.3	4.9	2.0	—	17.6	5.0	5.9	3.9	—	9.1	4.9
India	14.4	16.9	13.4	6.1	7.0	11.6	5.6	9.2	26.6	11.8	8.8
United States	13.9	15.4	12.2	5.3	17.4	16.7	12.9	14.3	—	14.6	14.6
Canada	11.0	9.2	5.0	5.1	23.5	16.2	18.8	23.0	27.1	11.0	19.3
Australia	7.2	7.8	4.9	3.0	5.5	5.0	2.2	2.4	14.2	7.0	3.2
Finland	16.3	22.8	21.7	—	6.7	24.9	12.8	9.9	36.0	14.5	15.8
South Africa	13.3	2.5	8.8	4.2	24.9	4.4	2.0	1.8	15.8	9.4	2.6

Source: Computed from Appendix.

CHART I. Membership Involvement and Duration of Strikes
Annual Averages, 1948–1956

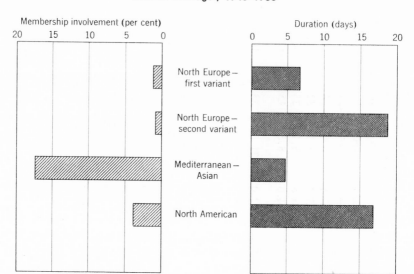

There remain three countries—South Africa, Australia and Finland —which we have not placed in any category.

From a purely behavioral standpoint, it would not have been difficult to classify them. Work stoppages almost never take place in South Africa, and last only about two days when they do occur. The same is true in Denmark, Germany, and other countries of the North European Pattern—First Variant. Australia's frequent brief conflicts are characteristic of the Mediterranean-Asian Pattern. Strike activity in Finland is quite similar to that in the United States: involvement is moderately high and duration of strikes is rather long. In both countries some 14 or 15 per cent of union members have gone on strike annually during the most recent decade, and stoppages have averaged fifteen or sixteen days.

The South African, Australian, and Finnish strike statistics "fit" well enough, but the explanations do not. As we shall indicate presently, the four patterns are associated with characteristic configurations of labor-management relations, political structure, and government policy. Countries in the Mediterranean-Asian group, for example, have weak and unstable labor movements, bitter leadership conflicts, flimsy collective bargaining systems, and ineffective political action on the part of labor. None of these conditions prevails in Australia. There are good explanations for the Australian pattern of strike activity, but some of them are special explanations. The same is true of the South African and Finnish patterns. Although every classification is something of a Procrustean bed, too much stretching and straining would have been needed to squeeze these countries into our regular categories, and we prefer to regard them as special cases. This does not create a serious problem, for we do not state that our classification is universally applicable. We do believe it is helpful in understanding industrial relations in many of the advanced industrial societies of the Western world.

Membership Loss Ratio and Employee Loss Ratio

Ratios of lost working time in proportion to union membership and non-agricultural employment are not emphasized in our analysis. However, they do give some indication—although a most imperfect one—of the relative impact of strikes on the economy.[3]

The decline in man-days of idleness in relation to the number of union members is remarkable. During the 1920–29 period, at least two days per year were lost for every union member in each country studied; more than eight days per year were lost in Norway, Sweden, and Finland. Between 1948 and 1956 there were two days of idleness annually per union member only in India, the United States, and Finland. At the other extreme there are seven countries with losses averaging *less than one-quarter day per member:* Denmark, the Netherlands, the United Kingdom, Germany, Norway, Sweden, and South Africa. Truly the strike has withered away in Northern Europe.

The employee loss ratio measures man-days of idleness in relation to the number of wage and salary earners. The movements of this ratio are affected by changes in degree of organization and are difficult to characterize. Suffice it to say that during the recent decade the relative loss in the majority of countries has been running below the 1927–47 period, despite the fact that workers are much more highly organized.

These measures, as we have noted, give a rough indication of the economic impact of strikes. Considering the vast amount of attention and emotion which strikes have engendered, the impact seems remarkably small. In not a single country has the average been as high as one day per wage and salary earner per year, and in the majority it has been less than half a day. We cannot think of any other major source of loss —including unemployment, industrial accidents, and the common cold— having a smaller relative effect. It is not the economic effects of strikes in general, however, but the political effects of particular strikes and groups of strikes that have been most significant.

TABLE 5. Membership Loss Ratio

Working Days Lost per Hundred Union Members, 1900–1956, Annual Averages for Three-Year Periods

	1900–1902	1903–1905	1906–1908	1909–1911	1912–1914	1915–1917	1918–1920	1921–1923	1924–1926	1927–1929	1930–1932
Denmark	152.0	222.5	123.0	201.4	107.0	79.8	226.6	386.8	464.9	8.0	45.2
Netherlands	—	—	—	—	236.5	97.8	174.4	354.5	291.7	115.9	132.7
United Kingdom	—	—	—	323.5	557.5	74.4	283.1	614.8	1039.1	74.4	129.3
Germany	—	284.5	210.0	239.4	173.3	51.4	251.9	225.3	350.3	190.6	54.2
Norway	—	721.6	684.1	972.7	385.2	477.5	482.6	1590.5	2510.4	651.3	1891.7
Sweden	—	1170.7	451.6	2837.3	302.6	253.7	1105.8	1050.6	455.7	417.5	371.7
France	613.6	426.8	569.9	423.0	215.8	—	1461.9	540.5	224.5	240.1	235.1
Italy	—	—	—	—	—	—	—	—	—	—	—
Japan	—	—	—	—	—	—	—	—	—	247.4	245.2
India	—	—	—	—	—	—	—	—	—	19088.2	949.2
United States	—	—	—	—	—	—	—	—	—	419.3	212.4
Canada	—	—	—	1537.7	559.3	252.9	528.9	431.9	477.0	58.3	61.5
Australia	—	—	—	—	166.8	410.8	424.5	140.7	140.5	256.1	79.1
Finland	—	—	—	1300.2	1381.9	930.0	577.2	438.0	317.9	893.1	31.1
South Africa	—	—	—	110.9	1345.4	28.0	378.1	580.1	6.2	6.8	26.7

TABLE 5 (Continued)

	1933–1935	1936–1938	1939–1941	1942–1944	1945–1947	1948–1950	1951–1953	1954–1956	1900–1929	1930–1947	1948–1956
Denmark	14.1	220.7	1.5	6.9	101.3	1.1	0.4	49.8	203.7	64.9	17.1
Netherlands	37.9	12.2	9.1	—	53.0	17.6	2.5	7.7	212.6	51.7	10.4
United Kingdom	28.5	38.3	17.0	29.1	29.0	18.5	19.9	32.5	434.4	45.2	22.5
Germany	—	—	—	—	—	6.2	18.5	18.7	221.3	—	15.1
Norway	148.6	211.8	243.9	—	16.0	17.0	13.0	19.7	941.8	542.2	16.2
Sweden	257.0	101.1	11.3	11.8	345.2	5.7	29.8	4.5	893.9	183.0	13.3
France	122.8	—	—	—	164.9	228.5	162.1	98.8	415.7	175.5	171.2
Italy	—	—	—	—	—	136.8	64.2	73.3	—	—	85.8
Japan	96.2	46.3	421.0	—	107.9	88.0	147.5	64.1	—	170.8	110.1
India	1183.4	2242.7	1127.1	597.0	1057.1	505.3	177.0	159.5	—	1192.8	315.2
United States	510.9	304.9	193.5	77.6	479.2	290.6	228.8	163.4	—	296.4	235.6
Canada	138.8	118.6	76.7	100.7	336.9	98.2	149.2	132.1	445.4	138.9	129.7
Australia	42.1	92.4	99.8	63.0	143.6	111.0	61.8	—	261.9	86.7	86.4
Finland	185.9	173.9	138.7	—	99.0	762.8	57.8	91.9	810.4	125.7	579.8
South Africa	23.1	5.3	1.6	12.6	134.8	5.5	4.2	—	315.2	38.1	5.0

Source: Computed from Appendix.

TABLE 6. Employee Loss Ratio

Working Days Lost per Hundred Non-agricultural Employees, 1927–1956, Annual Averages for Three-Year Periods

	1927–1929	1930–1932	1933–1935	1936–1938	1939–1941	1942–1944	1945–1947	1948–1950	1951–1953	1954–1956	1927–1947	1948–1956
Denmark	—	20.1	6.1	91.1	0.7	3.4	55.7	0.6	0.3	1.4	30.1	0.7
Netherlands	53.7	58.8	19.4	5.3	3.9	—	21.7	7.5	1.5	3.2	25.4	4.2
United Kingdom	49.9	38.7	8.1	11.9	5.8	12.5	13.4	8.9	9.5	13.5	16.9	10.6
Germany	—	—	—	—	—	—	—	2.6	8.3	5.7	—	5.9
Norway	—	36.6	25.6	92.4	112.8	—	8.5	9.4	7.5	41.3	53.1	19.1
Sweden	42.4	155.1	118.3	48.0	5.9	6.5	190.9	3.3	18.2	2.8	85.1	8.1
France	—	40.5	23.0	—	—	—	141.3	125.6	57.0	22.1	59.1	68.2
Italy	—	—	—	—	—	—	—	118.0	51.6	54.9	—	69.4
Japan	7.0	8.4	3.1	1.3	—	—	44.5	46.2	61.8	25.3	8.0	44.5
India	—	—	—	—	—	—	148.8	76.2	27.8	34.6	148.8	47.7
United States	49.3	27.5	68.6	57.5	47.8	21.2	151.9	93.3	75.9	55.6	60.5	75.0
Canada	7.8	9.4	21.2	21.2	13.4	22.9	92.6	33.3	45.2	43.4	26.2	40.3
Australia	274.6	45.9	21.4	29.0	38.4	39.8	87.4	68.6	39.7	37.0	58.4	48.5
Finland	167.3	1.3	11.9	19.0	17.1	—	44.3	216.7	15.2	25.4	43.5	162.0
South Africa	0.8	2.2	2.0	0.6	0.2	1.9	21.7	0.9	0.5	0.5	4.8	0.6

Source: Computed from Appendix.

NOTES TO CHAPTER 3

1. Omitting the World War II period.

2. A. M. Ross and D. Irwin, "Strike Experience in Five Countries," *Industrial and Labor Relations Review,* 4 (April 1951), p. 333.

3. "Statistics on man-days of inactivity do not provide a reliable basis for measuring the magnitude of economic loss because of strikes. On the one hand, the substantial indirect effects of certain strikes are not included, for example, curtailment of output in automobile plants when steel supplies become exhausted. On the other hand, there is sufficient slack in the economy to absorb the effect of most strikes without enduring loss of any great consequence. Employers may build up inventories in anticipation of the strike or step up production to fill delayed orders after it has been terminated, or consumers may obtain the goods from competing producers in the area or in some other area. In general, the less durable is a commodity (and the less adapted to stockpiling) and the more nearly is the whole market area included in the scope of a strike, the greater is the likelihood that a real economic cost is involved." [A. Kornhauser, R. Dubin, and A. M. Ross (eds.), *Industrial Conflict* (New York: McGraw-Hill Book Co., 1954), p. 7 (editorial matter).] It might be added that there is more slack in a wealthy economy than in a poor or underdeveloped economy.

CHAPTER 4

Problems

of Analyzing

Industrial Conflict

At this point some explanations are called for. We must define the
reasons for the general decline in strike activity throughout the industrialized world, and particularly in the Northern European countries;
and we must explain the differences in patterns of industrial conflict
from one group of countries to another. We shall undertake the first
task in Chapter 5 and the second in Chapter 6.

To bring forth general propositions about industrial conflict in so
many parts of the world is certainly a rash and dangerous enterprise.
Let the reader be assured that we have pondered upon the risks and
pitfalls.

At least five difficulties ought to be discussed. (*a*) Every country
is unique in its national culture, historical background, political institutions, and economic environment. (*b*) The fact that the fifteen nations
became industrialized as early as the first part of the nineteenth century
and as late as the middle of the twentieth, and that their wage and salary
earners have become unionized at very different points of time, raises

large problems of interpretation. We are tempted to assume that every country moves through a common cycle of development, but unfortunately such an assumption is not valid; the time dimension makes a great deal of difference. (c) There is the hazard that transient fluctuations may be misconstrued as long-run changes. Something or other is happening at any given time—war, postwar inflation, depression, recovery, etc.—and all these events have their influence on industrial relations. (d) Statistics on union membership and wage and salary earners are not very reliable in some countries; strike statistics are sometimes inaccurate; and we have not hesitated to make estimates and interpolations where we had sufficient foundation. (e) Dealing with ratios, averages, and percentages compounds the risk, for such measures are abstractions at best and are confusing and misleading if handled carelessly.

Still we think a study of this kind is worth doing, and could not be carried out except in the face of the aforementioned difficulties.   It might be desirable to explain here why we do not regard them as fatal.

(a) To begin with, what about the diversities among the fifteen countries? The answer is that, for the most part, we must concentrate on features which are subject to comparison and differentiation rather than those which are singular and incomparable. And the justification is that we are endeavoring to comprehend industrial conflict as a world-wide phenomenon rather than to group the uniqueness of individual countries.

C. G. Jung discusses a similar problem in his latest book, where he distinguishes between knowledge of men in general, which is the task of descriptive psychology, and the understanding of an individual man, which is the purpose of psychoanalysis. He points out on the one hand that "man, as a member of a species, can and must be described as a statistical unit; otherwise nothing general could be said about him." But on the other hand, "it is not the universal and the regular which characterizes the individual, but rather the unique. He is not to be understood as a recurrent unit but as something unique and singular which in the last analysis can neither be known nor compared with anything else." [1]

In concentrating on matters that make it possible to analyze the strike "as a recurrent unit," we must necessarily pass over much that is colorful and interesting about particular countries. We say nothing of the stolid Scandinavian character and the volatile Latin temperament because we are not equipped to make any systematic study of cultural differences in personality as they might bear on industrial conflict. We lay no stress on the fact that many early white settlers of Australia were sent to that island because of their rebellious nature. And so on.

In several instances, however, we have resorted to singular explanations to account for the fact that strike activity in a given country has been substantially greater or less than would have been expected on other grounds. Every observer of Australian industrial relations, for example, points out that the majority of strikes have taken place in coal mining and longshoring and that these trades all have been "strike-prone" almost everywhere. Again, we have thought it essential to mention the pronounced abhorrence of disorder in the postwar Bundesrepublik and the prevalent docility of German workers. In the case of South Africa the virtual absence of strikes must be explained by a factor —repression and the fear of repression—which, although not unique in the world, is certainly unique among the countries we have studied.

(b) Next, what about the fact that different countries have entered the process of industrialization and unionization at such different periods of time? There is real danger in taking it for granted that history will repeat itself. Some students of economic development have erroneously assumed that the newer countries should rely on the same sources of capital, government policies, etc., that the older countries utilized in the nineteenth century. An assumption that labor relations in the newer countries will go through the same process of evolution as in the older countries would be equally dubious and is not necessary to our argument.

This point applies particularly to the "underdeveloped nations" of Africa and Asia which have undertaken to industrialize under forced draft. It would be a great mistake to assume that they will necessarily pass through the same cycles of industrial conflict as the European and North American countries have done. There are almost 275,000 union members in Egypt, for example, but strikes have virtually disappeared under the Nasser regime. Israel has perhaps 350,000 unionists; from 1948 through 1955 the number of strikers averaged only about 9,000 and man-days of idleness only 50,000. Strike activity has been relatively high in India, but we have seen a dramatic reduction since independence was gained. In some of the newer countries that have not undertaken ambitious programs of economic development, such as Ceylon and Vietnam, industrial conflict has not been so muted.[2]

If the data for these countries were less fragmentary, we would probably have identified a fifth pattern of strike activity known as the Economic Development Pattern. The membership involvement and loss ratios are as low as in the Northern European group. This has come to pass not after a full century of collective bargaining but at the very threshold of industrial growth and organized employment relations.

In many of the older industrial nations, the emergence and absorption of unrest has followed a common course. Economic growth created a class of industrial wage earners. Their protest was originally impulsive and unstructured. Gradually trade unions achieved a prescriptive monopoly over the expression of protest, and as "merchants of discontent" sought to deal with the employers. The employers resisted at first, but eventually became reconciled to collective bargaining. Orderly procedures, binding contracts, and other appurtenances of the business system were adopted; use of the strike was restricted and rationalized.[3] As they gained experience in bargaining, employers and unions achieved a better understanding of each other, learned to harmonize their objectives, and brought more conciliatory leaders to the fore. Richard A. Lester has described the accommodation process as it has worked out in the United States. As one phase of this process:

> The use and character of the strike has also altered in many union-management relationships. As relations continue, resort to striking is likely to be less frequent, and any strikes generally are less severe or emotional. . . . With increasing professionalization, the negotiations are more intelligent, reasoned and moderate.[4]

This is the point that labor and management in the United States have reached. In the Northern European countries the process has moved to another point, at which industrial conflict virtually disappears from the scene. The reasons why this course has been adopted and the circumstances that have made it possible will be explained in the chapters that follow.

It should not be assumed, however, that American labor relations will necessarily continue along the European path. On this question Lester observes:

> There has been an assumption that collective bargaining in the United States would more or less follow patterns developed in other democratic countries, like England and Sweden, in which unions became well established and accepted by management much earlier than here. However, distinctly American developments make any close conformity unlikely.[5]

And by the same token, it should not be assumed that the newer African and Asiatic nations will necessarily repeat the experience of the United States and the European countries.

Several years ago Clark Kerr and others pointed out that whereas labor protest always emerges in the course of industrialization, protest can take different forms and can be handled in different ways. "A crucial factor is the locus of the control or 'management' of protest," they pointed out. ". . . There are rival contenders in the struggle to direct, control, suppress or manage labour protest. Among these contenders

are employers, union officials, political leaders, government adminis-
trators, military cliques and the leaders of religious sects." Furthermore, there are various "relationships between labour protest and other
social and political forces such as anti-colonialism, communism, anti-
clericalism and nationalism." [6]

It seems evident that in the newer nations such as India and Egypt,
labor protest has been "managed" in different ways from those of the
older countries. Capitalism as such has been less often the object of
protest; foreign capital and influence have been more frequently cen-
sured. Once national independence has been gained, labor movements
have been either successfully enlisted in programs of economic planning,
or brought under government domination, or suppressed. In contrast
to the laissez-faire policies of an earlier period, the new governments
have moved in aggressively to settle disputes and terminate stoppages.
Thus, anti-imperialism, nationalism, and government intervention have
combined to obviate the familiar cycle of industrial conflict.

It may be that the effect is only temporary. Perhaps the new countries of Asia and Africa will eventually move into the path taken by
the old countries of Europe and North America. So far, however, there
is little evidence to this effect.

(c) Third, can we be certain that we have identified a significant trend?
This question really incorporates two issues. (1) Are we justified in
saying that strikes have grown shorter and less frequent in numerous
countries during the first six decades of the twentieth century? (2) Can
we be confident that the trend will continue into the future?

(1) It might be argued that the prevalence of peace and quiet on the
industrial scene can be explained by the high profits, the inflation of
wages and prices, and the persistence of full employment during the
postwar period. The theory behind such a proposition would not be too
clear; it has traditionally been believed that industrial warfare is accelerated, rather than diminished, in periods of prosperity.[7] However, the
tranquilizing effects of the cold war on internal conflicts and the domi-
nance of conservative politics in the Western world might be invoked
in order to strengthen the argument.

Disentangling long-run changes from cyclical or other temporary influences is a familiar problem of interpretation. We have not resorted
to any involved statistical maneuvers, but we are satisfied that we are
dealing with more than the reflection of transient postwar influences.
The tendencies have been more persistent than that. In practically all
the countries studied (with the exception of the Mediterranean-Asian

group, where the brief and massive work stoppage is used as a protest demonstration), membership involvement has been declining for almost sixty years now. The duration of strikes has been greatly curtailed in every nation for which there are records covering the early decades of the century. In the majority of countries the process of curtailment has been steady and gradual rather than spasmodic.

There have been many big wars, small wars, cold wars, inflations, deflations, prosperities and depressions since 1900. Social and political tendencies have appeared on the scene, blossomed, and died away. Strike activity continues to decline. Under these circumstances there is every reason to believe that some basic and persistent influences have been at work. In the following chapter we shall endeavor to identify and describe these influences.

(2) The trend that has become so apparent during the specific historical period under discussion is certainly subject to change. The influences on strike activity have been basic and persistent, but they are not necessarily irreversible. As we shall indicate in the next chapter, strike activity has declined because of developments in employer policy, bargaining structure, government activity, and labor programs. If these underlying influences should change their direction, presumably industrial conflict would increase once more. We do not expect any basic reversal of trend, but we recognize that predictions of the future stand on a different plane from explanations of the past and present. The predictions are necessarily somewhat speculative whereas the explanations ought to be supported by evidence. We shall return to this question in the final chapter, which is written in a more ruminative tone than the remainder of the book.

(d) Turning now to our figures on strike activity, union membership, and non-agricultural employment, we cannot claim a high degree of reliability for many of them. If our conclusions rested on only a few statistics, or on a bare preponderance of conflicting evidence, they would certainly be questionable. Fortunately, however, this is not the situation. Instead, we have a large mass of data, most of it pointing in the same direction. Critical scrutiny of the data might suggest possible biases, but these could not be large enough to jeopardize our finding that strikes have become shorter and less frequent.

To be sure, there are many purists in the social sciences who insist that no one should ever make a statement until he can demonstrate it with precise and accurate mathematical proof. The trouble with this position is that the propositions which can pass such a rigorous test are generally the most trivial ones. When methodology and methodologists are permitted to run rampant, significant issues are often barred from discussion. Many of the really important problems in social science must be handled in a descriptive and qualitative fashion. What is more, even a little informed intuition often helps.

In analyzing industrial conflict we are relatively fortunate in that we do have a great deal of quantitative data. Much of the material is not as exact as we would like, but we must do what we can with what we have. As we see it, the important thing is that despite the inaccuracies, there is sufficient corroboration to indicate that we are dealing with basic changes in strike activity, and not merely with statistical shadows and fantasies.

(e) Finally, we should comment on the use of averages, ratios, and percentages which we have devised as comparative measures of strike activity. The use of averages should not be objectionable if it is made clear that they are only meant to indicate central tendencies. How else can a pointless mass of detail be made manageable? If history were not boiled off into oversimplifications, both the writers and the readers would drown in minutiae.

For example, we show that the average duration of strikes in Australia is about two days. Of course, there are quite a few longer ones. In 1956–57, for example, 76 per cent of strikes lasted two days or less, 12 per cent lasted three days to a week, and 12 per cent more than a week.[8]

We state that the strike in the United States is still a real trial of economic strength between workers and employers, basing this proposition on the fact that average striker has been away from his job about fifteen days during recent years. Obviously this does not mean that all strikes last fifteen days. Actually a great many are shorter; in 1957, 42 per cent lasted less than one week and 22 per cent lasted "one week and less than one-half month." These are not the significant disputes, however, and do not define the character of industrial conflict in the United States. The longer stoppages account for most of the man-days of idleness; 80 per cent were incurred in strikes lasting more than one-half month.[9]

One more example will suffice. In later chapters we point out the characteristic strike in the Mediterranean-Asian group is not a test of staying power dealing with basic terms of employment but a brief demonstration over working conditions, rank and file grievances, political issues, arbitration awards, and so forth. Still, there are many disputes over basic terms of employment just as there are many that last more than a few days. In about 30 per cent of Indian strikes from 1947 to 1953 the issue was "wages and allowances." Similarly, 24.9 per cent of Australian strikes in the 1930–50 period involved "wages and hours." [10]

Thus, although statistical measures conceal much of the variety and complexity of human affairs, they do indicate what is characteristic, prevalent, and significant.

NOTES TO CHAPTER 4

1. C. G. Jung, *The Undiscovered Self* (Boston: Little, Brown, and Co., 1958), pp. 9–10.

2. Statistics in the foregoing paragraph are from International Labor Office, *Yearbook of Labor Statistics* (Geneva: 1956), pp. 454–59; and U. S. Department of Labor, *Directory of Labor Organizations,* volumes for Asia and Australia and for Africa (Washington: 1958, mimeo.), *passim.*

3. See Arthur M. Ross, "The Natural History of the Strike," in A. Kornhauser, R. Dubin, and A. M. Ross (eds.), *Industrial Conflict* (New York: McGraw-Hill Book Co., 1954), pp. 23–36.

4. Richard A. Lester, *As Unions Mature* (Princeton: Princeton University Press, 1958), pp. 121–22.

5. *Ibid.,* p. 125.

6. Clark Kerr, F. H. Harbison, J. T. Dunlop, and C. A. Myers. "The Labour Problem in Economic Development," *International Labour Review,* 72 (March 1955), pp. 13–14.

7. See Albert Rees, "Industrial Conflict and Business Fluctuations," in Kornhauser, Dubin, and Ross, *op cit.,* pp. 213–20.

8. Australian Department of Labour and National Service, *Industrial Disputes in Australia* (Melbourne, 1958), p. 15.

9. U. S. Department of Labor, Bureau of Labor Statistics, *Analysis of Work Stoppages, 1957,* Bulletin 1234 (Washington, 1958), p. 23.

10. Australian Department of Labour and National Service, *op cit.,* p. 22.

CHAPTER 5

The Withering Away
of the Strike

In this chapter, we endeavor to explain the general decline in strike activity throughout much of the industrialized world. We are referring primarily to the Northern European countries—Denmark, Netherlands, United Kingdom, Germany, Norway, and Sweden—where both membership involvement and duration of strikes have markedly diminished. To a lesser extent the discussion applies also to the United States and Canada, where the decline in strike activity has been more moderate. In addition, we will note some developments in a few of the other countries we have studied.

In our opinion there are three primary reasons why the strike has been going out of style. First, employers have developed more sophisticated policies and more effective organizations. Second, the state has become more prominent as an employer of labor, economic planner, provider of benefits, and supervisor of industrial relations. Third, in many countries (although not in the United States) the labor movement has been forsaking the use of the strike in favor of broad political endeavors.

One further point should be mentioned as a possibility rather than stated as an established fact. It may well be that rank-and-file union

42

members are not so predisposed towards strikes as they formerly were. This question was raised rather sharply in the United States during 1959, when journalists and public-opinion experts conducted attitude surveys among the members of the United Steelworkers of America and reported a notable lack of enthusiasm over the possibility of a strike.

Whether the inherent propensity to strike has declined is a psychological issue and we are not equipped to consider it authoritatively. Despite the popularity and prestige of interdisciplinary research, there is still some virtue in knowing what one is talking about. The phenomena we analyze in this volume are behavioral, not psychological. Generally the strike reflects worker dissatisfaction, to be sure; but it is not essential to our line of argument to state that dissatisfaction has decreased. Industrial discontent is only a raw material. Strikes may or may not be fashioned out of it. The economic and institutional context of employment relations will determine the gradient or channel in which discontent is directed.

Nevertheless, the possible decline in the psychological propensity to strike is an interesting issue. We shall discuss it briefly before turning to other matters, but we do so in order to open up the issue, not to close it.

Are Workers Less Inclined to Strike?

Many psychologists would insist that labor unrest is a more or less constant factor because of its subjective character. They hold that discontent is a relative matter depending on the difference between expectations and achievements. As the level of attainment rises, the level of anticipation moves up at least as rapidly.

> We have seen that man's needs are almost constantly growing and proliferating—the achievement of one goal merely sets the stage for a higher level of aspiration. . . . A wage rate is psychologically inadequate, no matter how large in absolute amount, if it results in a wide discrepancy between the worker's level of aspiration and his level of achievement.[1]

Evidence supporting this point of view is not difficult to find. The dogged pursuit of constantly more demanding middle-class consumption standards can be cited. The husbands vie for overtime opportunity and take second jobs. The wives stay at work until the children come, and return to work when the children are old enough for school. If materialism shows any signs of flagging the advertising industry moves in to repair the damage.

Some cogent arguments can be offered in rebuttal, however. The first would run somewhat as follows: Although discontent is the normal condition of mankind, the specific content of discontent does change from time to time. Whereas Northern Europeans and North Americans are as dissatisfied as ever, they tend to be disturbed more about personal, sexual, and other non-economic problems. (Compare the enrollment in economics and psychology courses.)

Extreme poverty has been greatly reduced in these countries. Economic inequality has declined as a result of the income tax and other social policies of government. Snobbery and bitterness have mellowed,[2] whereas they remain harsh in other parts of the world. The suffering and deprivation of the nineteenth century factory worker, which novelist and historian have described so poignantly, are probably of a different order from the rather technical and relativistic grievances of the present-day union member. Although there may not be any great number of people who achieve personal fulfillment in work, at the same time it can be argued that workers do not hate their jobs and their bosses as passionately as they formerly did.

In this connection Richard A. Lester observes that

> high levels of employment, continually rising living standards, and more equal distribution of income have brought significant changes in the structure of our economy and in union programs. . . . Class lines in this country have become more blurred in recent years as the number of semi-skilled, white collar, and technical jobs have expanded relative to unskilled employment, and as differences in family incomes have narrowed for such reasons as the compression of wage differentials, the wage-earning wife, and highly progressive tax rates.[3]

The characteristic passivity and dependence of the present-day unionist in regard to collective bargaining and strike decisions can be related to these developments. Labor unrest must not only be rationalized and restrained,[4] but also instilled and cultivated. There are three groups in the modern union: the officials, a minority of activists, and the passive majority. The activists can be counted on to exhibit militant sentiments, but the passive majority must often be indoctrinated. In well-organized unions they are ready and willing to be educated as to the necessity of a strike. When the signal is given they are prepared to commence hostilities. When a cease-fire is ordered, they ratify the settlement and return to work. They are cooperative, but they are passive. Of course, there are exceptions, but generally the members look to the leaders for the tactical and strategical decisions that are necessary to secure the bread-and-butter benefits they expect.[5] Furthermore, whereas the national union formerly exerted a cautious and conservative influence, today it must frequently take steps to ensure that local unions do not make agreements undercutting national objectives. No longer can it be taken for granted that the national representative will be "softer" than the local official.

Thus it can be argued that class antagonisms and spontaneous inclinations to strike have declined. There are related influences connected with the new style of life in Northern Europe and North America. Families with middle-class mores and living standards resist any extended interruption of income. Strange as it may seem, the pressure to meet installment payments and support an elevated consumption level is greater than the pressure to maintain cash income at the margin of subsistence. Furthermore, the strike served as a respite from long and unremitting hours of work in older times but no longer does so. As late as World War II the holiday motif was unmistakable, particularly in the first few days of a strike. With forty-hour weeks, paid vacations, and paid holidays, this function has largely atrophied.

Finally, we can point to the growing prominence of white-collar and professional employees in the labor force and the labor unions. It will generally be agreed that these groups, as well as female workers, are disinclined to strike. There is an evident correlation between patterns of strike activity in various countries and the relative importance of white-collar workers in their labor movements. Where the white-collar workers make up a large proportion of union membership, either the strike weapon is seldom used or else stoppages are typically brief.

We find that in Denmark, more than half of the white-collar employees and foremen are enrolled in unions. In Norway about one-fifth to one-third of the salaried workers are union members, the exact proportion depending on whether certain groups such as railway clerks and marine engineers are considered salaried. To ensure adequate representation of the white-collar group, an association of salaried workers exists as an "advisory body" within the central confederation of labor. It is said that approximately 50 per cent of the "eligible" or organizable white-collar employees in Sweden have accepted membership. Typically these salaried workers belong to separate unions, and the salaried unions have their own federation.

White-collar unionism is quite extensive in the Netherlands. It is difficult to estimate the exact percentage of salaried employees belonging to unions, for the reason that the statistics on government and public utility employment do not show any breakdown between white-collar and manual categories. There are some 800,000 salaried employees; in 1956 approximately 390,000 employees of state and local governments and public utilities belonged to unions, and the white-collar union membership in private industry was about 126,000. Thus, perhaps half of all salaried employees are unionized, and in any event a substantial proportion are.

In the United Kingdom the white-collar workers are fairly well organized, especially the government servants, teachers, and employees of banking and insurance companies. Employees in the distributive trades are organized in substantial numbers, but not overwhelmingly. All in all, white-collar unionism in Britain is much greater than in the United States but probably weaker than in Scandinavia.

The German salaried employees and civil servants are fairly well organized. Both groups have established their own unions and federations, apparently desiring to preserve their separate identities apart from the manual workers. The salaried employees' federation now includes nearly 500,000 members.

White-collar unionism is also well developed in the countries characterized by frequent, brief strikes of the "demonstration" type. This is the one area in which French unions are solidly established. The bulk of the members of the anti-Communist Force Ouvrière, and a substantial proportion of the Catholic Confédération are in civil service and salaried unions. For that matter the Communist-led CGT also has strong unions in these fields. Perhaps half of the white-collar employees are organized. In Japan, white-collar unionism is the backbone of the labor movement. Salaried workers play a leading role in the widespread "enterprise unions," which are limited to the employees of a single plant. Furthermore, approximately one-third of all union members are government servants. And in India, insofar as any unionism is strong, this can be said of white-collar unionism. In fact, most of the 800,000 members of the Socialist-sponsored federation (the second largest group) are postal and communication workers, government employees, and teachers.

Significantly, the importance of white-collar unionism is much less in Finland, Canada, and the United States, the only countries studied in which strikes are relatively frequent and also relatively long. The salaried union federation in Finland has only about 65,000 members, representing about one-fifth of all salaried employees. Although there are no good Canadian statistics on this point, we can estimate that no more than 10 per cent of the white-collar workers in that country belong to unions. In the United States the Bureau of Labor Statistics calculates that approximately 2,500,000 white-collar employees are union members—less than 15 per cent of all unionists and a much smaller proportion of wage and salary earners in the white-collar trades.[6]

Employer Policies and Organizations

After the foregoing digression on subjective inclination to strike, we turn to developments in employer policies, government activities, and union programs.

The profound changes in managerial attitudes toward the worker and toward the union are so well understood that it will not be necessary to dwell on them at any length. For this reason we shall content ourselves with a few reminders, primarily from the experience and literature of the United States. To document the matter exhaustively with respect to eight separate countries would seem a rather tedious and pointless exercise.

The "metamorphosis of the employment relationship" has been so great that Lester calls it a "revolution in industrial employment."

> Around employment has grown a network of employer obligations and employee rights that involve not only the dignity and welfare of the individual worker but also the security and well being of members of his family . . . the pre World War I "commodity concept" of employment has been displaced by a post World War II "welfare concept" of employer-employee relations.[7]

The change has been so pronounced that modern employers are criticized not for hardhearted indifference but rather for oppressive solicitude. Obviously the new emphasis has not been limited to the United States, although it may have been carried farthest here. "Human relations," along with automation, has been a favorite topic of the numerous Northern European visitors who have made the circuit of American universities during the past decade.

"Rightly or wrongly," say Brown and Myers, "there is a pervasive belief in the existence of a positive correlation between the degree of 'morale,' 'job satisfaction,' or 'loyalty,' on the one hand, and the productive efficiency of the enterprise on the other hand. At the very least there is widespread acceptance of the proposition that prevention of dissatisfaction pays off." [8] And though many "human relations" efforts may have been fatuous or misdirected, it is evident that the whole "welfare concept" of employment has contributed toward lessening the incidence of strikes.

Likewise, it is well established that employers in the older industrialized countries have generally accommodated themselves to unionism and collective bargaining. Once regarded as subversive and insurrectionary, the union is now accepted as a permanent, and perhaps even a welcome, part of the enterprise. Resistance has fallen away at different times—fifty years ago in the United Kingdom, forty years ago in Sweden, twenty years ago in the United States—but in most of these countries the basic organizing struggle is fairly ancient history.

The change in employer attitudes has not stopped there, however. Building amicable relations with the union is generally regarded as a primary duty of management. Some years ago the European employers who visited the United States routinely pointed out the contrast between their own propitiatory policies and the more primitive approach of their American brethren. The contrast becomes weaker and weaker, however. Most corporations want directors (or vice-presidents) of industrial relations who can get along with the union and keep the peace. Their duties include "acceptance of the (frequently long drawn out) ritualistic procedures of the bargaining process, recognition that the same substantive results of bargaining may be reached by paths which, alternatively, build up the union leader or throw him to the wolves. . . ." [9] In other words, they understand the more sophisticated requirements of a live-and-let-live policy.

There are cross currents, to be sure. "Boulwareism" in the United States is one example. But these are not in the mainstream of development. The pronouncements of the National Association of Manufacturers should not be mistaken for the labor policy of American management at the operating level. "Perhaps the institutional needs of an organization like the NAM can be met only by maintaining an immutable philosophical position on such issues as unionism, where the identity of the adversary is clear." [10] Much more indicative is the obliging manner in which the auto companies bent over backwards to preserve the amenities during the summer of 1958 while the union elected to work without a contract.

There have been interesting personality changes in the type of men chosen for top positions in industrial relations. Just as the buccaneering railroad magnates of the nineteenth century have passed into limbo; just as the highbinding bankers and brokers of the 1920's have been replaced by a tamer, soberer, and less imaginative generation; so have the personnel and labor relations managers become blander, less excited about fundamental principles, more interested in practical results, more conciliatory. In fact, they are criticized more often today for wanting peace at any price than for excessive belligerency.

These changes in employer attitudes and policies could not have occurred if the unions had not adjusted themselves to the values and customs of the business community. Again we speak primarily from observation of American practice, but there is no doubt that the statement is accurate as to other countries. Although the Northern

European unions are politically affiliated with socialist parties, in their bargaining relations they are properly classified as business unions. The revolutionary aspirations formerly professed by many unions have disappeared along with the *mystique* of the syndicalist general strike. Like the American unions, they have accepted the doctrine that collective bargaining procedures should be reasonable and orderly; that a bargaining agreement is a binding contract; and that strikes, when they do occur, should be conducted so as to minimize unnecessary damage to the industry, inconvenience to the community, and loss of public opinion.

In the process of accommodation, numerous supposedly irreconcilable conflicts of principle, which at one time were fruitful sources of industrial warfare, have been reconciled. Some forty years ago, Robert F. Hoxie, a pioneer student of the labor movement, concluded that trade unionism and scientific management were incompatible. Since then job evaluation, time study, and other appurtenances of scientific management have been absorbed into collective bargaining systems both here and abroad, and today we seldom hear of any alleged incompatibility except in debates among trade union intellectuals. At one time unionism was regarded as a serious threat to industrial discipline, and discipline did break down in many newly organized plants. But where industrial relations have matured, discipline has been reintegrated into collective bargaining. Principles of due process and consistency have been introduced, and on the other hand many employer concepts of shop administration have been accepted in union circles. This is particularly true as to various obligations of the employee—to render continuous service during the period of an agreement, to meet established production standards, to obey instructions from supervisors, and to observe shop rules.

Organization among employers has played an important part in reducing strike activity. Multi-employer bargaining has become predominant in many industrialized countries, and even in the United States, the stronghold of individualism, multi-employer contracts cover about one-third of all represented workers.

Now it is not universally agreed that multi-employer bargaining is conducive to industrial peace.[11] We believe that it is, however. For one reason, employers as well as workers now have experienced professional leadership. Just as unions eliminate improvident emotional gestures by the rank and file, likewise employer associations exclude reckless or primitive attitudes to which small businessmen in particular are subject. The specialized skills of negotiation are made available, so that face and prestige, as well as money, are disposed of in a workmanlike fashion. The knowledge that any strike will be large and expensive serves as a deterrent to both sides, to the extent that employers are able to hold their organization together and prevent fragments from being split away.

Furthermore, employers within an industry do not have to worry about suffering a competitive disadvantage when all of them are subject to the same demands. The unions are not able to "whipsaw" employers by playing one off against another. At the same time the unions tend to be less aggressive since different branches are not competing to make the best showing within the industry.[12]

Role of the State

A second reason for the general decline in labor-management conflict is the heightened activity on the part of the state as operator of public enterprise, economic planner, protector of labor, and supervisor of industrial disputes. As laissez-faire policies have gone out of fashion and governments have assumed a more influential role in the economy, the strike has been pushed into a less prominent position.

The amount of socialized industry in the Western countries is not very great, but is still large enough to affect the incidence of strikes. Railroads, coal mines, electric power, the telephone and telegraph industries, airlines, radio broadcasting, and other utilities are frequently under public ownership. Occasionally certain financial and manufacturing establishments are socialized. In addition, regular civil service employees now constitute a sizable proportion of the labor force in these countries.

Strikes against public enterprises are not unknown, it is true, but brief demonstration strikes are more common than real contests of economic strength, and political solutions are even more likely. Moreover, the unions are frequently implicated in the administration of nationalized industries.

Where the state plays an active role in economic planning, it has a strong motive to ensure that its plans are not frustrated. This motive has been important in the United Kingdom and Scandinavia since World War II, and in the "underdeveloped nations" which are endeavoring to industrialize rapidly. In these newer countries the governments have also been successful in appealing to sentiments of nationalism and patriotism in order to forestall industrial conflict.

Through protective legislation and social security programs, the state disposes of issues that might otherwise be the focus of labor-manage-

ment conflict.   Americans are likely to underestimate the real importance of this point.   The legal minimum wage does not determine
the actual wage of very many organized workers in the United States.
Our fringe benefits are worked out privately.   In other countries the
minimum wage is often highly significant, and there may be national
or state legislation dealing with paid holidays, paid vacations, maternity
leave, sick leave, and related matters.   We have a negotiated social
security system which is perhaps the equal of our government program.
Other countries do not.

Government programs for terminating labor disputes must be discussed at somewhat greater length because opinions differ as to the
effect of such programs.

Space does not permit any exhaustive listing of dispute-settlement
techniques, but a few examples can be given.   Conciliation services
are provided wherever collective bargaining is practiced.   This is the
extent of the American government's program in normal cases, although additional procedures are provided for some exceptional kinds
of disputes.   Other countries have moved further along various lines
as appeared most expedient.   Thus Finland, Germany, and the Scandinavian countries have labor courts to interpret collective bargaining
agreements.   Recommendations by Danish mediators are frequently
enacted into law.   In Germany, the minister of labor can "extend" a
privately negotiated agreement to a whole industry once 50 per cent
of employees in the industry are covered by it.   There is a similar system in the Netherlands.   Australia has its famous compulsory arbitration machinery about which so much has been written.   The United
Kingdom has its statutory wage boards.   There was compulsory arbitration in that country between 1940 and 1951, and the arbitration machinery has been preserved, by agreement of the parties, in certain
industries.   Compulsory mediation is practiced in Canada and Norway.
Finally, in those nations with highly centralized collective bargaining
systems, the government generally exerts a powerful though informal
influence in "peak associations" of management and labor.

How much these techniques have contributed to reducing industrial conflict cannot be stated exactly.   Some authors minimize their
significance and say that their only effect is to impede the development
of mature bargaining relations and prevent the emergence of a stable
equilibrium of power between labor and management.   It is pointed
out that the government procedures can be discounted and manipulated
by sophisticated representatives, that the government cannot feasibly
prohibit strikes in a democratic society, that all the procedures in the

world cannot produce agreement where there is no desire to agree, etc. The futilitarian view is oversimplified, in our opinion. The effect of these procedures on the frequency and the duration of strikes depends upon their relationship with the country's collective bargaining system. If they obstruct and impede collective bargaining, the net result may well be to increase industrial conflict. If they support the collective bargaining system, however, or provide a workable substitute for it, they can serve to reduce strike activity.

A few examples of the varying relationships between dispute-settlement procedures and collective-bargaining systems may help to clarify this point. Under postwar mediation statutes in Canada, cooling-off periods are imposed and a compulsory two-stage conciliation procedure is invoked in virtually all labor disputes. At the second stage the conciliation boards must submit their own recommendations for settling disputes. According to Stuart Jamieson and other observers, this requirement obstructs the bargaining process, makes strikes more difficult to settle, and help to explain the fact that the average duration of strikes has been rising in Canada, in contrast to the trend elsewhere.

> Where unions and employers are compelled by law to submit their disputes to such procedure, the effect is often to circumvent or distort the process of collective bargaining. In many cases the representatives of the parties to a dispute take rigid positions beforehand, refuse to make any substantial concessions necessary to reach agreement, and then depend upon the conciliation board to get them "off the hook." More frequently, perhaps, collective bargaining does not really begin until after the lengthy and complicated conciliation procedures required by law have been completed. Each party saves its main ammunition for the conciliation board, in the hope of getting a majority recommendation that will support its case against the other party.[13]

A very different relationship between dispute-settlement procedures and collective bargaining is found in some of the Northern European countries with highly centralized bargaining structures. Private agreements are "extended" throughout whole industries by means of legislation, or the recommendations of mediators are enacted into law. These programs should not be thought of as eliminating the need for agreement. It is undeniable that agreement is the keystone of a functioning collective-bargaining system. At some level there must be some individuals, representing labor and management in some capacity, who must agree. But in these highly integrated systems it is not enough that a few individuals find themselves in accord. The accord must be effective. Often there are numerous and heterogeneous groups within the employer community and the labor movement, with somewhat differentiated interests and highly differentiated opinions, and the problem is to bring all these groups into line. To make a proper adjustment in the basic wage of the German steel industry, let us say, is not terribly difficult from a purely intellectual standpoint. To gain acquiescence is another matter altogether, and for this purpose the decision must have sufficient status, solemnity, and legitimacy. It is here, we believe, that the function of extended settlement procedures in the centralized bargaining structures is to be found.

One reason why the propensity to strike has declined so greatly in India appears to be the widespread use of the government's conciliation and arbitration machinery. As we point out in Chapter 9 many trade unions have "outside leaders," consisting of doctors, lawyers, etc., who furnish guidance on behalf of the Congress Party. When a dispute arises, the outside leader attempts to work out solutions with the employer. If he is unsuccessful, the controversy can be taken to a government conciliator, who in turn is empowered to submit it to compulsory arbitration. These procedures cannot be described as supporting collective bargaining. Instead they supplant it, or at least alter it to the point where "most of the bargaining takes place between the government and the employers rather than between employers and employees." [14] Nevertheless, they seem to work.

The program of the National War Labor Board in the United States during World War II is another case in point. Under the sanction of the no-strike, no-lockout pledge, the Board arbitrated more than 20,000 industrial disputes. This program might be defined as extremely centralized bargaining among the labor, industry, and public members of the board; or instead it might be regarded as a substitute for bargaining. At any event, there were virtually no official strikes until the end of the war; the average duration of strikes was 57 per cent lower in 1942–44 than in 1939–41; and loss of working time in proportion to union membership dropped correspondingly. In contrast, the National Wage Stabilization Board was not successful either in stabilizing wages or in preventing strikes during the Korean War. There was insufficient sanction from the parties: labor did not really accept wage control, and industry would not consent to governmental adjudication of disputes.

American railway labor legislation furnishes another example. The Transportation Act of 1920 was not properly related to the collective bargaining system of the industry, but was imposed from the outside. "The Act failed in its purpose, the Railroad Labor Board lost caste, its decisions were openly flouted by both the employers and the employees, until the whole enforcement machinery of the Act broke down." [15]

In contrast, the Railway Labor Act of 1926 was developed by the parties themselves as an extension of their own bargaining relationship, and enacted by Congress at their own request. Although the act has been a most imperfect instrument, for the most part it has been successful in preventing major strikes.

Finally, the compulsory arbitration procedures in Australia have had very different effects from one industry to another, depending on the general context of industrial relations in these industries. Kenneth Walker points out that

> in some industries circumstances favor peaceful relations in any case, and in some the intervention of arbitration has provided a stabilizing influence on the pattern of industrial relations. In others again, arbitration may exacerbate bad relations. . . . Probably the most that can be said is that where the conditioning circumstances would predispose the parties to be intransigent in any case, the arbitration system tends to encourage this attitude and provides further opportunity for its exercise.[16]

Thus the effect of government dispute-settlement programs on the volume of strike activity is complicated and not subject to generalization. But sustained and purposeful human effort generally achieves its objectives to some extent, and we see no reason to doubt that the repeated efforts of governments throughout the world to reduce overt manifestations of industrial conflict have had a certain amount of success.

Clearly the state plays a vastly different role in labor relations today than in the nineteenth century when the strike assumed its classical form. In his excellent study *Strikes* Knowles remarks:

> There is a third party which has been acquiring a dominant interest in industrial affairs. The increased participation of the State in these matters has brought it into touch with the Unions more intimately than ever before. To an increasing extent it has come to protect the worker; to an increasing extent it employs him. Not only are its functions tending to overlap with traditional Trade Union functions; not only has it become the biggest employer of labor; but Unions are acquiring something of a niche in the edifice of administration.[17]

Knowles is speaking of the United Kingdom, and is describing a situation that obtains only partially in the United States. In other countries it holds more completely, however, and it may well be on the wave of the future.

Abstention from Strikes

In suggesting that unions are abstaining from the strike weapon, we do not imply that the right to strike is unimportant, nor that the threat of a strike is ineffective, nor that picket-line struggles are being dropped from union myth and ritual, but only that the actual use of the strike as a conventional implement is dwindling. All the changes described above are working in that direction, but there are further reasons connected more closely with the strike itself.

To begin with, strikes are expensive to the union and its members. It is true that from the standpoint of the economy as a whole, they constitute a minor source of economic loss in most countries. But the forfeiture of all cash income is not a minor matter for the individuals directly involved and cannot be considered a convenient method of achieving one's objectives. It could certainly be expected that unions would endeavor to develop better methods, particularly as real incomes rise. As we have noted, the worker who is endeavoring to maintain a middle-class scale of consumption seems to have less tolerance for interruptions of income than the worker living at subsistence level.

The outcome of work stoppages generally has not been favorable to the unions. Picking the winner of a strike is notoriously difficult, but the attempt has been made in a number of countries, and the statistical results are sufficiently similar to invite attention. K. Forchheimer has studied these statistics for the United Kingdom, France, Germany, Sweden, and the United States, covering several decades in each instance. He concludes:

> Considerably less disputes ended "in favour of the workers" than "in favour of the employers" in all countries with the exception of the United States; the differences are even greater when we examine the number of workers involved in them. On the average not more than 20–30 per cent of the *disputes* ended with a workers' success in the European countries; and the share of *workers involved* in them is considerably smaller, in Sweden not more than 7 or 8 per cent on the average.[18]

Forchheimer points out that the percentage of victories is not a conclusive measure of success, for the reason that the largest number of strikes are in the "compromise" group. Obviously it is impossible to state whether compromise strikes are generally worthwhile to the union. Two additional facts are significant. First, the larger strikes were less successful than smaller strikes in each of the five countries. Second, the trend over time was adverse to the unions.

> One would perhaps expect that the percentage of compromises would rise more or less steadily during the last decades, that the results in favour of the workers would increase proportionally and those in favour of the employers would decrease. But the movements as shown by our figures are different. In the main industrial European countries (in the United Kingdom, in Germany and also in France) the share of *employers' victories* is

slightly falling only until about 1919 or 1920, but rising distinctly after-
wards; compromises show an opposite movement, rising only up to about
1920, then falling.[19]

In Sweden, however, the trend was contrary, showing a steady increase
in compromises at the expense of employer victories. Forchheimer
states that the American figures are difficult to interpret, because of
changes in statistical methods during the period studied. "The figures
such as they are suggest a rise in the percentage of compromises . . .
and a fall in workers' victories." [20]

Actually the Bureau of Labor Statistics changed its· classification of
results several times before giving up the attempt altogether in the
1940's. About all that can be said is that (a) American unionists have
had considerably better luck in strikes than European unionists; (b) the
proportion of workers' victories was considerably higher in the late nineteenth century than ever since; and (c) long strikes have at all times
been less successful than short strikes.[21] The following tabulation for
1927–36 is representative:

Results of Strikes Ending 1927–36, in Relation to Their Duration

Percentage of Strikes Resulting in

Duration	Substantial Gains to Workers	Partial Gains or Compromises	Little or No Gain to Workers	Other
Less than 1 week	39.7	19.3	35.5	5.5
1 week and less than ½ month	39.2	26.4	29.9	4.5
½ and less than 1 month	36.3	27.1	32.0	4.6
1 and less than 2 months	26.2	24.7	43.0	6.1
2 and less than 3 months	24.8	30.1	39.1	6.0
3 months and over	21.9	25.8	48.2	4.1

Source: Florence Peterson, *Strikes in the United States, 1880–1936* (Washington: U. S. Department of Labor, Bureau of Labor Statistics, 1938), p. 77.

Strikes lasting more than a month yielded substantial gains in only
one-quarter of the cases. Almost half brought few or no gains. Now it
is true that the great majority of strikes (about 75 per cent) last less

than a month. Those lasting more than a month, however, account for the bulk of man-days of idleness. In 1927–36, more than 70 per cent of man-days were consumed in these longer strikes.[22] In other words, if man-days of idleness can be considered as the workers' investment in strikes, then 70 per cent of the investment was sunk into relatively unprofitable enterprises.

Needless to say, we are not presuming to criticize the strike policies of unions nor to suggest that other decisions would have been preferable under the circumstances. These facts merely show that unions have had a motive to find other ways of achieving their purposes. They indicate particularly that unions would endeavor to avoid *long* strikes.

Knowles presents a detailed analysis of strikes in the United Kingdom. Workers fared worse in the 1930's and 1940's than prior to 1920. The proportion of compromise settlements declined over the years. Employers were winning more than half the strikes in the later period. Here also the short strikes have been more successful than the long ones. Knowles warns that the figures are difficult to interpret, and do not prove that union bargaining power was in a decline. They do prove, however, that strikes as such were not especially fruitful.[23]

Furthermore, the unfavorable aftereffects of strike waves and general strikes have probably inhibited major reliance on the strike weapon. These episodes have often been succeeded either by rapid loss of membership or the enactment of regulatory laws. In the United States, union membership declined greatly after the strike waves of 1885–86 and 1919–20; and the strike wave of 1945–46 was a major element in the passage of the Taft-Hartley Act. The Swedish general strike of 1909 led to such great membership losses and such a severe decline in the number of collective agreements that the prestrike levels were not surpassed for nearly a decade. The British general strike of 1926 was followed by the Trade Disputes Act. The aftermath of the massive Communist strikes in France and Italy during the late 1940's should also be noted. Claimed membership in France, which stood at 7,000,000 in 1947, fell off to 4,400,000 in 1949 and 2,200,000 in 1955. Similarly the number of Italian unionists dropped from 9,000,000 in 1948 to fewer than 6,000,000 in 1956.[24] Thus, overuse of the strike weapon has often brought on its own retribution.

As a result of this experience, union ideology concerning industrial conflict has changed. A strong syndicalist strain was present in some of the nineteenth century labor movements. Wholly aside from its short-run tactical function, the strike was considered useful in sharpening the inherent revolutionary potential of the workers and increasing

the bitterness between the classes, thus hastening the day of the cata-
clysmic general strike which would open up the era of socialism. All
this has passed, and syndicalism is dead. Modern unions, except for
those under Communist leadership, practice vigorous economy in the use
of the strike, and have turned to political action in order to achieve
broad economic and social changes.

Our final point is that labor political action, labor parties, and labor
governments have helped pave the way toward renunciation of the
strike.

Through political action, labor is offered the opportunity to gain its
objectives without sacrificing income. As noted earlier, going without
pay for an unpredictable period of time is certainly an awkward method
of prosecuting one's aims. It could have been expected that more
convenient techniques would be sought.

Political action is more dignified and respectable than industrial
conflict, which inevitably resembles guerilla warfare and often brings
annoyance and inconvenience to the general public. It is more in keeping with the social status of the union official once he has been accepted
into the "power elite" in his country, and more in line with the middle-
class orientation of workers in advanced industrial societies.

Clearly the instrumentalities of the state are more powerful than the
apparatus of collective bargaining. This is no place to review the
perpetual controversy as to whether unions can influence the level of
money wages, the level of real wages, and the distribution of income
through collective bargaining. What is, must be, the philosopher says;
but many economists are unconvinced. Just as some scientists have
shown that a bumblebee is incapable of flight and a baseball cannot be
thrown in a curve, likewise some economists have demonstrated that
unions cannot affect wages. To avoid misunderstanding, let us say
that in our opinion, unions do raise the level of money wages, and do
redistribute income between unorganized and organized workers. That
they can raise real wages and change the distribution of income between
labor and property owners has not been established.[25] But these issues
need not be decided here, for it is clear that the state can influence the
worker's economic welfare more powerfully through tax policy, public
spending, economic planning, and social welfare legislation than the
unions can affect it through collective bargaining. And as Clark Kerr
has shown, the efficacy of these programs in redistributing income cannot be doubted.[26]

American workers, it is true, have had greater industrial strength and
lesser political strength than European workers. Their industrial strength

has been greater because employers are more poorly organized than in Europe, because productivity has risen so rapidly, and because American firms are less dependent on the world market. Their political strength has been lesser because of the "voluntaristic" tradition and the complexities of the federal system. These differences help to explain why American unions still rely strongly on industrial action.

What Knowles calls "the shifting of the strategical field from that of mere wages and working conditions to include the most comprehensive political objectives" [27] could not have occurred without the necessary theoretical basis in twentieth century economics and the corresponding development of govermental techniques. Nineteenth century Socialism presented a detailed indictment of the capitalist economy but was vague as to remedies. In the post-Keynesian era this condition no longer prevails.

Thus, changes in employer policies, dispute-settlement techniques, government functions, and union programs have combined, in a context of relatively stable union membership, to reduce the level of strike activity. There are countervailing pressures, to be sure: "shop steward revolts," unofficial strikes, and other forms of insurgency within the ranks of labor; corresponding movements in the employer community; disturbances of power relations between management and labor resulting from economic and political changes, and so on. But these unsettling influences have clearly been weaker than the tranquilizing forces.

NOTES TO CHAPTER 5

1. David Krech and Richard S. Crutchfield, *Theory and Problems of Social Psychology* (New York: McGraw-Hill Book Co., 1948), p. 542.

2. See J. Kenneth Galbraith, *The Affluent Society* (Boston: Houghton Mifflin, 1958), Chapters III–VIII, pp. 21–121.

3. Richard A. Lester, *As Unions Mature* (Princeton: Princeton University Press, 1958), p. 42.

4. G. D. H. Cole, *A Short History of the British Working Class Movement 1789–1848*, Vol. 1 (London: George Allen and Unwin, 1925), pp. 12–110, *passim;* and John R. Commons, et al., *History of Labor in the United States,* Vol. 1 (New York: MacMillan, 1918), pp. 109–55, 412–16.

5. A. M. Ross, *Trade Union Wage Policy* (Berkeley: University of California Press, 1948), Chapter 2, pp. 22–44.

6. For data on white-collar unionism in the United States, see *Directory of National and International Labor Unions in the United States,* U. S. Department of Labor, Bureau of Labor Statistics, Bulletin 1222, 1958, p. 12. Sources of information on union membership in the other countries are listed in certain of the notes at the end of Chapters 7 through 11.

7. Richard A. Lester, "Revolution in Industrial Employment," *Labor Law Journal,* 9 (June 1958), p. 439.

8. Douglas V. Brown and Charles A. Myers, "The Changing Industrial Relations Philosophy of American Management," *Proceedings of the Ninth Annual Meeting, Industrial Relations Research Association* (Madison, Wisc., 1957), p. 89.

9. *Ibid.,* p. 93.

10. *Ibid.,* p. 95.

11. Adolf Sturmthal expresses the contrary opinion in "Some Comments on 'Strike Experience in Five Countries,'" *Industrial and Labor Relations Review,* 6 (April 1953), pp. 391–94.

12. See Clark Kerr and L. H. Fisher, "Multiple-Employer Bargaining: The San Francisco Experience," in R. A. Lester and Joseph Shister (eds.), *Insights Into Labor Issues* (New York: MacMillan Co., 1948), pp. 419–25; and R. A. Lester and E. A. Robie, *Wages Under National and Regional Collective Bargaining* (Princeton: Industrial Relations Section, Princeton University, 1946).

13. Stuart Jamieson, *Industrial Relations in Canada* (Ithaca: Cornell University Press, 1957), p. 119.

14. Oscar A. Ornati, *Jobs and Workers in India* (Ithaca: Cornell University Press, 1955), pp. 176–77.

15. T. R. Fisher, *Industrial Disputes and Federal Legislation* (New York: Columbia University Press, 1940), p. 167.

16. Kenneth F. Walker, *Industrial Relations in Australia* (Cambridge: Harvard University Press, 1956), p. 365.

17. K. G. J. C. Knowles, *Strikes* (Oxford: Basil Blackwell, 1952), pp. 90–91.

18. K. Forchheimer, "Some International Aspects of the Strike Movement: The Results of Labour Disputes," *Bulletin of the Oxford University Institute of Statistics,* 10 (September 1948), p. 295.

19. *Ibid.,* p. 297.

20. *Ibid.,* p. 300.

21. See Florence Peterson, *Strikes in the United States, 1880–1936* (Washington: U. S. Department of Labor, Bureau of Labor Statistics, 1938), pp. 34, 40, 68–81; and annual bulletins on work stoppages issued by BLS for years subsequent to 1936.

22. Average of annual percentages. Peterson, *op. cit.,* p. 52.

23. Knowles, *op. cit.,* pp. 240–62.

24. As noted in Appendix A, we use Italian union membership statistics which are based on inflated union claims.

25. For various points of view on the unionism-and-wages controversy, see Paul H. Douglas, *Real Wages in the United States, 1890–1926* (Boston: Houghton Mifflin Co., 1930), pp. 95–141; John T. Dunlop, "Productivity and the Wage Structure," in Lloyd A. Metzler and others, *Income, Employment and Public Policy: Essays in Honor of Alvin H. Hansen* (New York: W. W. Norton and Co., 1948), pp. 341–62; Joseph W. Garbarino, "A Theory of Interindustry Wage Structure Variation," *Quarterly Journal of Economics,* 64 (May 1950), pp. 282–305; Arthur M. Ross and William Goldner, "Forces Affecting the Interindustry Wage Structure," *Quarterly Journal of Economics,* 64 (May 1950), pp. 254–81; Walter A. Morton, "Trade Unionism, Full Employment and Inflation," *American Economic Review,* 40 (March 1950), pp. 13–39; Harold M. Levinson, *Unionism, Wage Trends and Income Distribution* (Ann Arbor: University of Michigan Press, 1951); Milton Friedman, "Some Comments on the Significance of Labor Unions for Public

Policy," in David McCord Wright (ed.), *The Impact of the Union* (New York: Harcourt, Brace and Co., 1951), pp. 204–34; Lloyd G. Reynolds, "The General Level of Wages," in G. W. Taylor and F. C. Pierson (eds.), *New Concepts of Wage Determination* (New York: McGraw-Hill Book Co., 1957), pp. 239–59; and Lloyd Ulman, "Marshall and Friedman on Union Strength," *Review of Economics and Statistics,* 37 (November 1955), pp. 384–401. These are only a sample.

26. Clark Kerr, "Trade Unionism and Distributive Shares," *American Economic Review,* 44 (May 1954), pp. 279–92.

27. Knowles, *op. cit.,* p. 61.

CHAPTER 6

Influences

on Relative

Strike Activity

In the preceding chapter we undertook to explain the decline in strike activity which has occurred in numerous countries. But this decline has not proceeded evenly, nor has it been experienced everywhere. As we have seen, there are four distinctive patterns of industrial conflict among the countries we have studied systematically, and three of the countries are best described as special cases. Presumably there are reasons why strikes in Denmark are so unlike those in Finland, why industrial conflict in the United States is a different matter from that in France. The purpose of the present chapter is to identify these reasons by describing the main influences on relative strike activity with varying incidence in the different nations.

A similar attempt was made in "Strike Experience in Five Countries." There several factors were stressed as tending to aggravate industrial warfare: employer resistance, "voluntary choice between membership and non-membership," organizational and jurisdictional conflict, internal leadership rivalries, Communist unionism, single-firm bargaining, and the absence of a labor party. In general, the strike was seen as "a response to difficulties that are encountered by unions in acquiring organizational stability and by union leaders in attaining personal . . . security." And it was held that "these difficulties are the result of competition and freedom of choice in various forms: power conflicts with employers, ambiguous loyalties on the part of workers," etc.[1]

This interpretation worked well enough for Australia, Canada, Great Britain, Sweden, and the United States. All of these countries have similar institutions, including a long-established and well-financed labor movement. All of them put primary reliance on collective bargaining as the main instrument for defining terms of employment. A broader interpretation is necessary, however, for countries in which the whole environment of labor-management relations is different, such as Japan, India, France, and Finland.

For example, "Strike Experience in Five Countries" held that "continuous voluntary choice between membership and non-membership is conducive to agitation and strikes" because "issues are sharpened, grievances promoted, and commotions created in order to keep members in good standing"; but "when, in contrast, union membership is guaranteed, either by contractual arrangement with employers or social pressure and habit among wage earners, apathy and quiescence can be permitted to set in. . . ."[2] This interpretation is valid where the act of joining the union represents a significant decision, membership is a formal status, and the dues are relatively high. But we find many countries in which union membership is a different kind of phenomenon. The work force of an enterprise joins up more or less as a group, the dues are nominal and are not systematically collected, the line between membership and non-membership is a hazy one, and the worker is not called upon to make a considered, individual decision. The environment is so different that the question of individual choice cannot be analyzed in the same way.

The leading influences in relative strike activity which are amenable to comparison between one country and another appear to be the following:

1. *Organizational stability*
   (*a*) Age of the labor movement.
   (*b*) Stability of membership in recent years.
2. *Leadership conflicts in the labor movement*
   (*a*) Factionalism, rival unionism and rival federations.
   (*b*) Strength of Communism in labor unions.

3. *Status of union-management relations*
   (*a*) Degree of acceptance by employers.
   (*b*) Consolidation of bargaining structure.
4. *Labor political activity*
   (*a*) Existence of labor party as a leading political party.
   (*b*) Labor-party governments.
5. *Role of the state*
   (*a*) Extent of government activity in defining terms of employment.
   (*b*) Dispute-settlement policies and procedures.

What is the relationship between these influences on relative strike activity, on the one hand, and the reasons for the decline of industrial conflict in several countries (which were discussed in the preceding chapter), on the other? The answer is that the two classifications overlap to a considerable extent but are not entirely congruent. They differ because Chapter 5 deals principally with Northern Europe and North America, whereas Chapter 6 also covers the Mediterranean-Asian group, Australia, Finland, and South Africa. We must, therefore, have a classification that will explain a broader range of phenomena than we discussed in Chapter 5.

Have we included all the factors that affect the volume and duration of strikes in these fifteen countries? We have not, but only those that are amenable to a comparative analysis. As noted in Chapter 4, every country—like every individual—is essentially unique, but we must concentrate on features that are subject to comparison rather than those that are singular. We have made a few exceptions, but only a few; if each country had been analyzed in its own terms, no generalizations could have been attempted. Furthermore, we could not investigate two or three possible influences because the data were not available. It is possible, for instance, that differences in the industrial structure or "industry mix" have a bearing on relative strike activity.[3] Actually the distribution of non-agricultural employment among the major economic divisions (mining, manufacturing, etc.) is quite similar in most of the countries. To deal with a more detailed industrial classification would have introduced so many complications that it could not feasibly be done within the confines of this study.

Although these influences on strike activity are described separately, they should not be thought of as independent variables. Actually, much depends on how they fit into the total system of industrial relations in each country. When we state, therefore, that a certain factor is conducive to industrial peace or industrial conflict, we mean that it has such an effect in the context where it is typically encountered. The importance of context will be discussed further in the final chapter.

Organizational Stability

In discussing the paucity of strikes in some of the newer countries where nationalism, anticolonialism, and economic planning are prominent factors, we warned against the concept of a universal cycle of union development. Nevertheless, there has been a common cycle of growth in most of the older countries which are studied in this monograph. The early years of the labor movements have been marked by friction, hostility, and confusion. With the passage of time, organizations have become more solid and secure, control over the rank and file has been cemented, and accommodative relations with the employers have been established.

Thus the chronological age of a labor movement may have an important influence on the incidence of industrial conflict. Older movements are more likely to have completed their struggles for existence, recognition, and security, and to be integrated into their national economies. Once this point has been reached, bargaining machinery can be developed to handle economic issues without frequent work stoppages.

Age alone does not tell the full story. Rapid changes in membership can initiate new struggles for worker allegiance and for recognition and acceptance. "Organizing periods" are not always limited to the early years of a labor movement. Membership fluctuations may take place at any time. Pronounced fluctuations are generally conducive to industrial conflict as the unions strive to organize and absorb new members and to settle the most pressing grievances, or struggle to limit their losses and recapture their territory.

Leadership Conflicts

Factionalism encourages the prosecution of issues because the vested officials must protect their position against upstarts lower down in the ranks, while the upstarts must demonstrate that the members are being sold down the river by a tired, indifferent or corrupt Old Guard. In contrast, the only threat to the established officials in a one-party union lies in shop steward revolts at the bottom of the pyramid. Such revolts, which take the form of outlaw strikes, can be choked off quickly if internal discipline is sufficiently effective and relations with employers are good.

Rival unionism is a potent cause of strikes where rivalry is pursued on the basis of comparative militancy in pressing grievances and comparative gains in collective bargaining. A labor organization must attempt to match the achievements of its rival or rivals and must secure even greater benefits, if possible, regardless of the amount of resistance to be overcome. In the absence of competition for members, the pressure to use bargaining gains as economic weapons is not so great.

In many countries the concepts of bargaining unit and exclusive bargaining agent do not apply. Several organizations may be operating inside what we in the United States would consider a single bargaining unit. Moreover, these organizations may be affiliated with rival federations or trade union centers. Rivalry among unions under these circumstances is even more intense. The striving to outdo a competitor exists not only from one contract negotiation to the next, but from day to day in the plant as well. That stable union-management relations are difficult to construct under these circumstances would seem obvious.

The union structure most conducive to the elimination of industrial conflict is a unified national movement with strongly centralized control. Under these conditions the central leadership can consciously substitute other tactics for the strike and can restrain the exercise of power by strong subordinate unions.

Finally, where the Communist faction has substantial strength in the labor movement, strike activity is usually stimulated—particularly the use of massive demonstration strikes. In the Communist view, the worker's grievances are not to be settled conclusively within the framework of capitalism. Strikes have an agitational purpose; for although the eventual seizure of power is to be accomplished by military or political means, the "inherent revolutionary potential of the workers" must be developed and their awareness of class differences sharpened in the meantime. Economic gains resulting from strikes are useful to prove the effectiveness of leadership but cannot be allowed to underwrite any lasting reconciliation. When Communists operate as a minority group within unions, and have failed to achieve top leadership, settlements by the established officials must be denounced as sellouts. It follows that strikes are unlikely to wither away in any democratic country so long as Communists have majority control or strong minority influence within important unions.

We are not stating, however, that Communist leadership will inevitably employ the strike for agitational purposes. Much depends on the party strategy at the time; much depends also on the membership base. The bargaining policies of Communist-led unions in the United States have generally been indistinguishable from those of other unions. Disinterested in ideological unionism, the members have expected a bread-and-butter approach and their expectations have been rewarded. Those left-wing leaders who have survived for any substantial period have practiced the same business unionism that is condemned so heartily in Marxist literature. The same can be said of left-wing union leaders in the United Kingdom.

Status of Union-Management Relations

There are two main types of industrial conflict. The first is basically organizational even though wages and other economic issues may ostensibly be involved. It has dominated the early states of labor-management relations in many countries, where the unions have struggled to win their place in economic society and employers have striven to retain their traditional authority. This phase has come to an end where employers and unions have attained an acceptable balance of power and prerogatives. The usual description is that employers have "accepted unionism and collective bargaining," although the process is actually more complicated than that.

Concededly "acceptance" is not capable of measurement and is difficult to discuss except in stilted terms. It is sufficiently obvious that as long as unions are permitted to strive for power but are thwarted in their every bid, only conflict can result.

The second type of industrial conflict is essentially economic and persists after collective bargaining has become "institutionalized" and the parties have found ways and means of living together. But as we have seen, even this kind of conflict has virtually disappeared in some countries where the collective bargaining system has become tightly organized and controlled.

There also are two degrees of centralization in the structure of collective bargaining. Industry-wide bargaining between industrial unions and employer associations constitutes the first degree. It is not necessary that master negotiations cover the entire industry; the resulting agreement can be extended by force of law or by voluntary action. Nor is it necessary that there be a formal industry association with power of attorney. Unless the number of firms is large, informal employer committees can accomplish the same result.

We have already indicated in the previous chapter the reasons why multi-employer bargaining is conducive to industrial peace. Professional leadership eliminates reckless and emotional behavior; the costliness of large strikes serves as a deterrent to both sides; employers are less inclined to resist because they are not in danger of being whipsawed and will not suffer a competitive disadvantage within the industry; unions are less aggressive because intraunion competition is eliminated. The United Kingdom is a good example of a country with this type of bargaining system. Unauthorized or unofficial strikes (the counterpart of local-union strikes in a decentralized bargaining structure) are always a possibility, but in the nature of the case they are generally brief gestures of protest.

The second degree of centralization is economy-wide rather than merely industry-wide. The labor market is regulated and disciplined as a whole. It is in this state of affairs that the strike is most likely to wither away. In some of the newer countries, governments are moving to organize and discipline the labor market through an alliance with the unions and under the banner of nationalism and anticolonialism. In some of the older countries of Northern Europe a thoroughly consolidated bargaining structure has been created under private auspices. "Peak associations" or federations of management and labor have been the means of integration. The officers of such federations represent the broadest possible constituencies and are the farthest removed from parochial pressures. Of course, this fully centralized system will not work without the highest degree of subordination and discipline within the federations.

Labor Political Activity

In the preceding chapter we observed that labor parties and labor governments have contributed toward relinquishment of the strike by providing a political alternative. We noted that the powers of the state over income distribution and other aspects of economic welfare are clearly stronger than the possibilities of collective bargaining, and that political action is more convenient, dignified, and respectable than industrial conflict.

It remains to point out that the existence of a labor party with close trade union affiliations is perhaps the greatest deterrent to the use of the strike. We are not speaking of just any labor party, however, but rather of one which is capable of imbuing the unions with a feeling of political responsibility. The party must have tasted political power, or at least must be sufficiently potent to be seen as a serious contender for power. And there must be a reasonable prospect of achieving labor objectives through government action. We emphasize the last point because the existence of strong labor parties has not eliminated industrial conflict in postwar Finland and in Australia. In the first case the economic environment has been too hostile for successful reliance on the political mechanism, and in the second case the constitutional powers of the federal government are too weak. The federal form of government in the United States and Canada, with much power located in the states and provinces, has inhibited successful political action and helps to explain why unions have relied so heavily on industrial action.

Why is labor political action a deterrent to strikes? First, strikes are injurious to the political fortunes of the labor party. Middle-class votes must be attracted if the party is to be successful, but the middle-class voter is antagonized by strikes and tends to blame them on the unions. Second, worker unrest is channeled off into the political sphere. Demands that would otherwise be made upon the employer are directed against the government instead. If the labor party comes into power, the deterrent effect is even stronger. The trade union officials, having invested heavily in the party, are disinclined to do anything that would have the effect of sabotaging its program. Moreover, large-scale strikes are always embarrassing to the administration in power; and if industrial paralysis seems to be threatened, unpleasant repressive measures may become inevitable. All of this means that the trade union leader who wishes to cooperate with party officials, or is himself such an official, will show maximum restraint in the use of the strike.

Role of the State

We showed in the last chapter that greater participation by government as entrepreneur, economic planner, guardian of labor, and supervisor of union-management relations has been partly responsible for the declining frequency of strikes. We indicated also that labor protest against public employment policies or compulsory arbitration awards is more likely to take the form of brief demonstrations than actual trials of economic strength.

All governments have not assumed these new functions to an equal extent, however. The amount of socialized industry in the United Kingdom, for example, is greater than in Canada. The Scandinavian countries have implemented programs of central economic planning to an unusual extent during recent years, generally under the leadership of labor party governments. France, Italy, and Japan rely on legislation for defining many conditions of employment that are determined by collective bargaining elsewhere. Australia has an elaborate system of compulsory arbitration, whereas the government of the United States remains aloof from most industrial disputes except for offering mediation services.

Influences on Strike Activity and the Four "Patterns"

In Chapter 3 we classified most of the countries we have studied under four patterns of industrial conflict, and in the present chapter we have attempted to describe the principal influences on relative strike activity. It is now time to bring these two classifications together.

We think that a significant association can be shown between national patterns of strike activity, on the one hand, and the condition of the labor movement, union-management relations, and political institutions

CHART II. North European Pattern: First Variant
Membership Involvement: Workers Involved as a Percentage of
Union Membership

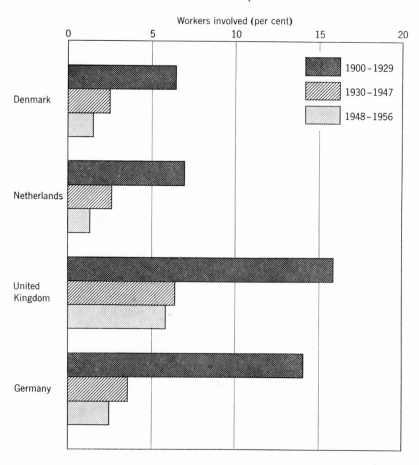

CHART III. North European Pattern: First Variant
Duration of Strikes: Working Days Lost per Striker

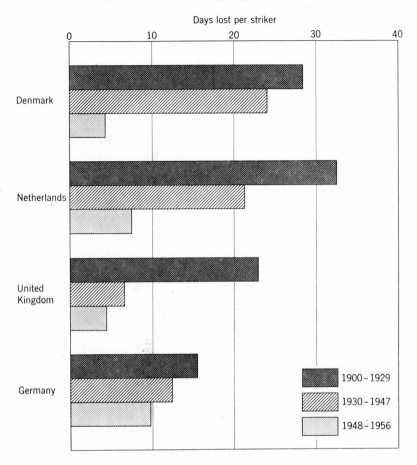

on the other. In the nature of the case only a broad and general association can be expected, however. There are so many unique and special
causes at work in particular countries that a perfect correlation is out of
the question. In fact, if a simple and mechanical relationship could be
established, there would be reason to suspect that we were dealing with
shallow and verbal categories rather than with real distinctions.

Having sounded this caveat, we may turn to the four patterns of industrial conflict. What is said below will be discussed in much greater
detail in the remaining chapters of this volume.

The North European pattern—first variant

This pattern, found in Denmark, the Netherlands, the United Kingdom, and Germany, is characterized by a nominal propensity to strike and a low or moderate duration of strikes. These countries have mature labor movements with firm and stable memberships. (The postwar German labor movement, as Kerr has noted, is a revival of the pre-Hitler movement with remarkably little change.) Leadership conflicts are subdued: there is one dominant central federation in Denmark, the United Kingdom, and Germany. (It is true that three federations have coexisted in the Netherlands for upwards of four decades, but their com-

CHART IV.   North European Pattern: First Variant

Membership Loss Ratio: Working Days Lost per Hundred Union Members

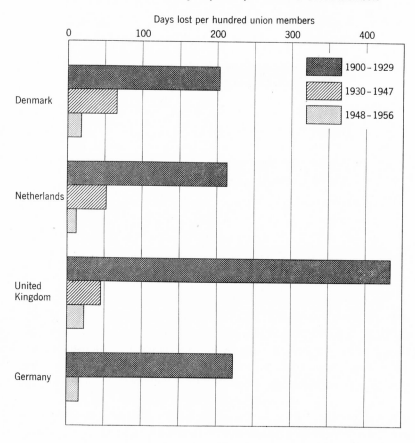

CHART V.   North European Pattern: Second Variant
Membership Involvement: Workers Involved as a Percentage of
Union Membership

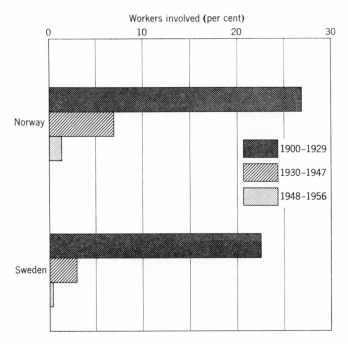

petition has not been so vigorous as to provoke industrial conflict.)   The
Communist faction has been notably weak in all four countries.

By virtue of industry-wide negotiations and the influence of central
federations, collective bargaining structures have become highly centralized, although the degree of consolidation varies from one country
to another.   Industrial unions and industry associations do the negotiating in the United Kingdom, for example, whereas much power is concentrated in the Danish and Dutch central federations.   There are strong
labor or social democratic parties, which have organized or at least
participated in the government, except in postwar Germany.

There is a fair amount of public enterprise in the United Kingdom,
but not a great deal in the other nations.   Neither is there much reliance
on the state for defining important conditions of employment.   On the
other hand, all four governments have had active programs of interven-

tion in bargaining disputes.   Compulsory arbitration was practiced in
the United Kingdom until 1951, and the machinery was retained on a
voluntary basis in a number of key industries.   In Denmark the legislature has frequently intervened, generally by enacting mediation proposals into law.   An official Board of Mediation in the Netherlands has
authority to approve, modify, or disapprove collective agreements, extend their provisions to employers and workers not directly covered, and
set wages directly in some cases.   The "extension" system is also used
in Germany.

The North European pattern—second variant

This pattern is defined by very infrequent but long stoppages.   The
labor movement, the bargaining system, and political context in Norway
and Sweden are similar in most pertinent respects to those in Denmark,
the Netherlands, the United Kingdom, and Germany.   The only significant difference we have identified is that Norway and Sweden generally
maintain a hands-off policy in labor-management controversies, whereas

CHART VI.   North European Pattern: Second Variant
Duration of Strikes: Working Days Lost per Striker

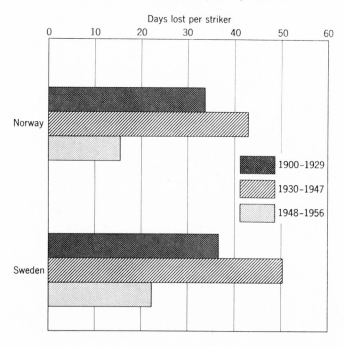

CHART VII.   North European Pattern: Second Variant
Membership Loss Ratio: Working Days Lost per Hundred Union Members

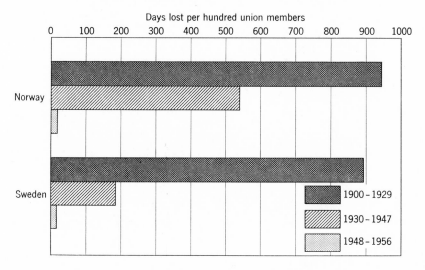

more active intervention has been practiced in the other countries.   This is not a very convincing explanation of the remarkable disparity in average duration of strikes.   Differences in the "industry mix" may be significant, and doubtless additional causes are at work.

The Mediterranean-Asian pattern

This pattern includes France, Italy, Japan, and India.   Participation in strikes is very great but duration is short.   Labor movements entered the phase of mass organization, or reorganized from scratch, subsequent to World War II.   Union membership does not involve an important personal or financial commitment and has often been an ephemeral phenomenon.   Rival unionism and internal leadership conflicts have been endemic; there has been a powerful Communist faction in each of these countries, which has made chronic use of the massive demonstration stoppage as an agitational tool.

Labor-management relations, like the labor movements themselves, are weak and unstable.   The unions have not really been accepted by employers and are not in a position to negotiate on an equal basis.   Although the forms of multi-employer bargaining are used in some of these countries, the subject matter of bargaining is rather insubstantial.   The significant conditions of work, for the most part, are either set by the government or remain within the employer's control.   The unions are normally too poor to undertake long strikes.

All these countries have two or more left-wing parties affiliated with different branches of the labor movement.   They are bitterly divided, however, a far cry from the unified labor or social democratic parties of Northern Europe.   As a consequence, conservative governments have occupied the stage during the past decade.   No single labor party has come sufficiently close to political power that the strike policy of its affiliated unions has been affected.   (In recent years, however, collaboration between the Congress Party and the largest group of Indian unions has had a definite influence on strike activity.)

There is a surprising amount of public enterprise in France, Italy,

CHART VIII.   Mediterranean-Asian Pattern

Membership Involvement: Workers Involved as a Percentage of
Union Membership

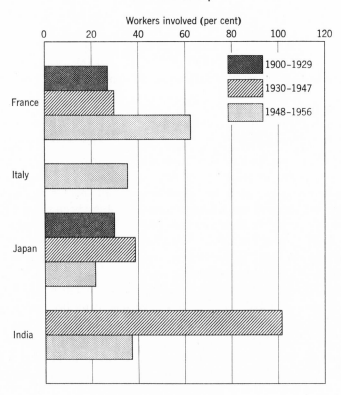

CHART IX. Mediterranean-Asian Pattern
Duration of Strikes: Working Days Lost per Striker

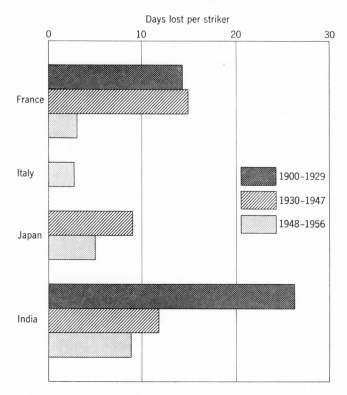

Days lost per striker

Japan, and India.   Moreover, as noted above, many important terms of employment are defined by the state rather than collective bargaining; unionism is so weak in the industrial sphere that unrest is focused on the political process.   Thus labor protest is frequently directed against the government, a further reason for the popularity of brief demonstration strikes.

The North American pattern

The North American pattern, found in the United States and Canada, is characterized by a moderately high propensity to strike as well as a relatively long duration.   Insofar as large-scale organization is concerned, the labor movements are younger than those in Northern Europe but older than those in the Mediterranean-Asian group.   There were

CHART X. Mediterranean-Asian Pattern
Membership Loss Ratio: Working Days Lost per Hundred Union Members

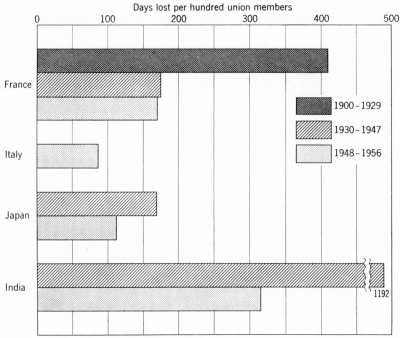

wide swings in union membership until the 1940's, but the intensity of organization has become more stable in recent years.

The status of union leadership is likewise in transition. Historically, rival unionism, jurisdictional conflict, and internal leadership struggles have all been prevalent in the United States and Canada. Communist influence was significant in numerous unions between 1935 and 1950. But with the expulsion and atrophy of the Communist unions, the development of no-raid agreements, and the merger between AFL and CIO, there has been a notable tendency for jurisdictional lines to stabilize. Furthermore, political rivalry inside unions has diminished as the organizations have become more stable and the leaders have grown older. It is possible, however, that technological changes will revive the conflict between craft and industrial unionism and encourage competition over the growing army of white-collar workers.

The major employers in the United States and Canada generally resisted unionism until the latter part of the 1930's.   In subsequent years labor organizations have increasingly been accepted and incorporated into the industrial system.   Here again the situation is midway between the Northern European countries, where collective bargaining became "institutionalized" early in the present century, and the Mediterranean-Asian group, where collective bargaining is still weak and undeveloped. Bargaining structure in the United States and Canada is more decentralized than in any other country we have studied.   About five-sixths of all labor contracts in the United States are negotiated in single-employer units, and most of the multi-employer contracts cover local areas only.   Canada's collective bargaining system is very similar.

Political processes in the United States and Canada, like bargaining structure, are consistent with relatively frequent and rather long industrial disputes.   The important conditions of employment are determined privately rather than by government: the minimum wage laws are not very significant from a practical standpoint; paid vacations, holidays,

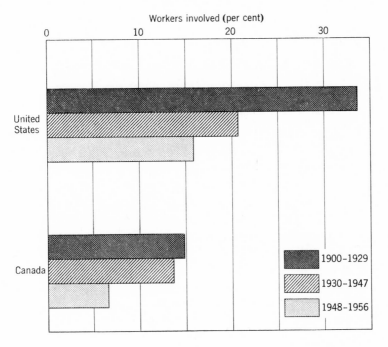

CHART XI.   North American Pattern
Membership Involvement: Workers Involved as a Percentage of
Union Membership

CHART XII.   North American Pattern
Duration of Strikes: Working Days Lost per Striker

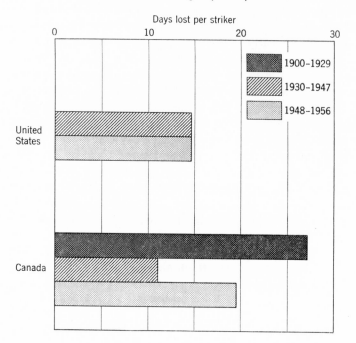

CHART XIII.   North American Pattern
Membership Loss Ratio: Working Days Lost per Hundred Union Members

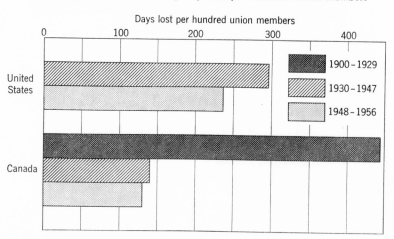

etc., are not covered by legislation; and even a private system of social security has developed. A successful labor party has not emerged in either country, and the central orientation of the labor movement is industrial rather than political. Finally, although compulsory mediation is practiced in Canada, the United States maintains a laissez-faire policy towards most types of industrial disputes.

The relation between economic and political institutions, on the one hand, and strike activity on the other has been sketched out in a preliminary fashion. To establish this relationship in greater detail will be the task of the next five chapters.

NOTES TO CHAPTER 6

1. A. M. Ross and D. Irwin, "Strike Experience in Five Countries," *Industrial and Labor Relations Review*, 4 (April 1951), p. 336.
2. *Ibid.*, p. 337.
3. See Clark Kerr and Abraham Siegel, "The Inter-Industry Propensity to Strike —An International Comparison," in A. Kornhauser, R. Dubin, and A. M. Ross (eds.), *Industrial Conflict* (New York: McGraw-Hill Book Co., 1954), pp. 189–212.

CHAPTER 7

North

European Pattern

—First Variant

Denmark

Denmark[1] fits well into the North European pattern of long-established, peaceful labor relations. The incidence of industrial conflict has been very low, with only occasional eruptions such as those of 1925, 1936, 1946, and 1956. With less than half of one per cent of non-agricultural workers participating in strikes in a typical year, and with stoppages averaging only three days in length, ratios of lost time might be recorded more easily in minutes per man-year rather than the usual man-days.

Of central importance is the fact that Danish unions and employer organizations became highly centralized, and formally undertook to recognize and deal peaceably with each other, at a very early date. After the failure of a large-scale lockout in 1899, the employers' confederation and the labor federation concluded a permanent agreement providing for mutual recognition and the curbing of industrial warfare. In the years following the "September Agreement," as it is now known, the unions and employers' associations have erected, bit by bit, their system for determining wages and working conditions. Many features of Danish industrial relations—unsymmetrical bargaining units, encompassing cities and regions and differing from industry to industry; a complicated procedure for ratifying agreements; the persistence of numerous separate unions clinging to historical craft jurisdictions; the elaborate negotiating procedure and private dispute-settlement apparatus—are characteristic of a collective bargaining system that has evolved gradually, rather than being imposed suddenly. The private collective bargaining system has achieved semiofficial stature and the two major federations have become quasi-public institutions.

Both union and employer groups have bargained from positions of strength. As early as 1900 the unions had enrolled 75 per cent of the adult male workers in manufacturing and handicrafts, and 22 per cent of the females. By 1930, more than 40 per cent of all non-agricultural workers in Denmark were union members. The degree of organization exceeded 50 per cent in 1944, and has ranged between 55 and 60 per cent of non-agricultural workers in the years following.

The Danish labor movement is and always has been quite unified. It has not been marked with the ideological and religious differences that have torn other national labor movements into bitterly competing groups. A single confederation, De Samvirkende Fagforbund i Danmark, has included nearly all Danish unionists since just before the turn of the century. Furthermore, the Federation of Labor plays an important role in collective bargaining. The national unions undertake preliminary bargaining with the appropriate employer associations. Issues unsettled after six or seven weeks of bargaining at the industry level are submitted to the peak organizations for further negotiation. Walter Galenson points out that major changes in terms of employment are thus shifted to the Federation of Labor and the Employers' Association. The Danish system, he concludes, "amounts to national collective bargaining. . . ." [2]

Although there have been jurisdictional conflicts among the Laborers' Union, the Municipal Workers' Union, and the craft unions, such conflict has been quite subdued. Undoubtedly contributing to this restraint is the fact that all unions are members of the single central confederation, and that the confederation has had an effective jurisdictional disputes board for many years.

The Communists, who contribute greatly to the ideological rivalry in other labor movements, have never been a very significant factor in Danish politics or labor affairs. Before World War II, they were a tiny minority; their greatest vote was achieved in the 1939 elections, and amounted to only 2 per cent of the total. The Communists did make considerable gains during the war, and won about 12 per cent of the vote in the 1945 elections, but they have again slipped back into obscurity.

The employers have likewise been highly organized. Their associations, usually organized by industry, bargain over all terms of employment. A strong confederation of employers' associations, the Dansk Arbejdsgiverforening, was formed at the end of the last century. Affiliates are forbidden to conclude agreements covering the usual subject matter of collective bargaining without the approval of the executive committee. In addition, the "recommendations" of the Dansk Arbejdsgiverforening "are followed more or less literally by its affiliates." [3] Participation in the peak negotiations described above further enhances the power of the central association.

A very high proportion of Danish employers, especially the larger ones, are members and submit to the discipline of the associations. Although the employers and the central confederation resist union demands with skill and vigor, they have scarcely ever opposed unionism and collective bargaining as such, and have followed conciliatory policies almost from the time of their inception.

Danish bargaining structure, although not so tightly controlled as in the Netherlands or Norway, may be considered relatively centralized. Collective bargaining agreements are typically negotiated between national unions and employer associations, covering an industry throughout the nation or in a particular region. Moreover, two very large unions, the laborers and the metal workers,[4] act as pattern setters in collective bargaining and thus encourage uniformity of settlements. The growing tendency to refer major issues, and many lesser questions, to the central organizations on both sides also contributes to centralization.

Another characteristic of the North European pattern found in Denmark is a strong labor party. Although perhaps the mildest of all European socialists, the Danish Social Democrats are nonetheless a labor party, closely allied with the Danish union movement and perhaps slightly dominant over it. Walter Galenson points out:

> At the local level, institutional cooperation is secured through affiliation of the socialist club with the central trades and labor council. Nationally, the Federation of Labor has as one of its constitutional purposes "to cooperate with the Social Democratic Party in order jointly to further labor legislation"; in addition, the party elects two members to the executive committee of the Federation. In reciprocation the Federation elects one member to the executive committee and one to the small and powerful council of the party.[5]

Conceding that it is difficult for a non-participant of inner council meetings to decide whether the unions dominate the party, or vice versa, Galenson nonetheless concludes, "To an outsider, there are reasons for believing that the preponderance lies with the party."

The Danish Social Democrats have not only been a strong party for most of this century, but have governed, as the leading partner in coalitions, for most of the time since 1929. Thus, although the Social Democrats have never enjoyed an absolute majority, the Danish labor movement has flourished for nearly thirty years under governments specifically friendly to unions in which they have had considerable voice.

The labor-dispute policies of the Danish government reinforce the tendency to eliminate strikes and lockouts. It is true that the state does not play a significant primary role in determining conditions of employment either as an employer on its own account or through detailed labor legislation. The amount of public enterprise in Denmark is not great, probably the least of any Scandinavian country. Perhaps this results from the moderate outlook of the Social Democratic party and the need for cooperation with conservative parties in order to govern. Furthermore, although the customary social insurance system is in effect, vacations, holidays, and other fringe benefits regulated by the government in many countries are determined privately in Denmark.

The state does intervene actively in settling labor disputes, however. Secondary disputes under existing contracts must be adjudicated by the Labor Court or referred to industrial arbitration machinery. There is no permanent arbitration system for primary disputes over the terms of agreements, but since 1933 there has been a tradition of direct government intervention in all major controversies. Most frequently, the legislature enacts the state mediator's settlement proposal into law. Occasionally, however, an *ad hoc* compulsory arbitration board has been empaneled to settle the specific dispute.

Thus the major influences in Denmark appear to be (*a*) maturity of relationships, (*b*) organizational stability, and (*c*) control of bargaining by the central federations, reinforced by the intervention in major disputes of a government friendly to labor. As it will appear, the situation in Norway, Sweden, and the Netherlands is essentially similar.

The Netherlands [6]

Clearly the strike has withered away in the Netherlands. During the 1947–56 decade only about one per cent of trade union members, and half of one per cent of non-agricultural employees went on strike in the average year. Moreover the typical striker has lost only about seven working days during the period subsequent to World War II. There appear to be three strategic factors in the disappearance of industrial conflict: a highly centralized collective bargaining system, extensive intervention by the government in the bargaining process, and a Labor Party which has participated in the government continuously since 1945.

Consolidation of bargaining structure is the outstanding feature of industrial relations in the Netherlands. Industry-wide collective agreements are negotiated in detail by representatives of the employer associations and the unions. In some industries, permanent joint machinery exists for continuous collective bargaining and dispute settlement. More important, however, is the participation of the government and the Foundation of Labor, a private group.

The labor relations law of postwar Netherlands authorizes the government Board of Mediators to establish rules and procedures for wage determination and to supervise collective bargaining. All collective agreements must be submitted to the Board of Mediators, which may approve, modify, or disapprove them. Furthermore, the board may extend the provisions of these contracts to other groups of employers and workers who have not signed them, giving the force of law to the negotiated provisions. In some cases, wages may be set directly by the board.

Labor and management are not really superseded in establishing terms of employment, however. The Board of Mediators is required by statute to consult with the Foundation of Labor. The foundation is a permanent body consisting of top representatives from the employer associations and the union federations, created to advise the government on wage issues, social insurance, and similar questions. The foundation decides some issues as a matter of national policy, and sets limits on other issues within which industry-wide agreements are negotiated. Disagreements arising from contract negotiations are unofficially mediated by the foundation. Negotiated agreements are referred simultaneously to the foundation and to the government Board of Mediators. The latter then takes appropriate action upon them, usually following the advice of the Labor Foundation. The influence of the foundation is so great that one writer has observed, "The establishment of the Foundation had the consequence of virtually transferring collective bargaining from the industrial to the national level." [7]

The unique structure of wages in the Netherlands is the result of this highly centralized system of collective bargaining. In the postwar reconstruction period, the government, unions, and employers decided to replace a wage structure built from numerous separate determinations with one based on "social justice." The wage system so conceived began with a "social minimum" wage for the unskilled male adult worker. Appropriate differentials reflecting skill and geographical factors were then added. Uniform standards of job evaluation and time study were adopted at the national level, and eventually covered three-fourths of the employees. National wage policy then sought to maintain the level of real wages and to restrain inflation. Although slight deviations from this rationalized structure were permitted in 1956, when wage increases were permitted to vary slightly from industry to industry, depending on ability to pay, the basic policy still stands.

The parties to the centralized bargaining system are strong and stable union and employer groups which reconciled their ideological differences and accommodated themselves to each other many years ago. Dutch workers began to organize in large numbers about the time of the First World War, although the Socialists' federation had been established even earlier in 1906. Membership grew steadily to nearly 700,000 by 1920, when it began to decline. After losing about one-fourth of its members, the union movement resumed its growth in the late 1920's. For the past twenty-five years, membership has been either stable or increasing slowly, roughly keeping pace with the expansion of the labor force. About 41 per cent of non-agricultural employees were enrolled in 1930–32, and the same proportion in 1954–56. Thus the Netherlands has had a substantial degree or organization and relatively stable union membership.

Although not formally unified, the union movement has been free of bitter rivalry in recent decades. There have been three major union federations for about forty years. The Socialist federation is the largest, but the Catholic and Protestant federations together have slightly more than half the total union membership.[8] There were periods of enmity in earlier years, but following World War II the three groups adopted a policy of close collaboration. They established a Council of Trade Unions, presenting a united front in national negotiations within the Labor Foundation. Relationships were strained in 1954, when both Catholic and Protestant churches reaffirmed their edicts banning their communicants from membership in Socialist unions, but close relations still persist among the federations.

In many countries, as we have noted, the most serious threat to labor unity has been the Communist group. Left-wing elements have been present in the Dutch labor movement since its earliest days, but always as small minorities. The contemporary Communist labor federation, Eenheidsvakcentrale, is unrecognized either by the government, the employers, or the other labor organizations. For a short time after World War II, the Communist Party enjoyed considerable strength in parliamentary elections, winning approximately 10 per cent of the seats in 1946. Communist voting strength gradually declined. In the 1956 election, the party was reduced to 4 seats out of 75 in the First Chamber and 7 out of 150 in the Second Chamber of Parliament.

Employer organization is generally parallel to that of the unions. There are three federations of employers—Catholic, Protestant, and non-sectarian. Unlike their counterparts in the union movement, however, the Catholic and Protestant employer federations are quite small. The non-sectarian federation, Centraal Sociaal Werkgevers-Verbond (CSWV), includes about 80 per cent of all Dutch employers.

As in other countries, employers in the Netherlands stoutly resisted unions in the early days of the labor movement. Employer opposition subsequently waned, and unions and collective bargaining were firmly entrenched and accepted by the late 1920's. Collaboration between employer and union groups, with strong government support, began in 1927 with the statute regulating collective bargaining. It was strengthened in 1933 when laws were passed permitting the government to set wages in some sectors of the economy. By 1937, labor-management-government relations had begun to assume form along lines quite similar to those prevailing at present.

Political institutions in the Netherlands have played an important part in the development of labor relations and the elimination of industrial conflict. Political parties, like union and management groups, are divided along religious as well as ideological lines. The two largest parties, both about the same size, are the Labor Party and the Catholic Party. There are three others linked to Protestant churches, although with varying degrees of attachment, as well as a Liberal Party and a Communist Party.[9]

The participation of labor in government is typical of the Northern European countries where strikes have virtually disappeared. In the Netherlands, this participation has been chiefly through the Labor Party. Originally called the Social Democratic Labor Party, it rapidly achieved prominence after being established in 1894. As early as 1913, the party held about one-fifth of the seats in Parliament. It participated in the government for the first time in 1939 and has participated in all postwar governments. Indeed, since 1948 the prime minister has been from the Labor Party.

The Catholic Party, with which the second largest union federation is affiliated, has also participated in the government on equal terms with the Labor Party since World War II. Furthermore, one or more of the Protestant parties have also been included in every postwar government, although as relatively minor partners.

In summary, the Netherlands has the highly centralized bargaining system, the stable and non-rivalrous unionism, the tradition of employer-union cooperation, and the participation of labor in political power that are associated with industrial peace in Northern Europe. The role of the government reinforces the tendencies worked out in the private sphere. Government intervention appears to be a device for conferring official status and sanction upon the joint decisions of the central union and employer groups. This is a most interesting example of a cartelized collective bargaining process, one that is conducted with a minimum of friction.

The United Kingdom [10]

As in the other Northern European countries, rates of participation and losses of working time have declined steadily in the United Kingdom over the four and a half decades covered by our study. The number of workers involved in strikes as a per cent of union membership has dropped from a 1911–29 average of more than 16 per cent to slightly less than 6 per cent in the 1948–56 period. At the same time strikes have grown much shorter. The 1911–29 average was 23 days lost per striker; the 1948–56 average was only 4.3 days lost. Working days lost per union member each year similarly declined from 4.3 days in the 1911–29 period to 0.2 days in the years since 1948.

Strike participation rates in the United Kingdom have been significantly higher than elsewhere in Northern Europe, it is true. As already mentioned, nearly 6 per cent of British union members were involved in strikes annually between 1948 and 1956, compared with only 1.4 per cent in Denmark, 1.3 per cent in the Netherlands, 2.6 per cent in Germany, 1.2 per cent in Norway, and 0.3 per cent in Sweden. However, the British participation rates are lower than those of any country outside of Northern Europe, except South Africa. Taking everything into account, we can properly classify the United Kingdom in the group of countries characterized by low participation rates and brief stoppages.

The substance of the matter is that British labor has largely abandoned the strike as a tactical instrument in pressing its purposes. The age and stability of unions, the sophistication of employers, the improvement of bargaining machinery, the activities of government, the political aims of the labor movement and the success of the Labour Party are all involved. The "unofficial strike"—a protest directed against union leadership rather than employers—is the safety valve in the system, and accounts for the fact that the propensity to strike is not so low as in Denmark, the Netherlands, etc.

To begin at the beginning, Britain is the birthplace of trade unionism. A hard core of 500,000 members had been organized by the 1870's, and the first "permanent" million had been enrolled by 1890, when Sidney and Beatrice Webb were writing *Industrial Democracy*. Union membership reached approximately 4,000,000 by 1914, and never declined below that point, even during the Great Depression. Thus British workers were unionized on a substantial scale about the turn of the century, some thirty-five years earlier than in the United States.

British unionism not only has a long history, but has been relatively stable as well. Although there were occasional setbacks, membership grew steadily from the late 1880's to 1917. A great explosion of unionism began in 1918 and culminated in 1920, when more than 8,000,000 workers had been enrolled. As in nearly all the industrialized countries, unionism was weakened during the 1920's. Approximately 3,500,000 members had been lost by 1933. Growth resumed in the mid-thirties, however, and has persisted to the present time. Throughout this period, the degree of organization has remained relatively high. Prior to World War II, the proportion of non-agricultural employees enrolled in the unions was never less than about 30 per cent, and subsequent to the war it has been in the neighborhood of 50 per cent.

In the present century the unions themselves have been secure, but at times there have been pronounced leadership rivalries. British unionism had a haphazard growth, with a wide variety of structural forms. Jurisdictional or "demarcation" conflicts were common at one time, and sufficiently troublesome to inspire the Webbs' unrealistic proposal that unions abandon the concept of job property rights in favor of a "common rule" protecting all workers. During the 1920's, however, the Trade Union Congress (TUC) established a committee to arrange peaceable settlements of jurisdictional disputes. This procedure has worked fairly well, and the recent history of national unions with overlapping claims has been characterized by peaceful coexistence and relative freedom from bitter rivalry. The unchallenged status and growing strength of the TUC has contributed to this condition.

In the 1930's the Communists endeavored, although not with great success, to gain control over local trade councils as well as local Labour Party groups. During World War II they renewed their efforts inside the unions, and by 1947 had achieved substantial control over four of the seventeen largest unions, and considerable influence within six others.

At that time the top leadership of the TUC was openly expressing its concern over the strength of the Communists inside the unions. Communist influence has declined during the most recent decade, however, and is now weak.

All in all, the trade union movement of the United Kingdom may be described as fairly unified. To be sure, it is fragmented into many unions with overlapping jurisdictions, and has a national union center less powerful than those of Germany, Norway, or Sweden. On the other hand, there is much less organizational and ideological conflict than in France, Italy, and the Asian countries. The overwhelming majority of members are in unions affiliated with the TUC and adhere to a common philosophy of unionism. Another type of leadership rivalry has been more significant: the power struggles between shop stewards and other militant elements in the local branches, on the one hand, and the genteel and conservative top leadership of unions on the other. The resulting unofficial strikes account for a large proportion of all work stoppages in the United Kingdom and help to explain why the participation rates are higher than in other countries of Northern Europe.

British employers resisted the unionization of their workers long and vigorously during the nineteenth century, using repressive legislation as well as economic force. Unionism and collective bargaining were generally accepted by the first decade of the present century, however, and in the subsequent period their existence as permanent institutions has never been challenged.

As in so many European countries, British employers formed themselves into associations and federations. Unlike the Scandinavian and German employers, the British never organized a strong central or economy-wide federation. The typical employer group dealing with labor matters is a regional or industrial association—the National Federation of Rayon Yarn Producers, the Engineering and Allied Employers' National Federation, the National Association of Port Employers, and so on. Employer organization is complicated; in some industries there are numerous craft or trade bodies, local federations, and national federations. In other industries, the employers have formed national associations which are federated with similar bodies in related trades. The employer groups differ widely not only in breadth of jurisdiction, but also in size, method of organization, etc.[11]

The collective bargaining system, as might be expected from the nature of the unions and the employer associations, exhibits considerable diversity in negotiating machinery, geographical scope, and industrial coverage. The typical labor-management agreement is a multi-employer instrument, often national in scope, covering an industry, a group of skilled crafts within an industry, or occasionally a complex of industries. In some instances all the terms of employment are set forth in a national agreement. In other cases local negotiations are used to fill in some of the details. Notwithstanding these variations, the British collective bargaining system may unequivocally be described as multi-employer and frequently industry-wide.

Joint Industrial Councils and the various Wages Councils further complicate the system. The Joint Industrial Councils, recommended by the Whitley Committee during the First World War, were intended to be permanent organizations, dealing not only with normal collective bargaining issues, but also with broader matters of labor-management cooperation. Several trade unions and industrial groups may be represented on a council. These Whitley Councils lost union favor for a period but regained support, through the medium of the "Mond-Turner conferences," after the general strike of 1926. During World War II the Joint Industrial Council system expanded once more. K. G. J. C. Knowles has noted the pacifying effect of the councils:

> True, from the point of view of strike action, a large Union may be a very strong force; but its strength may not be correspondingly great in the context of joint organization and procedure, where it works as one section out of many, and where the strike weapon has been implicitly or explicitly forsworn.[12]

The government has played an important role in reducing the incidence of industrial conflict. The Wages Councils are statutory bodies which regulate the terms of employment of some 4,500,000 workers in retail trade, catering, agriculture, and similar activities. Wages Councils are descendants of the Trade Boards, established originally to promulgate minimum standards in these industries where unionism was weak, employees had no individual bargaining power, and working conditions were poor. Some industries have Joint Industrial Councils and Wages Councils as well as private negotiating procedures.[13] Government ownership of industry is also a significant factor. Public enterprise in Britain is somewhat more prominent than in Western Europe: coal mines, railways, medical services, some of the air lines, radio broadcasting, electric power, telecommunications, and other utilities are publicly owned. The steel industry was nationalized by Labour and denationalized by the Conservatives. Of course, strikes in the nationalized industries are not unknown; but labor leadership, being represented on the governing boards and having a stake in nationalization generally, is even more desirous of preventing stoppages in the government sector than in private industry.

In addition, from 1940 to 1951, strikes and lockouts were prohibited and a thorough-going system of compulsory arbitration was in effect. The fact that this system survived for six years after the war is dramatic evidence of the renunciation of strikes in the United Kingdom. Even when the statute that banned industrial conflict and required arbitration was repealed, arbitration machinery was retained in a number of industries by agreement between the unions and employer organizations.

Thus far we have been dwelling on the maturity of the labor movement, the development of a centralized collective bargaining structure, and the role of government in order to explain why union leadership has seldom initiated strikes, "has been more active in preventing, restricting and curtailing strikes than in encouraging them, and has tended increasingly to assert that they were clumsy, outmoded and unnecessary even in the last resort." [14] But there are additional explanations, particularly the association of trade unions with the Labour Party and the shift of emphasis from industrial to political objectives.

The relations between labor unions and the Labour Party are well understood in the United States and need not be described in detail. Unions began supporting candidates successfully in 1874, when two MP's were elected with labor votes. The present Labour Party was established in 1906, and may be considered a descendant of the Labour Representation League of the 1870's, Keir Hardie's Independent Labour Party of 1893, and the Labour Representation Committee at the beginning of the century. The Labour Representation Committee, like the Labour Party which succeeded it, was formally supported by the Trade Union Congress as a vehicle for political expression. The Labour Party participated in the government in 1924, and again from 1929–31, although with unhappy results on both occasions. Seriously damaged by the depression and by internal dissension, Labour was unable to lead the government until after World War II. The Labour Party had a majority government from 1945 until 1951, however, and, although not governing since, has remained a serious contender for national leadership.

We return to Knowles to emphasize once more that abstention from the strike has been accompanied by increased emphasis on political activity, social legislation, and central economic planning as alternatives to "sectional" labor-management conflict in particular industries.

From the middle of the nineteenth century, however, the development of the Trade Union movement in Britain has been away from the position of a "purely economic" organization struggling for the right to bargain with employers and at times venturing into Opposition politics, to a leading position in the State—with its bargaining rights fully confirmed and free to concentrate on the widest political objectives: a development from "irresponsible" independence of employers and Government to "responsible" dependence. The special reasons for Trade Union support of the Labour government—and therefore for discouraging strikes so as not to alienate public sympathy—are obvious and need not be stressed again; but, quite irrespectively of the Labour government being in office, the objectives—and therefore the strategy—of the movement have immensely broadened. So long as political methods of achieving social and economic objectives remain open to the workers, strikes are not likely to return to official favor.[15]

It may well be that if the same type of analysis were made in other countries where the strike has been withering away, the same conclusions would emerge.

The causes we have emphasized thus far account satisfactorily for the low level of strike activity in the United Kingdom. But as we have noted above, the propensity to strike is considerably greater than in other countries of Northern Europe. This fact must also be explained; and the explanation seems to lie in the unofficial strike, which corresponds to the "outlaw strike" in the United States. Although British unions are not using the strike as a normal tactical instrument, there are numerous unofficial stoppages. In fact, most strikes in the United Kingdom have been of this type during recent years. They are frequent enough to explain the relatively high rates of participation; and since they usually lack support above the branch (or local) level, and do not involve fundamental labor-management issues, they typically last only a few days. It is not clear, however, why this conflict between militant local elements and conservative national leadership is much more common in Britain than on the continent of Europe.

Knowles observes that:

> The removal of conflict to a remote national level, out of range of local clamour, and the fighting of industrial battles on a symbolical plane by expert negotiators armed with formulae in the privacy of a Joint Industrial Council rather than with the crude weapons of the picket line, has widened the cleavage between the trade union hierarchy and the rank and file.[16]

Thus the typical strike in Britain is not a test of strength between union and employer, but rather an internal union protest against the vested leadership. The meaning of the strike is quite different from what it is in Scandinavia and the Netherlands, or in the United States for that matter. The protest strike against union leadership in Britain, like the protest strike against the government in France, Italy, and Japan, is characteristically short. Here is the explanation for an average duration of only four days during the past two decades.

Knowles states that "the resistant, militant element in the union," who are responsible for unofficial strikes, "although they have always given life and enthusiasm to the movement, have proved less and less able to dominate it" [17]; and in the final sentences of his book he dwells once more on the significance of unofficial strikes:

> For many years now [strikes] have been less and less an instrument of Union policy, and increasingly a weapon of rebellion against Union authority—and sometimes State authority. Socially, however, they still fulfill the function (in some ways an increasingly important function) of calling immediate attention to weaknesses in the working of the ever-more-complex machinery by which industry is regulated; statistically, they provide a certain measure of these weaknesses, and, more generally, of the distrust felt by rank-and-file workers of the system of regulation as a whole. In a society which is democratic in aim, this should be enough to justify, in principle, their being permitted to occur, and also to act as a spur to the elimination of their causes by every possible means.[18]

Germany [19]

Unionism and collective bargaining were defunct in Germany for more than twelve years prior to their revival after World War II. Therefore our analysis must be confined chiefly to the postwar decade. The most prominent feature has been the low level of strike activity, roughly comparable to that in the Netherlands. The proportion of union members and of non-agricultural employees who have gone on strike has been quite nominal, only a fraction of what it has been in the United States, for example. The average duration of strikes during the postwar period has been ten days—higher than in the United Kingdom, but lower than many other Northern European countries.

The combined effect of lower participation rates and shorter length of stoppages has been a negligible loss of working time. Only Denmark, the Netherlands, and South Africa have lower loss ratios than Germany. During the postwar years the German ratios have been only one-tenth as great as those of the United States.

In some ways this situation was to be expected. German unions enjoy organizational stability, and include many white-collar workers. Unionists generally support the Social Democrats, one of the two major political parties; and like their English counterparts, have chosen to concentrate their efforts in the political rather than the industrial sphere. Collective bargaining is highly centralized, and the negotiated results are given additional status when they are extended throughout industry by ministerial decree. In addition, important terms of employment are dealt with in state or federal legislation.

On the other hand, there are two reasons why the low level of strike activity in Germany is rather surprising. First is the long suspension of unionism and collective bargaining between 1933 and 1945. We might well assume that the task of reviving them after twelve years would be equivalent to starting from scratch and would be accompanied by the usual organizing conflicts. Second, the Social Democratic Party has never participated in the government of the Bundesrepublik, and therefore the unions have never experienced the sobering and chastening effects that are felt when an affiliated political party carries political responsibility.

Here some additional factors, emphasized by Clark Kerr in his perceptive essay on "Collective Bargaining in Postwar Germany," make up any deficiency in the argument. Kerr shows that employer organizations are really much stronger than unions, despite the relatively high degree of organization in Germany. He describes the docility of German workers and their opposition to strikes, the modesty of union demands and their emphasis on codetermination. Finally he shows that the renewal of unionism and collective bargaining after World War II was not a beginning from scratch but rather a reconstruction of things as they were in 1933 with remarkably little change.

It will be convenient to contrast unionism, collective bargaining, and government policies in contemporary Germany with those in the pre-Hitler period, in order to explain the virtual disappearance of strike activity.

The pre-Hitler union movement, although mature in years, suffered sharp membership fluctuations and was splintered into rival factions. Many unions had been founded by the end of the 1860's. Although expansion was thwarted by employer antagonism and government repression during the 1870's and 1880's, union membership increased steadily from 270,000 in 1891 to three million in 1912. There was a sharp decline after the beginning of World War I, but the union movement expanded tremendously in the wave of postwar unrest, attaining a peak membership of 9,000,000 in 1920. Once more a process of attrition began, and by 1926 total union membership was almost halved. Thus instability was a pronounced feature of the pre-Nazi labor movement.

Disunity was another characteristic. The liberal or Hirsch-Dunker unions were always a relatively small segment, averaging scarcely 2 or 3 per cent of the total membership. More important were the Catholic unions. Ideologically opposed to the Socialists, Catholic unions represented about 10 per cent of the total labor movement between the 1890's and 1933. The great majority of German unionists, however, were affiliated with the Socialist-dominated Free Trade Union federation, the ADGB. The Communists were a vocal minority within the ADGB until 1923, and exercised considerable influence within the trade unions and works councils. They withdrew from the federation in 1923, but continued to solicit support from members of the Socialist unions until 1933. In addition there were the syndicalist unions, Freie-Arbeiter Union, with a peak membership of 200,000 in 1922, and the confederations of salaried workers and civil service workers.

In contrast, the union movement in postwar Germany is unified and highly centralized. The question of its actual strength will be discussed later, but we may note that the proportion of the non-agricultural labor force enrolled in unions has varied between 40 and 45 per cent since 1945. Stability is suggested by the steady growth of membership each year since 1947, without declines or wide fluctuations in the annual increment. Unity has been a primary objective of postwar labor leadership, and has unquestionably been attained. Nearly all German unionists are affiliated with the national center, the Deutsche Gewerkschaftsbund (DGB). The existence of separate federations of salaried workers' unions and civil service workers does not seriously impair labor unity.[20] The Communists, a strong minority in the Weimar period, have been greatly outnumbered and overshadowed by the Social Democrats in the contemporary labor movement. Attesting to the great centralization of the postwar German labor movement is the fact that all unionists are organized into only sixteen multi-industrial unions, the four largest of which have about 60 per cent of the members.[21] Furthermore, decision-making power is concentrated at the top. Kerr observes,

> By 1950 . . . power had risen, like cream in milk, to the top. This may be illustrated in several ways: (1) All basic social, economic, and political policy is made at "Dusseldorf" [DGB headquarters]; whereas the employers speak with several voices, the trade union movement speaks with one. (2) The national DGB within its own organizational structure and the national office of each industrial union in its jurisdiction can remove any elected or appointed trade union official at lower levels or veto his election or appointment. Although this power is circumscribed and is sparingly used, it exists. (3) Financial expenditures are concentrated at the higher levels.[22]

Turning to union-management relations, we cannot properly describe them as "mature" in the Scandinavian or British sense. Employers aggressively opposed unions in the early years, and were able to confine them to small and medium-sized companies in competitive industries.

After World War I the Weimar government supported unionism, and collective bargaining became widespread. Employer resistance grew stiffer as Germany's economic distress became greater during the 1920's. The eight-hour working day was abandoned, and employers were pressing for wage reductions when the Nazis abolished unionism. Although collective bargaining is again widespread, we cannot speak of mutual acceptance and accommodation between strong and self-reliant parties. As in the 1920's, the employer associations are much stronger than the unions, which do not appear to have massive support at the grass roots and consequently lack aggressiveness.

The employers in present-day Germany are well organized. The basic unit is the association covering a single industry in a single state. There are regional federations, multi-industrial federations, and a comprehensive national federation, the Bundesvereinigung der Deutschen Arbeitsgeberverbände. In Germany, unlike the Scandinavian countries, power is dispersed among the employer associations rather than being concentrated in the national federation. The German associations, however, do have effective authority to bind their members and enforce discipline.

As in most European countries, multi-employer bargaining is prevalent. Typically, one of the large multi-industrial unions negotiates with an employers' association to define minimum standards of employment for a single industry within a state. In a few instances, such as privately owned railroads, the bargaining unit is nation-wide. Some bargaining units are less than state-wide; the textile industry in North Bavaria furnishes an example. Finally, there are negotiations cutting across industry lines, as in some of the metal trades.

The German practice of "extension" serves to enhance the centralized character of the collective bargaining system. The federal minister of labor may extend the terms of a privately negotiated agreement, giving it the force of law, provided that 50 per cent of the workers in the industry are covered by the negotiated agreement and that the extension is deemed to be in the public interest.

These master contracts are supplemented by local works' council and plant rules agreements. The works' councils, elected by all plant employees, lead a separate existence from the unions. However, the unions may offer slates of candidates, and, according to Philip Taft, "the old union-works' council relationship, with the council as the extended arm of the union, has reasserted itself." [23] The functions of the works' councils include administration of agreements, settlement of grievances, and similar matters, which are handled by local unions in other countries.

The weakness of the trade unions at the grass roots, resulting from their lack of local functions and the absence of contact with the rank and file, is one of the important reasons why strikes have been so infrequent in Germany. Another reason is that unions are not aggressive in collective bargaining. Because of their modest bargaining power, and their desire to have agreements regarded "in the public interest" and therefore eligible to be extended, they have negotiated only minimum terms of employment. Actual wages and other working conditions are often more favorable than those required by the master agreements. Thus, whereas employers have not sought to repress the unions or withhold concessions altogether, the unions have not attempted to achieve great gains.

In this connection Kerr observes that German workers and union members, as well as other elements in the population, are generally opposed to strikes. Not only do union leaders mention the reluctance to strike, but a poll taken by the U. S. Military Government confirms their views:

> The support of strikes by union members or union sympathizers rises in no case higher than 38 per cent, and indeed for all the groups examined in this report rises nowhere higher than a 41 per cent minority. . . . Disapproval of strikes—both economic and political—is widespread sentiment among all major elements of the German population.[24]

The political affiliation and orientation of the unions and the intervention of the government in labor relations remain to be described. Separate socialist political groups—one led by Lassalle and the other by Bebel and Liebknecht—were founded in the 1860's. They merged at Gotha in 1876. After a period of government repression, the Social Democratic Labor Party re-emerged in the 1890's and rapidly attained major party stature. By 1914, the Social Democrats were winning one-third of the votes cast in parliamentary elections. Immediately after World War I, however, the party split over goals and methods; the left wing withdrew to form a separate party which eventually became the Communist Party. The revisionist majority, continuing under the Social Democratic name, participated in coalition governments through most of the period until the rise of Hitler.

In the post-World War II period, the Social Democrats have again resumed their place as a major political party. There are no dissident factions and the Communists do not furnish any significant competition. Although the union groups have made formal professions of political neutrality, the fact is that most union leaders support the Social Democrats. The stated goals of the Labor Federation are almost identical with the platform of the party.

Despite its failure to win parliamentary control, German labor has continued to place primary emphasis on political and legislative goals, particularly codetermination. Kerr has explained the rationale of codetermination as follows:

> Groping for the solution to an immense problem, the labor movement accepted codetermination as the gigantic compromise—a compromise among ideologies, among conflicting political and social pressures. It reflected also a consideration of the mistakes of the past, the realities of the present, and the fears of the future. Codetermination was conceived as the decisive step toward the "people's economy." Viktor Agartz, head of the DGB research institute (WWI), stated its purpose to be, not primarily economic reform, but rather a change in the "social and political structure of the German people.". . . It was hoped that, through codetermination, economic and political power could at last be separated in Germany; and that the social worth of the workers would be raised by opening to them access to the status symbols of society—managerial authority—and they would thus become more attached to democracy.[25]

Obviously the decision to seek representation on governing boards of the enterprises is inconsistent with any substantial reliance on the strike as a tactical instrument. Some of the government policies have the same effect. The procedure by which collective agreements are extended throughout an industry clearly has a moderating influence on union demands, since the agreements will not be deemed in the public interest if they are too irksome to the unrepresented employers. The other significant point to be noted is that state or federal laws in Germany deal with some matters, including paid holidays, health insurance, dismissal procedure, and annual vacations, which are subject to collective bargaining in the United States.

In summary, postwar Germany has had the relatively stable, unified and highly centralized union movement, the consolidated bargaining system, and the necessary minimum of employer acceptance, which are usually associated with a fairly low level of strike activity. Reinforcing this tendency, and perhaps of even greater importance, are the unions' weakness at the local level, popular aversion to strikes, and the orientation of the labor movement toward political goals, particularly codetermination.

NOTES TO CHAPTER 7

1. Walter Galenson, *The Danish System of Industrial Relations* (Cambridge: Harvard University Press, 1952); Orla Jensen, *Social Services in Denmark* (Copenhagen: Det Danske Selskab, 1948); "Postwar Economic Problems in Denmark:

Employment, Wages and Public Finance Policies," *International Labour Review,* 53 (March–April 1946), pp. 211–20; John P. Umbach, "Labor Conditions in Denmark," *Monthly Labor Review,* 59 (November 1944), pp. 945–61; Leonora L. Stettner, "Wage Pressures and Inflation Controls in W. Europe," *Monthly Labor Review,* 79 (June 1956), pp. 664–70.

2. Galenson, *op. cit.,* p. 120.

3. *Ibid.,* p. 82.

4. The laborers' union is overwhelmingly the largest affiliate of the federation, with about 36 per cent of the total membership in 1955. The metal workers' union is much smaller, but is nonetheless one of the major Danish unions. Membership statistics are published in the *Yearbook of the International Free Trade Union Movement* (London: for the International Confederation of Free Trade Unions, 1957), pp. 217–21.

5. Galenson, *op. cit.,* pp. 44–45.

6. B. C. Roberts, "National Wage Policy in the Netherlands," *Economica,* 24 (August 1957), pp. 191–204; P. S. Pels, "The Development of Collective Employment Agreements in the Netherlands," in A. Sturmthal (ed.), *Contemporary Collective Bargaining in Seven Countries* (Ithaca: Institute of International Industrial and Labor Relations, Cornell University, 1957), pp. 98–127, and "The Labour Foundation in the Netherlands," *International Labour Review,* 75 (May 1957), pp. 437–49; John P. Windmuller, "Postwar Wage Determination in the Netherlands," *The Annals of the American Academy of Political and Social Science,* 310 (March 1957), pp. 109–22; "Factors in Labor Peace in the Netherlands," *Monthly Labor Review,* 81 (April 1958), pp. 412–13.

7. Roberts, *op. cit.,* p. 192.

8. In 1956, the Nederlands Verbond van Vakverenigingen (NVV) had approximately 500,000 members, the Catholic federation, Nederlandse Katholieke Arbeidersbeweging (KAB) had about 350,000 and the Protestant federation, Christelijk Nationaal Vakverbond (CNV) about 200,000 members.

9. The distribution of parliament seats resulting from the 1956 elections was:

	1st Chamber	2nd Chamber
Labor Party	22	50
Catholic Party	25	49
Anti-Revolutionary (Protestant)	8	15
Christian Historical (Protestant)	8	13
Liberal	7	13
Communist	4	7
Political Reformed (Protestant)	1	3

10. Allan Flanders and H. A. Clegg (eds.), *The System of Industrial Relations in Great Britain* (Oxford: Basil Blackwell, 1954); K. G. J. C. Knowles, *Strikes —A Study in Industrial Conflict* (Oxford: Basil Blackwell, 1952); Herbert Tracey, *The British Trade Union Movement* (Brussels: International Confederation of Free Trade Unions, 1954); Allan Flanders, "Great Britain," in Walter Galenson (ed.), *Comparative Labor Movements* (Englewood Cliffs, N. J.: Prentice-Hall, 1952), pp. 1–103.

11. H. A. Clegg emphasizes this diversity in Flanders and Clegg, *op. cit.,* especially pp. 216–22.

12. Knowles, *op. cit.,* p. 72.

13. Allan Flanders in Flanders and Clegg, *op. cit.,* pp. 287–94.

14. Knowles, *op. cit.*, p. 150.

15. *Ibid.*, p. 296.

16. *Ibid.*, p. 30.

17. *Ibid.*, p. 61.

18. *Ibid.*, p. 296.

19. Clark Kerr, "Collective Bargaining in Postwar Germany," in Adolf Sturm-thal (ed.), *Contemporary Collective Bargaining in Seven Countries,* pp. 168–211, and "The Trade Union Movement and the Redistribution of Power in Postwar Germany," *Quarterly Journal of Economics,* 68 (November 1954), pp. 535–64; Philip Taft, "Germany," in Walter Galenson (ed.), *Comparative Labor Movements,* pp. 243–312; W. H. McPherson (chairman), "German Experience with Codetermination: A Panel Discussion," *Proceedings of the Eighth Annual Meeting of the Industrial Relations Research Association, 1955* (Madison: 1956), pp. 118–49; Erich Roll, "Germany" in H. A. Marquand (ed.), *Organized Labour in Four Continents* (London: Longmans, Green and Co., 1939), pp. 61–116; J. F. J. Gillen, *Labor Problems in West Germany* (Historical Division, Office of the U. S. High Commissioner for Germany, 1952).

20. Both groups are fairly well organized, and both desire to preserve their separate identities apart from the manual workers. The salaried employees' federation, Deutsche Angestellten Gewerkschaft, now includes nearly 500,000 members.

21. Clark Kerr, "Collective Bargaining," pp. 176–77.

22. *Ibid.*, pp. 182–83.

23. Taft, *op. cit.*, p. 309.

24. From Opinion Surveys Branch, Information Services Division, Office of Military Government (United States), *German Attitudes toward Economic and Political Strikes,* May 1949, quoted in Kerr, "Collective Bargaining," p. 189.

25. Kerr, "The Trade Union Movement and the Redistribution of Power," p. 555.

CHAPTER 8

North

European Pattern

—Second Variant

Norway [1]

Norway conforms to the North European pattern in that the proportion of non-agricultural employees involved in strikes, and the loss of working time per employee, are very low. Stoppages in Norway, however, are much longer than in other Northern European countries. Although present-day strikes are shorter than those of an earlier period, nevertheless the average duration was fifteen days in the 1948–55 period, compared with three days in Denmark and six days in the Netherlands.

An important feature of the contemporary collective bargaining system is the strong, unified labor movement. But the gradual evolution of craft unionism through many peaceful decades, which has characterized Danish labor history, has not taken place. Instead, there were sharp ideological rivalries within the Norwegian labor movement, particularly during the 1920's. Left-wing leadership led the Norwegian Labor Party into the Communist International in 1921, whereupon the more moderate Social Democrats withdrew to form their own party. "Titoist" or revisionist tendencies of the Norwegian left-wing leadership resulted in the withdrawal of the Labor Party from the Comintern in 1923, whereupon yet another group of dissidents seceded and created a third party in the name of labor—the pro-Russia Communists. The Social Democrats reunited with the somewhat modified Labor Party in 1927; and as the ideology of class struggle and revolution was gradually supplanted by an evolutionary emphasis on peaceful attainment of goals, the leadership and program of the Norwegian labor movement grew more moderate.

Political rivalry was reflected in the unions as well, but in a muted fashion. Inasmuch as union locals are affiliated with the Labor Party, with considerable overlapping of leadership, intraparty struggles were certain to be felt in the union sphere. Thus there existed factions within the union federation struggling for ascendancy. Unlike the unsuccessful groups in the political arena, those in the union federation did not secede from the union center, nor did the successful faction endeavor to drive them out. Although the majority faction desired to reorganize Norwegian unionism along industrial rather than craft lines, and even into regional syndicates, it did not impose its views when it won control by a bare majority in the mid-twenties, but instead offered to compromise.

Despite the internal conflicts of the twenties, Norway thus has had only one national union federation, which has included a very high proportion of all unionists within its ranks. Moreover, the federation traditionally has been strong and highly centralized. Edvard Bull notes that strike funds were centrally controlled from the outset, and that the national unions frequently have been too small to support well-staffed secretariats with legal and economic advisors. He contrasts the functions of local and national unions and the federation in Norway with those in the United States, Britain, and France, concluding that "in Norway, the National Federation is indisputably the most powerful authority." [2] Furthermore, the union movement has been relatively free from sharp internal differences since the time of troubles in the decade following the First World War. Not only have ideological conflicts receded, but jurisdictional rivalry has been contained within bounds. The existence of a strong labor federation; the successful functioning of its "disputes committee," which was established in 1931 to settle jurisdictional differences; the close ties with the Labor Party; and the persistence of solidaristic sentiments have worked to keep rivalry subdued.

The Communist Party has not been an important divisive factor since 1923. After its secession from the Norwegian Labor Party in 1923, the Communist Party rapidly declined in size and influence. Discussing the amalgamation of the Labor Party and the Social Democrats in 1927, Galenson states that "unity was achieved in 1927, leaving outside the fold only the communists, who through desertions had already been reduced to a small and ineffectual sect." [3] Although the Communists regained some strength during World War II, winning 12 per cent of the vote in the 1945 national elections, they soon declined once more.

The Norwegian trade union movement is not only unified and controlled by a strong national center, but has enjoyed a loyal and stable membership. From small beginnings at the turn of the century, union membership increased steadily and fairly rapidly. Growth was accelerated during the second decade, and union membership reached a peak of approximately 142,000, in 1920, representing a substantial degree of organization in a country of less than 3,000,000 persons in which many employees were engaged in agriculture and other non-industrial pursuits. A sharp drop in membership occurred in the early twenties, but growth was quickly resumed. Losses in membership were regained by 1931, and membership continued to grow steadily until the German occupation in World War II. By 1948 nearly 60 per cent of wage and salary earners had been enrolled in unions. This proportion has been maintained up to the present. Thus, except for the economic and ideological difficulties of the early 1920's and the German occupation during World War II, Norwegian trade unions have enjoyed steady growth to a high degree of organization.

Acceptance of unionism and collective bargaining on the part of employers is another important element in stable industrial relations. Again, the Norwegian story is unlike the Danish. Instead of the "spirit of corporatism" found in Denmark almost from the beginnings of the modern collective bargaining system nearly sixty years ago, there was a long period of large-scale industrial disputes often tantamount to complete breakdowns in union-management relations. Vast strikes and lockouts were frequent, particularly in the years between 1920 and 1931. The 1931 series of strikes and lockouts resulted in a loss of approximately fifty-two working days per union member in that year, a ratio probably never matched in any other industrialized country. The outbreaks in 1921 and 1924 were similarly of massive proportions, and there was severe industrial unrest in 1920, 1926, and 1927. Perhaps because of exhaustion, or because the long deflationary period had come to an end, or because each side finally realized that the other could not be vanquished,[4] Norwegian industrial relations entered a peaceful phase.

The Norwegian counterpart of the Danish "September Agreement" of 1899 was the "basic agreement" of 1935. Capital and labor mutually recognized each other's right to organize and provided a uniform grievance procedure and bargaining apparatus. This formal agreement was concluded between representatives of the Federation of Labor and the central Confederation of Employers' Associations. Thus the struggle for existence and institutional security came to an end in 1935.

The basic agreement not only formalizes mutual acceptance, but illustrates the high degree of centralization of the Norwegian collective bargaining system. It is incorporated automatically into every agreement concluded by affiliates of the "peak" organizations; its regulations concerning election rights and duties of shop stewards, grievance procedures, balloting on agreements, and so forth, are thus made uniform throughout most of the economic structure.

Negotiations are generally conducted on a multi-employer basis, but consolidated bargaining structure does not stop there. In addition, the peak organizations have more power in determining employment conditions than do their counterparts in most countries. Not only does the Federation of Labor control strike funds and participate in signing the collective agreements, but "no collective agreement may be terminated, no wage demand raised, and no notice of strike given, unless the approval of the NFTU Executive Board is secured in advance." [5] The situation is similar on the other side of the table. According to Galenson, the representative of the Employers' Association does the active bargaining in industry-wide negotiations. "The power of the Employers' Association stems ultimately from the fact that neither an affiliate nor an individual member may enter into an agreement without the advance approval of its central board." [6] Thus the Norwegian collective bargaining system is one of the most centralized in the world.

Relations between the unions and the Labor Party, and changes in the role of government, have also contributed to the virtual elimination of strikes in the years since 1935. Founded in 1887, the Labor Party grew steadily—though not without trouble, as already described—to major party status in the late 1920's. Although it became the largest single party in Parliament in 1933, having just slightly less than a majority, the Labor Party did not take over the government for another two years, when shaky right-wing coalitions finally collapsed. The Labor Party governed in coalitions from 1935 until the beginning of World War II, led the government-in-exile during the war, won an absolute majority in 1945, and has governed exclusively ever since.

Working relations between the Labor Party and the Federation of Labor have always been close. Collective affiliation of union locals to the party and overlapping of leadership have previously been noted. Although Galenson emphasizes the autonomy of the industrial and political wings, he observes that "with few exceptions national trade union leaders are members of the Labor Party, while the party officialdom is largely drawn from trade union ranks." [7] This close identification has undoubtedly colored the labor relations scene, particularly in the postwar era when its absolute parliamentary majority has enabled the party to move ahead firmly with its own program of comprehensive national planning.

Sharing the same ideals and goals, the unions and the party have cooperated to attempt to regain prewar productivity standards, maintain a balance between desirable real wage levels and inflationary pressures, rationalize the wage structure by eliminating objectionable differentials, and guide the direction of industrial development through labor market controls. Implementing these efforts during the immediate postwar reconstruction period was the collaboration between the government and the unions, which was essential to make compulsory arbitration workable.

The effects of this close alliance in reorienting the outlook of the labor movement seem obvious. Under a system of national planning and pervasive economic regulation, the labor movement is able to influence the conditions of the working population by control over the price level as well as wages. Charged with responsibilty for the economy as a whole, the labor movement must carefully weigh the effects of its policies and goals upon employment, the price level, and the international competitive position of the export industries. It is forced to bear the preponderance of responsibility for maintaining industrial peace. High productivity and wage restraint have been added to its list of objectives.

In summary, then, Norway has had for more than twenty years a strong, secure, and unified labor movement, a well-developed and highly centralized collective bargaining system, and a political setting that gives the unions a direct interest in promoting cooperation and industrial peace.

Sweden [8]

Strike activity was very great in Sweden, as in Norway, for several decades after the beginnings of large-scale unionism and collective bargaining. The proportion of union members participating in strikes was among the highest in the world from the start of the century to the mid

1920's. Rates of involvement dropped sharply to a lower level for nearly a decade from the mid-twenties to the mid-thirties, and dwindled rapidly again during the closing years of the thirties, reaching a very low level in 1939. Participation in strikes has continued to be very low up to the present time, except for the 1945 metal workers' strike.

The duration of work stoppages in Sweden—man-days lost per worker involved—also was high in the early days of unionism. Unlike the involvement rates, however, duration has not declined over the years. In fact, strikes seem to have grown slightly longer. Stoppages being so infrequent, however, loss of working time has been very low during the past two decades, whether considered in relation to union membership or to the number of wage and salary earners.

A major element in industrial peace is the strength and stability of the union movement. Important components include the extent of organization, the attachment to their unions exhibited by rank and file members, the solidarity and unity within the union movement, and the extent of centralization of authority and disciplinary powers. These components will be observed one by one in their Swedish context.

Sweden ranks high in the first component of union strength—the relative size of the unionized sector of the labor force. The degree of organization, measured by total union membership as a per cent of all non-agricultural wage and salary earners, has been among the highest in the world, year after year, for at least the past three decades.

Attachment to unions on the part of rank-and-file members may be assessed as a first approximation by the relative stability of union membership. Almost from its inception, the Swedish union movement has gained membership steadily, without the wide fluctuations which have occurred in many countries. The most severe setback took place in the few years following the failure of the 1909 general strike, during which the unions lost nearly 50 per cent of their prestrike membership. Since that time, however, the only years in which union membership declined from the preceding year were 1921, 1922, and 1933. Each time the decline was small and was erased within one or two years.

A third important component of strength is the high degree of unity and internal solidarity. The present national trade union center—Landsorganisationen i Sverige (LO)—was founded in 1898 as a reformist-Socialist federation. It included only about half of the trade unionists in the country for the first few years, but rapidly achieved a preponderance of membership. The Svenska Arbetareforbundet, Swedish counterpart to the German Hirsch-Dunker unions, was established in 1899, but was eliminated in the aftermath of the 1909 general strike. An attempt also was made to form a Swedish equivalent of the Knights of Labor in the early 1900's, but this also failed after a few years. The only serious rivalry to the Socialist federation was offered by the Syndicalists, succeeded by the Communists after the First World War. These left-wing groups were always a small minority of Swedish unionism, however. During the years of World War II the Communists gained strength within the LO, especially in the Metal Workers' Union, but their importance dwindled rapidly after the failure of the 1945 Metal Trades strike.[9] Thus the overwhelming predominance of LO, the Socialist center, has never been seriously challenged since the earliest days of unionism.

Other threats to labor unity have been insignificant. Although the federation of salaried workers' unions created during the 1930's has grown to substantial size [10] it is not a divisive factor.

Jurisdictional rivalry, which has plagued some national union movements in place of religious and ideological rivalry, similarly has been quite insignificant in Sweden. The strength of the central federation and the emphasis on unity springing from the early victory of the Socialists have enabled Swedish labor to move, without strife, from craft to industrial unionism, and to realign jurisdiction along rational rather than historical lines.

A final component of union strength is centralization of control within the union movement. The Swedish national trade union center exhibits a significant degree of centralized power and control. Proposed strikes involving more than 3 per cent of the workers in an industry must have approval of the General Council of the LO before LO strike benefits can be paid. The LO officials have the right to supervise bargaining if two or more unions are affected. LO leaders or representatives participate in negotiations and may submit proposals on their own. Above and beyond these formal provisions, control of the central federation is strengthened by the long tradition of solidarity within the labor movement. Myers observes,

> The strongest pressure exerted by the LO on its affiliated unions is undoubtedly a moral one. The feeling of solidarity which has been characteristic of the Swedish labor movement tends to discourage actions by national unions which would embarrass the LO or the Social Democratic government.[11]

Another important element in national patterns of industrial relations is the policy of employers regarding unions and collective bargaining. In Sweden, as elsewhere, employers resisted unionism vigorously in the early days of worker organization. After only a few years of rapid union growth, the employers began to counterorganize. Strikes and strike threats were answered by large-scale lockouts. Despite this initial resistance to unions, collective agreements grew increasingly common as the years passed. Employers continued to oppose union demands, even to the point of conducting massive lockouts to press for wage reductions, but abandoned the attempt to eliminate unionism at some time early in the century. Norgren, discussing the launching of the employers' counteroffensive shortly after the creation of strong associations in the early 1900's, asserts that

> The employers' main and immediate objective in organizing was, of course, to halt the workers' forward push. But it is significant that in launching their counter offensive they did not try to destroy either the unions themselves or the bargaining institutions which union initiative had brought into being.[12]

An SAF pamphlet states that in 1906 the two sides reached an agreement whereby "the employers agreed to respect the workers' right to organize, while the workers recognize the employers' right of management and freedom to select the labour required." [13] Another SAF publication, however, refers to the 1909 general strike as "the last time the organizations tried to break each other in open strife." [14]

Even the employer attempts to "halt the workers' forward push" gave way during the twenties and early thirties. Tage Lindbom observes that the blacklists had fallen into disuse, and that the use of strikebreakers, formerly widespread, ceased after the Adalen clash in 1931.[15] A further step was the SAF policy, at the onset of the great depression in 1931, to seek the smallest possible wage reduction in an attempt to avert labor unrest and to keep future wage demands "within reason." [16]

The present era of mutual acceptance and good feeling began with the signing of the "Saltsjöbaden Agreement" in 1939. This basic agreement, frequently referred to as a general labor peace treaty, established a joint Labor Market Board to handle certain questions concerning dismissals, layoffs, and various work-stoppage problems. The agreement also established a negotiating procedure and included explicit provisions covering dismissals and layoffs. The basic agreement has subsequently been ratified by most of the constituent unions and employer associations.

A third major element in Swedish industrial peace, a consolidated bargaining structure, requires highly centralized employer and worker organizations. We have already noted that this requirement has been met on the labor side. The employers' central federation, Svenska Arbetsgivareföreningen (SAF), was established in 1902 and grew very rapidly in strength. It was able to organize large-scale lockouts in the early 1900's, and effectively contained the union offensives in the 1909 general strike. SAF now includes a large proportion of all Swedish employers, organized into forty-two industrial associations.

The federation has even greater centralized control than the labor center. The executive board of the SAF, composed of a full-time managing director and other members appointed by the affiliated associations, exercises broad powers. The bylaws require affiliates and members to obtain the board's approval before signing any labor agreement. Concerning the strong position of the board, Norgren writes,

> . . . in practice the executive board (or its constituent group, the executive committee) makes nearly all the important decisions. It plays an important role in terminating, drafting proposals for, and concluding agreements; in deciding on action regarding strikes; and in declaring and effectuating lockouts.[17]

The power to make decisions is supported by power to enforce them in order to maintain the position of the SAF. Substantial fines may be imposed by the board upon members and affiliates for breaking discipline. The SAF also offers positive inducements: regular strike benefits are paid, and if exceptional circumstances indicate the need, a substantial extra allowance may be forthcoming.

With strong federations on both sides, it has been possible to build a tightly controlled bargaining system. A major proportion of Swedish workers are covered by multi-employer, industry-wide contracts. Typically, negotiations are carried on by representatives of an industry association and a national trade union with approximately the same jurisdiction. Agents of the central federations may also participate on both sides of the table. As pointed out earlier, the employers' association involved in the negotiations has relatively little power for independent action, the authority to make final decisions being retained by the central employers' group. The trade union negotiators usually have more autonomy, but the central federation has the prestige and moral authority to be very persuasive.[18]

Tendencies toward greater centralization in bargaining have been appearing in recent decades. The negotiations leading to the Saltsjöbaden Agreement of the later thirties were a first step toward greater involvement of the peak organizations in negotiations. The central organizations agreed to the 1949–50 "wage-stop," and in 1952 they negotiated an across-the-board increase for all affiliated unions and associations.

The final cause of the disappearance of strike activity in Sweden is the political effectiveness of the labor movement. The Swedish unions were involved in the creation of the Social Democratic Party, and the two wings of the labor movement, industrial and political, have maintained close working relationships to the present time. Although a proposed requirement that unions desiring to join the LO must also affiliate with the Social Democratic Party met with opposition and was finally dropped in the early 1900's, union officials continued to urge affiliation and strong support. At the present time, there are no formal connections between the national union center and the party, but there is considerable overlapping of membership as well as close collaboration between the two groups.

The Social Democratic Party has been a major political force in Sweden almost since the beginning of the modern democratic state. The party and the unions were leaders in the movement for full manhood suffrage at the turn of the century. By 1914 the Social Democratic Party was the largest single party in the lower house of the Riksdag. It participated in a coalition government with the Liberals in 1917. During the 1920's the Social Democrats led coalition governments on several occasions. Winning strong support in the 1932 elections, but still short of an absolute majority, the party again took over the government in 1933. The Social Democrats were dependent on the Agrarians for a sufficient majority to enact their program during the thirties, and included the latter party in their government after the 1936 elections.

A national coalition government, including all the major parties but led by the Social Democrats, was formed in 1939 and was sustained for the duration of the war. In 1945, the Social Democrats formed a one-party government which lasted until 1951. They ruled in coalition with the Agrarians from 1951 to 1957, when they established a one-party government again. Thus, during the forty-one years from 1917 to 1958, since the adoption of the full parliamentary system in Sweden, the Social Democratic Party has led the government for a total of thirty-two years, much of the time as the sole governing party or with an absolute majority in the Riksdag. Clearly, the Swedish labor movement has been politically successful.

NOTES TO CHAPTER 8

1. Walter Galenson, *Labor in Norway* (Cambridge: Harvard University Press, 1949); Edvard Bull, *The Norwegian Trade Union Movement* (Brussels: International Confederation of Free Trade Unions, 1956); *Employment Policy in Norway* (Oslo: Norwegian Joint Committee on International Social Policy, 1950); Steve M. Slaby, *The Labor Court in Norway* (Oslo: Norwegian Academic Press, 1952); *The Trade Union Movement in Norway* (Oslo: Arbeidernes Faglige Landsorganisasjon i Norge, 1955); Mark W. Leiserson, *Wages and Economic Control in Norway* (Cambridge: Harvard University Press, 1959).

2. Bull, *op. cit.,* p. 42.

3. Galenson, *op. cit.,* p. 68.

4. Edvard Bull states, "The greatest labour conflict in the history of Norway ended indecisively. Both in the Confederation of Employers and the Federation [of Labor] there was the impression that both parties had now become so strong that nothing could be gained by wrestling in the old way: like modern warfare, there was only loss for all sides." Bull, *op. cit.,* p. 93.

5. *Ibid.,* p. 134.

6. Galenson, *op. cit.,* p. 86.

7. *Ibid.,* pp. 71–72.

8. Paul H. Norgren, *The Swedish Collective Bargaining System* (Cambridge: Harvard University Press, 1941); Sigfrid Hansson, *The Trade Union Movement of Sweden* (Amsterdam: The International Federation of Trade Unions, 1927), and *Employers and Workers in Sweden* (Stockholm: The Royal Swedish Commission, New York World's Fair, 1939); Charles A. Myers, *Industrial Relations in Sweden* (Cambridge: The Technology Press, 1951); *A Survey of Social and Labour Conditions in Sweden* (Stockholm: The Swedish Employers' Confederation, 1947); *Perspective of Labour Conditions in Sweden* (Stockholm: The Swedish Employers' Confederation, 1954); Tage Lindbom, *Sweden's Labor Program* (New York: League for Industrial Democracy, 1948); *This is LO* (Stockholm: Landsorganisationen i Sverige, 1952).

9. Charles A. Myers' comment on the 1945 strike, the most serious industrial dispute in Sweden since the twenties, is interesting on this point. "There was one outstanding exception to this attitude [hesitation by national unions to take action embarrassing to the government or to L.O.] in 1945, when communist elements in the Metal Workers' Union took advantage of postwar dissatisfaction over wage levels to urge a strike. Even though the officers of the Union and of the L.O. opposed the strike, they did not attempt to prevent it at all cost. The strike lasted five months, and failed to gain much against the united opposition of employers. But the strike 'taught the members a lesson,' for they learned that they could not successfully get more than the labor movement generally was able to get." Myers, *op. cit.,* p. 20.

10. The rapid growth of the salaried workers' unions, federated in the Tjänstemännens Centralorganisationen outside the LO, has resulted in a decline in the proportion of total union membership affiliated with the workers' federation. However, in view of the rather clear demarcation of jurisdictional lines, the overwhelmingly large size of LO and the absence of serious rivalry between the LO

and the TCO, it seems that the rise of the latter does not seriously impair the unity of the Swedish union movement.

11. Myers, *op. cit.,* p. 19.

12. Norgren, *op. cit.,* p. 67.

13. *A Survey of Social and Labour Conditions in Sweden,* p. 21.

14. *Perspective of Labour Conditions in Sweden,* p. 17.

15. Lindbom, *op. cit.,* pp. 9–10.

16. Norgren, *op. cit.,* pp. 301–02.

17. *Ibid.,* p. 41.

18. The difference in centralization within the two organizations was nicely illustrated by the observation in an SAF publication, "The employers' delegation has the power to put a final signature on the recommendation straight away if it is in line with SAF policy, but the labour delegation usually submits it to the contract conference or to a general vote of the union members." *Perspective of Labour Conditions in Sweden,* p. 36.

CHAPTER 9

Mediterranean-Asian

Pattern

France [1]

The six countries discussed in the preceding chapters are all characterized by a low propensity to strike. In some, stoppages are typically very brief; in others they are sufficiently long to constitute real tests of economic strength; but in every country the percentage of union members going on strike each year is small.

We now encounter a second group in which the pattern of industrial disputes is very different. Strikes are widespread, involving substantial proportions of union members and non-agricultural employees in most years. At the same time, the average duration of strikes is only a few days. France, Italy, and Japan clearly belong in the group. This pattern of strike activity has been generally characteristic of India, although strikes there have been somewhat longer than in other countries of the Mediterranean-Asian group. Australia also has many short strikes, but as noted previously, the explanations are so different that Australia is best classified as a special case.

No two countries are alike, let alone four, and least of all France, Italy, Japan, and India. Nevertheless, certain common conditions will be observed. We shall note weak, unstable, and decentralized labor movements, with severe leadership rivalries. Communists have held strategic positions of leadership. Employers have generally not accepted the unions in any full sense, nor has a solid collective bargaining structure been erected. Labor parties have not been so effective as to encourage relinquishment of the strike weapon. Legislation and other government actions have played a larger role than collective bargaining in defining major terms of employment. Under these circumstances the strike is most commonly a technique of massive demonstration and protest rather than a phase in the collective bargaining process.

It will be convenient to point out here that union membership statistics for all four of these countries are highly imprecise. Those for France, Italy, and Japan are generally exaggerated; those for India are understated. Our membership involvement rates are necessarily affected; but for reasons discussed in the Appendix, we do not think the inaccuracies are fatal.

We may begin with France. Involvement in strikes was already high in the days of the Popular Front, and remained high after the revival of unionism in 1945. The number of strikers reached 115 per cent of union membership in 1948. It has never been less than 36.1 per cent since 1946, and averaged 62.4 per cent for the 1948–56 period. Similarly, the proportion of non-agricultural employees going on strike has averaged about 25 per cent annually since the war. Clearly, French workers have been the most strike-prone of any in the world. On the other hand, the average duration of strikes, although fifteen to twenty days in prewar France, has been extremely short during the postwar period. It has declined steadily from about five days in 1945–47 to less than two days in 1954–56. During the latter period, it was the lowest of any country studied with the exception of South Africa.

The extremely high rates of participation offset the brevity of strikes, so that ratios of lost working time are relatively high. Idleness in relation to the size of the labor movement as well as the number of non-agricultural workers is greater than in most other countries. Only the United States, India, and Finland have higher loss ratios.

As we have suggested, this pattern of strike activity is often associated with a weak and unstable labor movement, which either has not attempted to establish viable bargaining relationships or has not been successful in doing so. The French labor movement, it is true, is one of the older ones. There were more than 1,000,000 union members as early as 1912. Unionism has been far from stable, however.

Membership of the central federation dropped from 2,000,000 to 600,000 members during 1920, for example. There was a four-fold jump in the mid-thirties, from 1,400,000 in 1935 to 5,500,000 in 1936. By 1940, however, membership had fallen below the 1935 level.

French unionism has been just as unstable in the postwar period. The intensity of organization has declined from 85 per cent of the non-agricultural wage and salary earners in 1945–47 to 28 per cent in 1954–56. In absolute numbers, membership fell from about 7,000,-000 in 1947 to scarcely more than 2,000,000 in 1955.[2] Other labor movements—those in Italy, Japan, and Finland, for example—have suffered relative losses since 1947, but none has lost so many members so quickly.

Thus the degree of organization in France was the highest in the world ten years ago and has since become one of the lowest of any country studied. Despite its long history, the French labor movement has not solved the problem of instability and has never gained a strong and permanent membership base.

Organizational and leadership rivalries have been persistent throughout French labor history. Unions and federations have been differentiated on political and religious grounds, but, in contrast with similar groupings in the Netherlands, have seldom practiced a policy of peaceful coexistence. Today there are three major federations: the Communist-led Confédération Générale du Travail (CGT), the Socialist-led Confédération Générale du Travail—Force Ouvrière (FO), and the Catholic Confédération Française des Travailleurs Chrétiens (CFTC).[3] Their affiliates have been designated as "representative unions" in a wide variety of industries. The concepts of majority rule and exclusive bargaining rights are not accepted in France, so that affiliates of two or even three major federations often have members in the same plant. Therefore, competition for prestige and membership is carried on not only in multi-employer bargaining negotiations and political affairs, but also at the plant level. As Adolf Sturmthal states,

> Every union endeavored to demonstrate that its competitor was "giving in" too readily to the employers, and the union representatives were reluctant to accept reasonable compromises out of fear of their rivals. To demonstrate that no better results could be obtained, the unions "tolerated" strikes with or without official approval. . . .[4]

Disunity and rivalry in French unionism have undoubtedly been aggravated by the Communists. As in many countries, the Communists first became prominent in France during the early 1920's, drawing strength from the success of the Russian revolution. When expelled from the CGT in 1923, they took more than half the membership and remained a strong factor in French unionism. The CGT was reunified in 1936, and Communist-led unions controlled about half the membership until their expulsion once more in 1939. The Communists took a leading role in the resistance movement during World War II, and obtained control of the CGT when it was re-established in 1945. The CGT, still Communist-controlled to the present date, is by far the largest national union center, having as many members as all other federations combined.

It can be taken for granted that where strikes are called as frequently as in France, the labor movement is not disciplined by a strong responsible political party. There has been no single labor party on the British or Scandinavian model. Divisions in politics have been similar to those in the union movement, with numerous parties specifically appealing for labor support, including the Communists, the Socialists, and the MRP.

The antiparliamentary position of the Communists and the relative weakness of the other parties have made labor governments in France a near impossibility. Only the Popular Front of 1936–38 and the first few postwar governments from 1945 to about 1947 were clearly labor governments. Although Socialists participated in some of the subsequent governments, they did not play an effective role, and French politics have moved steadily to the right during the past decade. All in all, political activity has not been an organizing and disciplining force in French labor relations.

Nor has an effective collective bargaining system been developed. Negotiations are somewhat centralized, usually involving local or regional employer associations and affiliates of two or three of the major union federations. There is very little national industry-wide bargaining as is prevalent in northern Europe, but negotiations at the plant level are also rare. Indeed, there has been little collective bargaining at all in France. Prior to 1936 the unions were not generally strong enough to challenge the employers' autonomy. Under the laws promulgated by the Popular Front government of the late 1930's, wages and working conditions were established by government-appointed arbitrators in nearly all cases. Free labor unions disappeared during the World War II. In the postwar period, the government closely regulated wages and labor-management agreements until 1950. Although stringent government controls were lifted in 1950, collective bargaining has remained rather restricted. In fact, most of the agreements are limited to wage rates, leaving all other subjects untouched.

Much of the weakness arises from the resistance of French employers to unionism and collective bargaining. In this connection Val Lorwin observes,

> Employer attitudes work against orderly bargaining and union responsibility. . . . On the employer side as on the worker side, labor relations still have the character of a class conflict rather than of an economic bargain.[5]

The employers have had superior organization, superior staff and superior bargaining strength. They have played organizations against each other, have refused to bargain on many issues, and generally have been successful in keeping the unions at bay. Adolf Sturmthal concludes that "in spite of high levels of profits in many branches of industry, French employers are rarely willing to make collective bargaining work." [6]

French workers and unions, unlike those in Germany, have not been agreeable to this subordinate position. Thus, the lack of full acceptance has thwarted the development of collective bargaining and has encouraged industrial conflict in the same way as in the United States during the 1930's.

The part played by the French government, if it has not weakened collective bargaining, has at least usurped many of its functions. The government has established terms of employment not only as an entrepreneur, but also through regulation of private industry. Since the time of the Popular Front in the 1930's, hours of work and paid vacations have been defined by statutes. Under a system of wage control between 1946 and 1950, no collective agreement could become effective without government approval. Although wage control was abandoned in 1950, the legal minimum wage has continued to wield an important influence on the whole wage level. It has not only been frequently adjusted, but has also—unlike the minimum wage in the United States—had the effect of elevating the entire wage structure. Quoting Sturmthal once more,

> In general, the increases [in the minimum wage] were fairly well reflected in the general wage structure. Contractual wages are so close to the legal minimum that changes in the latter provoke adjustments all along the wage hierarchy.[7]

Finally, the "social charges," such as family allowances, which constitute a major fraction of labor costs and earnings, are determined by legislation and not by collective bargaining.

The government's entrepreneurial role is likewise important. There is a surprising amount of public enterprise in France. Not only are the coal mines, railways, and public utilities under state ownership, but also a substantial share of the banking, insurance, automobile, aircraft, and airline industries. The government employs approximately one-fourth of all non-agricultural workers in France.

Under all these circumstances, French strikes in the postwar period have had the character of demonstrations, with political overtones, rather than economic tests of strength. The Communists, with their predominant hold on French unionism, have frequently used the strike as a device for political agitation. Protests have been directed against the Marshall plan, prosecution of the war in Indochina, the arrest of Communist leader Jacques Duclos, the activities of General Ridgeway, and so forth. Discussing non-economic elements in Communist-led work stoppages, Sturmthal asserts,

> From the summer of 1947 on . . . successive waves of strikes expressed at the same time the social dissatisfaction of the workers, the political struggle in France, and the friction between the Soviet Union and France.[8]

The other unions, too, employ the strike as a political tactic. The Socialist-inclined CGT-FO, for example, conducted demonstration strikes in 1949 to urge the abandonment of wage controls.

In summary, strike activity in France can be understood by reference to its setting. Union weakness, employer strength, and the rudimentary character of the collective bargaining system tend to preclude recourse to the economic strike as a test of staying power. The prominence of Communist leadership, the intensive organizational rivalries, and the major role played by a government not specifically friendly to labor, all encourage frequent resort to the demonstration strike. Finally, the economic and political institutions that explain the virtual disappearance of industrial conflict in Northern Europe have not developed in France.

Italy [9]

Italy and France have strong similarities in many aspects of life, including economic organization, political structure, labor-management relations, and industrial conflict. During the postwar period, rates of participation in both countries have been among the highest in the world. The number of strikes in France has been the highest in relation to union membership, whereas Italy has had the highest rates in proportion to non-agricultural employment. The duration of strikes has typically been very brief in both countries.

When we examine the two systems of industrial relations, we find many common attributes which are consistent with high participation rates and low strike duration. In Italy as in France, inflation has been a key issue since 1945. The labor movement is disunited and splintered into several confederations. Political radicalism is widespread. The Communists control the largest federation and have frequently launched large-scale strikes for political purposes. Employers are more strongly organized than workers and have never fully accepted unionism in the sense of becoming reconciled to permanent, stable, and close relationships. Labor lacks unity in the political field as well as in economic life, and has never assumed responsibility for organizing governments. Finally, the prevalent poverty, continual inflation and deep-seated class antagonisms are conducive to industrial discontent and frequent protests.

There are significant differences between the two countries, however. First, collective bargaining in Italy is more centralized. The agreements cover particular industries throughout the nation rather than in smaller regions. Second, the Italian government does not participate so actively as the French in defining terms of employment through legislation. Consequently, the collective agreements have more real importance in Italy. Third, the Italian labor movement, unlike the French, includes large numbers of agricultural workers. For this reason—and perhaps also because estimates of union membership have been even more inflated than in France—the Italian statistics showing intensity of organization are even higher.

Before explaining these matters further, we should furnish a few details concerning strike experience in Italy. Between 1948 and 1956, the number of strikers averaged 35 per cent of union membership annually. As noted earlier, this ratio was the highest of any country studied, with the exception of France, where it averaged 62 per cent during the same nine-year period. The proportion of strikers to non-agricultural employees has been higher in Italy, however, averaging about 28 per cent per year. This ratio is nearly six times as great as in the United States and seventy times as great as in Sweden! Thus the Italian rates of participation have been fantastically high.

As in France, strikes are generally very short. The average duration was three days in 1948–50, two days in 1951–53, and three days once more in 1954–56.

The Italian labor movement, like that of France, Japan, and India, has been weak and divided throughout its history. There has been a deep and chronic division between the advocates of evolutionary and revolutionary methods. Unions began to form in Italy, as in most of

Europe, during the late nineteenth century; but they were unimportant, having no more than a few hundred thousand members in a country of more than 30,000,000 people, until the end of the First World War. The labor movement flourished immediately after World War I, as it did elsewhere in Europe. Union membership rose to more than 1,000,000 in 1919, and more than 2,000,000 in 1920. At that point a process of attrition set in, the number of unionists shrinking by almost half. The rise of fascism virtually extinguished the unions; there were scarcely 200,000 members in 1924, and complete collapse followed soon after.

Twenty years later, with the fall of Mussolini, unions again flourished in Italy. As in Germany and Japan, they grew rapidly with the encouragement of the occupying forces. By 1948, approximately 9,000,-000 adherents were claimed. Once more there was a decline in membership in the 1950's, although not relatively so great as that of the early twenties. About 6,000,000 members were still listed in 1956,[10] and there is reason to believe that the actual total was considerably smaller.

Thus large-scale unionism has existed in Italy for a total of less than twenty years, and even these twenty years have been divided between two periods of time so widely separated as to destroy any continuity. For all practical purposes, Italy has a new union movement.

Italy resembles the other Mediterranean-Asian countries, and differs from those in northern Europe, in the character of union membership. Dues are nominal; affiliation and disaffiliation come easily, and represent collective rather than individual decisions.

Theory suggests and history supports the proposition that a disunited labor movement is not in a position to discipline and pacify the labor force. Italian unionism has not only been weak and unstable but also disunited. There are three major confederations, the Communist Confederazione Generale Italiana del Lavoro (CGIL), the Socialist Unione Italiana del Lavoro (UIL), and the Confederazione Italiana Sindicati Nazional dei Lavoratori (CISL), which is regarded as having close but unofficial ties with the Christian Democratic Party and the Catholic Church. The Communist confederation claims to be as large as the other two put together, and the Socialist group is small.[11] Affiliates of all three federations must be signatory to the major industry-wide agreements, and as we would expect, there is much rivalry and disagreement over terms of employment to be sought. Joseph LaPalombara devotes a chapter to interunion rivalry, chiefly between the CGIL and the CISL. An interesting example of the divisive effect is found in the 1953–54 wage negotiations, in which CISL took a more conciliatory line than

CGIL. As a result, CGIL was forced from the negotiations, and "for the first time in its proud history, CGIL was compelled by the free unions to sign a national contract it did not want and in the negotiation of which it had played no part." [12]

Interunion competition extends to the election and operation of plant grievance committees. Technically the plant committees are divorced from federation control, but the relationship is close. In most cases only the Communist and Catholic-oriented groups compete at the plant level, but in some areas there is rivalry between UIL and CGIL. Finally, the fact that the CSIL is fairly close to the Christian Democratic Party, whereas the Communists have not participated in governments and have sought to weaken their effectiveness, has sharpened the animosity between these two larger organizations.

The role of the Italian Communist Party in the labor movement has been similar to that of the French party. The Communists played a leading part in anti-Fascist strikes, sabotage, and armed resistance during World War II, especially in northern Italy. When a free labor movement was re-established, they emerged in firm control of the major unions as well as the CGIL, which remained the only national union center until 1948. Catholic and Socialist federations have subsequently been established, but as already noted, CGIL still retains an absolute majority of total membership.

The CGIL has been called the "labor arm of the Communist party" and has dominated Italian strike activity. There is no serious dispute that a large number of strikes have been political in character. The widespread and continuous strike movement of 1947–48 (a critical election year) was not only politically inspired, but in the minds of some observers, approached the status of an abortive revolution. Neither can it be denied that many Communist strikes have had the purpose of thwarting and hampering the Italian government. LaPalombara states that trade union objectives generally have been subordinated to political purposes.

> That is, CGIL leaders are presumed to owe their first loyalties to the parties and therefore are expected to direct the confederation in a manner consistent with the articulated needs of [the Communist and Nenni Socialist parties]. . . . It may be concluded that the Communists within CGIL are not free to pursue trade union ends viewed apart from the overriding goals of the Communist movement itself.[13]

It should not be thought, however, that CGIL strikes have been purely political in nature. The Communist-led unions have been conscious of the need to perform the everyday social and economic tasks of unions that are not inconsistent with their political goals. Thus they assiduously handle grievances, are active in local welfare programs, and so forth. J. C. Adams warns against oversimplifying CGIL strike policy and points out that the majority of strikes have involved local grievances, wages, and other economic issues.

> Many of the post-Fascist strikes were of a political nature, but because this type of strike received more attention in the press, the larger number of economic strikes is sometimes overlooked.[14]

Nevertheless, the political strikes have been larger in scope, as well as receiving more attention in the press. In any event, the fact remains that the average striker has remained away from work only two or three days. The typical Italian strike is clearly a demonstration rather than a trial of economic strength, regardless of its causes.

We turn now to the collective bargaining institutions in Italy. As in other countries where workers are unusually prone to strike, the economic and social context is conducive to industrial unrest. Italy is overpopulated; poverty is a general condition, particularly in the south. There is chronic unemployment, which never amounts to less than about 10 per cent of the labor force, and which is coupled with serious underemployment. Needless to say, the Italian economy was badly disorganized by the end of World War II; inflationary pressures have been chronic since that time, although the tight-money policy followed in 1947–50 was reasonably effective under the circumstances. The Italian social structure is similar to the French in that there are rigid class lines which lend credibility to the ideology of class struggle, and different from the German in that workers have not agreeably accepted a subordinate position in the interest of national unity.

At first glance, the Italian collective bargaining system appears to be well developed and quite centralized. All important negotiations involve large groups of workers and employers. At the top of the pyramid is a master agreement negotiated between the employers' federation and the several labor federations. This agreement covers basic wage rates, cost-of-living increments, family allowances, and shop-committee functions, and is renegotiated from time to time. There is further bargaining at the industry level, and, in some instances, supplementary negotiations are held in the plant or locality. These local agreements are rare, however, and often amount to no more than memoranda incorporating the terms of settlement of piece-rate or other local disputes.

Behind the façade of a highly centralized collective bargaining system are important weaknesses. One weakness is that the system is new. It is not the old well-entrenched institution developed gradually to meet the need of the unions and employers, as are the Northern European systems. Instead it was hastily slapped together, of materials borrowed from abroad or inherited from the fascist regime, and has existed for scarcely more than a decade. The unions were organized from the top down and do not have strong roots in the industrial establishments.

The state plays an important role in the labor market, although not so important as in France. There is considerable public enterprise, including not only those activities that are generally socialized in Europe, but also the production and distribution of petroleum and natural gas, and a complex of banks and industrial plants administered by the Institute of International Reconstruction. Family allowances amount to about one-third of wage payments. Paid vacations are required by law, as well as premium pay for work on four national holidays.

The most important source of weakness, however, is employer resistance. Observers of Italian labor relations agree that except for the period immediately after World War II, employers have been generally hostile to unionism and collective bargaining. Their opposition takes many forms. The Employers' Federation, Confindustria, often refuses to negotiate on certain issues. The absence of any agreement on plant grievance committees between 1948 and 1953, as a result of Confindustria's refusal to bargain, is a case in point. Resistance also consists of widespread and open disregard of negotiated agreements. Commenting on the weakness of local unions and their inability to improve on the minimum terms of the national contracts, LaPalombara observes,

> Much more common is the situation wherein the hundreds, perhaps thousands, of weaker local unions and leagues are pitifully unable to cope with managements that not only refuse to improve the terms of national contracts, but refuse to honor them at all.[15]

Finally, employer opposition is expressed in open attacks on unions. Maurice Neufeld shows in detail how the Motta Company, for example, completely eliminated the union from its plants.[16] A similar case is that of Falk, a large North Italian iron and steel producer. The Falk management is strongly paternalistic, Neufeld points out, and insofar as it deals with any labor organization at all, favors the Communist CGIL and ignores the CISL.

Plausible explanations for such curious industrial behavior were numerous, but the one repeated most often was based on the supposition that Italian industrialists were convinced that the Communist party would be outlawed sooner or later; then, once CGIL was destroyed, they would not have to deal with any unions at all. A simpler explanation was perhaps the most valid one; the management at Falk was convinced that the non-Communist unions could not escape the political issues of the day and that constructive labor relations were impossible.[17]

Certainly it cannot be said that Italian collective bargaining has anything like the stability and effectiveness of the Scandinavian systems, for example. The hostility of employers toward collective bargaining and the disunity in the labor movement makes such a result impossible.

The final ingredient in the industrial relations pattern of the Mediterranean-Asian countries is the ineffectiveness of labor parties. During the reign of Mussolini, of course, the government was openly hostile to unionism. Since the close of the Fascist era there has been not a unified labor party, but rather, three groups espousing the cause of the worker—the Communists, the left-wing or Nenni Socialists, and the right-wing or Saragat Socialists. The first two are closely affiliated with CGIL, and the third with UIL. Despite their considerable strength, they have not participated in governments, except that the Saragat Socialists were included in the later DeGasperi coalitions. Although the Catholic-oriented federation, CISL, has some influence in the ruling Christian Democratic Party, it certainly is not predominant. Furthermore, CISL represents only a minority of labor; the Communist and Socialist unions together have a larger following. Consequently, most Italian unions have always existed under governments showing varying degrees of unfriendliness, and have never felt obligated to restrain their militancy for reasons of political responsibility.

Japan [18]

For about two years after the armistice in 1945, involvement in strikes among Japanese unionists was only moderate. Beginning in 1948, however, Japan soon developed a pattern of strike activity remarkably similar to the French and Italian patterns: unusually high participation and very brief duration. About 21 per cent of union members, on the average, went on strike each year in 1948–50, 24 per cent in 1951–53, and 16 per cent in 1954–56. At the same time, Japanese strikes have been growing shorter. The average striker lost five working days in 1948–50, six in 1951–53, and only three in 1954–56.

Union membership statistics for Japan are probably somewhat inflated, although not so badly as the French and Italian statistics. For this reason the estimates of propensity to strike tend to understate the situation.

Japan exhibits in classic form the economic and political characteristics associated with this pattern of strike activity: weak and unstable unionism, disunity in the labor movement, employer resistance to unions, an ineffective bargaining system, a strongly political cast to industrial relations, and a government in which labor has little or no voice.

One of the principal features of Japanese unions is their newness; indeed, the labor movement, to a great extent, is a product of the occupation. Japanese workers, unlike those in Germany and Italy, were not organized to any substantial extent prior to their complete suppression by totalitarian governments. Some hesitant beginnings in the 1890's were completely suppressed in 1900. The government slightly relaxed its harsh policies about the time of World War I, but Japanese unions did not meet with any great success during the subsequent three decades. At the peak of their prewar strength in 1936, Japanese unions had only 420,000 members, scarcely more than 3 per cent of the non-agricultural labor force. After being barely tolerated for a few decades, Japanese unions were again suppressed by the government in 1940.

The great turning point came after World War II. The American Occupation not only permitted but encouraged unionism, and in conquence, membership in Japanese unions rose from nothing in early 1945 to more than 6,500,000 in 1949.

The latter year was the high-water mark of unionism. There was a sharp decline in 1950 and 1951 as the result of a campaign against Communism and of renewed employer resistance to dealing with unions. Although membership began to rise once more in 1952, and losses had been regained by 1957, the increase was not commensurate with the growth of the labor force. Consequently, the proportion of wage and salary earners enrolled in labor organizations has dropped each year from 56 per cent in 1949 to barely 40 per cent in 1957. Thus Japanese unionism is of recent origin and has not yet demonstrated staying power over any substantial period of time.

Another element of weakness is disunity in the Japanese labor movement. Rivalry among various ideologies and schools of thought has been endemic since the earliest days. The miniature labor movement of the 1920's was torn by struggles among socialist, syndicalist, communist, and other factions. Ideological conflicts were renewed after World War II in the absence of any common philosophy of unionism.

> Even though almost every conceivable labor ideology from abroad—British Fabian socialism, Soviet communism, French syndicalism, German codetermination, American business unionism—has been articulated within the Japanese trade-union movement since the end of the war, just as the foreign "isms" competed in the prewar movement, none of these philosophies has yet proved predominant in Japan.[19]

These ideological rivalries have often been expressed in competing union federations. As soon as unions were sanctioned by the American occupation, Communists and other left-wing groups established the Sanbetsu, which remained the largest federation until 1949, with approximately 1,500,000 members. The more conservative unionists created Sodomei, only about half as large as Sanbetsu. Internal conflict, employer resistance, government opposition, and pressure from the occupation authorities led to the virtual collapse of Sanbetsu in 1949. A new and larger federation (Sohyo), subsequently to be dominated by left-wing Socialists, was formed in 1950. Sohyo grew rapidly to about 3,000,000 members, chiefly through the adherence of unions that had withdrawn from Sanbetsu and Sodomei, and some that had not affiliated with any federation. Even earlier, a small federation dedicated to pure industrial unionism (Shinsanbetsu) had come into existence. And in 1954, yet another national union center (Zenro Kaigi) was established by conservative elements withdrawing from Sohyo together with remnants of Sodomei, which had remained independent to this time. Zenro claimed about 800,000 members.

Although the Communists had great strength in the labor movement during the early postwar years, and although the Communist strike is typically a massive mobilization for agitational purposes rather than a true economic conflict, the persistence of high frequency and short duration of strikes cannot be attributed to Communist leadership. Communist strength rapidly waned after the "red purge" of 1949–50. The Socialist federation, Sohyo, which had acquired a large proportion of Sanbetsu's membership, frequently followed the Communist line during its first few years, but subsequently developed a more moderate leadership. In the 1955 national elections the Communists polled only 730,-000 votes, barely one-quarter of their strength in 1949. Sanbetsu had dwindled to about 12,000 members by 1955, and had formally dissolved three years later. Therefore, the persistence of numerous brief work stoppages must be explained on other grounds.

One explanation is the continued weakness of the labor movement. Through all the organizational transformations a relatively few strong national unions—those of seamen and textile workers, for example— have retained their identity and have been able to shift easily from one federation to another, or back to unaffiliated status. But more typical of the Japanese labor movement are thousands of "enterprise" unions. An enterprise union includes nearly all the employees of a single company without regard to occupation. Enterprise unions with about 1,000,000 members are entirely independent, whereas another group, with approximately 1,500,000 members, is loosely associated in national unions but not connected with any federation. In a few instances involving the employees of nation-wide firms such as the railway express company, an enterprise union may also constitute a national union.[20] Thus the Japanese federations have been, and still are, weak and unstable alliances embracing only a portion of all union members. There is no strong center, no prevailing ideology, and no common front within Japanese labor.

The enterprise union is not only the basic organizational unit but also the principal collective bargaining agent. Industry-wide bargaining prevails in the maritime and textile unions, it is true; but as a general rule Japanese collective bargaining is conducted at the company level by the enterprise union. In addition to being decentralized, bargaining is limited in scope. The negotiations, although wordy and prolonged, frequently deal with little more than the size of summer and year-end bonuses, retrenchment problems, and rights of permanent employees. Many "collective bargaining contracts" merely rehearse legal guarantees of recognition and incorporate fringe benefits already provided by statute. Furthermore, almost one-quarter of all union members are not covered by any kind of collective agreement. Adding to the weakness of the collective bargaining system is the fact that a considerable proportion of Japanese unionists are employed by the government, and consequently are not in a position to do much bargaining. About one-third of all union members are enrolled in organizations of government employees, and government unions make up two-thirds of Sohyo, the largest federation. There are few countries with so much unionism and so little collective bargaining as Japan.

Contrasting with the weakness of unionism is the dominant position of the employer. Japanese employers were quite disorganized by defeat in World War II, and accepted unionism without murmur in the early years of the occupation. In 1949 and 1950, however, they reversed their position. They vigorously cut back the industrial work force following the economic reorganization and monetary reforms of the Dodge plan. They undertook a purge of Communists with the encouragement of the government and occupation authorities. Basic labor laws were revised. The employers generally took the initiative in all economic matters, including vigorous opposition to union demands. In this "no-contract" era, the number of collective bargaining agreements was reduced by almost one-half, and the number of workers covered by one-fourth.[21]

Although the no-contract period came to an end, the position of the union still is weak. The enterprise union faces the employer almost alone. Its affiliations with other bodies are loose and tenuous. It envisages only a limited role for itself—to safeguard the interests of the permanent employees. This restricted concept of the union's task is in line with a Japanese tradition of lifetime attachment to a single employer. The enterprise union is further weakened, as an independent force, by the importance of the company's white-collar employees and technicians in the affairs of the union. In fact, in some cases even the plant manager is a member.[22] Thus, typical Japanese unions have interests confined to one plant, recognize only a restricted range of issues, have limited powers, and are without outside support. Many are dominated by supervisory personnel.

A final explanation for the Japanese pattern of industrial conflict is found in the nation's political structure. As we have seen, strong labor parties with opportunities to participate in governments are generally found in countries where the membership involvement rate has fallen to a low level. Conversely, labor parties are ineffective or non-existent in the countries with higher rates of participation. Japan belongs in the second category. Socialist parties have been closely allied with union groups, but there has been neither the unity in labor politics nor the responsibility for the conduct of government which would significantly reduce the inclination to strike. There was nominally one Socialist party until 1951, but it was split into right and left factions. These two wings formally separated when the Communists went into decline, and in 1955 reunited once more into a rather shaky party.

Although the Socialists participated in the Katayama government for a brief period in 1947–48, they have been very much a minority since that time. The conservative parties have won at least twice as many seats in the Diet as have the Socialists. The same ratio has been maintained since the two Socialist parties merged into the Japan Social Democratic Party in 1955, and the two conservative parties simultaneously coalesced to form the Liberal Democratic Party. Thus except for a brief period in 1947–48, Japanese labor has not had a strong voice in politics nor a responsible part in government. Large demonstration strikes have been organized even after the decline of the Communists—to oppose the Peace Treaty, to resist Japanese rearmament, to protest nuclear explosions, to express dissatisfaction over specific government policies.

Summing up, Japan has a new, disunited, and weak union movement, a decentralized and ineffective bargaining system, and a political structure that does not encourage pacification of the labor force.

India [23]

The pattern of strike activity in India has basically resembled that in France, Italy, and Japan, particularly during the period prior to 1947. Changes have been in progress since independence was gained, and the resemblance is declining; but reviewing India's experience as a whole, we are still inclined to place India in the Mediterranean-Asian group.

During the British period, the propensity to strike was fantastically high, by far the highest in the world. The ratio between strikers and union members has greatly declined since 1947. In 1954–56 it was only one-fourth as great as in 1942–44 and one-seventh as great as in 1945–47. Nevertheless, the participation rates are still the highest of any country with the exception of France and Italy. Since 1927, the average number of strikers each year has been almost equal to average union membership. In some years there were many more strikers than union members. Although the membership figures are undoubtedly too low, it is evident not only that Indian unionists have been extremely prone to strike, but also many non-unionists have joined them, in a tradition of mass action which owes a great deal to the civil disobedience campaigns.

The average duration of strikes in India is longer than we would expect, significantly longer than the stoppages of two to five days which are characteristic of France, Italy, and Japan. The number of working days lost per striker has varied between four and seventeen, averaging about nine, during the past decade. Since 1935, the duration of Indian strikes has been approximately the average for all fifteen countries studied.

With widespread participation and moderately long strikes, the ratios of lost time in India have been very high; and although they have declined substantially in recent years, they are still among the world's highest.   During 1954–56, the ratio between loss of working time and union membership in India was exceeded only in the United States and in Finland.

In explaining the tremendous propensity to strike, we shall show that most of the conditions generally associated with this phenomenon are present in extreme form—new and weakly established unions, bitter rivalries in the labor movement, lack of centralized control on the part of national unions or federations, employer resistance to unionism and collective bargaining, and the absence of a solid collective bargaining structure—or, for that matter, even of systematic grievance machinery. Not only is the labor market ineffectively organized, but the workers exist in a condition of poverty much more profound than even prevails in Italy and Japan.

The recent decline in rates of participation can be accounted for primarily by the advent of the Congress Party government, its relations with the labor movement, its far-reaching program of dispute settlement in order to prevent interference with the five-year plans, and the favorable awards of the "adjudication" or compulsory arbitration authorities which began to provide modest improvements in real wages after about 1950.

As we have noted, the substantial duration of many strikes in India is not easily explained.   Three facts are significant, however.   First, the civil disobedience campaign prior to independence built a tradition of expressing protest by abstaining from work for long periods of time. Second, interunion rivalries are so extreme in some regions and industries that organizational chaos sometimes results.   Third, it can at least be suggested that Indian workers are accustomed to such deep poverty that they are better able to subsist without cash income than can other groups with higher living standards.

Substantial unionism is a comparatively recent phenomenon in India. Of course, some Indian unions, such as the Ahmedabad Textile Labour Association, have operated successfully for several decades, but these are rare indeed.   Prior to World War II unions had only a few hundred thousand members at most.   Even allowing for the overwhelming predominance of agriculture and primitive handicrafts in the Indian economy, the extent of organization was very slight.   Union membership increased substantially during the war, and has continued to grow during the years of independence as well.   Even today, however, unionization is not great.   Our statistics indicate that union members represented 16.5 per cent of the non-agricultural wage and salary earners in the latest year for which data are available.[24]   Only South Africa, among the countries studied, has such a low degree of organization. (Reasonable allowance for underreporting of Indian union membership does not alter the situation.) Furthermore, it should be kept in mind that the industrial labor force is only a thin veneer on a predominantly agricultural economy.

Indian unions are small, weak, and intensely competitive. They are local organizations of employees in particular industries only loosely federated at regional or national levels. In 1952–53, about 3,000 unions were registered.[25] Kennedy points out that many unions do not register, however, and estimates that there are about 5,000 in India.[26] Myers writes that the average registered Indian union had only 768 members in 1952–53. Furthermore, 65 per cent of the unions had less than 300 members each. The 12.8 per cent of the registered unions claiming more than 1,000 members included more than 76.4 per cent of the total membership.[27]

In addition to being very small, Indian unions are poorly staffed and financed. Membership in good standing is a "vague and elastic concept"[28] and dues are seldom collected. Myers illustrates this point by citing the case of the National Federation of Indian Railwaymen, which claims to be the representative federation in an industry of more than 900,000 employees. The Railway Federation had an income of 6,917 rupees in 1954–55, equivalent to about $1,400. Some 2,650 rupees, or $500, was expended on salaries covering "at the most the wages of two members of the clerical staff."[29] Myers also notes that the average annual reported income for all unions in 1952–53 was 1,906 rupees, or approximately $400. Furthermore, the bulk of the income of Indian unions comes not from regular dues but from voluntary donations. In an article written at the request of the Bombay Association of Free Trade Unionists, Kennedy found it necessary to emphasize that "there are strong reasons for abandoning the practice of depending on donations for regular union income. It is a sporadic, unpredictable, and highly uncertain form of income."[30]

As might be expected from their small size, ephemeral membership, and weak financial position, many Indian unions are rather temporary affairs. Kennedy points out that the "paper organization," with virtually no members, and the *ad hoc* union created to meet a specific objective and having no permanent existence are common types.[31]

Interunion rivalries also weaken the Indian labor movement. An important aspect of these rivalries is the absence of a single national trade union center. Since the middle of the 1920's, there have been several rival confederations at all times. Conflict between the Communists, the Congress Party nationalists, and other groups dominated the period prior to independence. At the present time there are four major federations. The Indian National Trade Union Congress, which had roughly 1,500,000 members in 1953, is controlled by the Congress Party. The All-India TUC, with 750,000 members, is Communist dominated. Another federation is the Indian Labour Association, sponsored by the Socialists and Praja Socialists, with 800,000 members in 1953. The smallest of these four groups is the United TUC, a left-wing but not overtly Communist federation, with slightly fewer than 400,000 members.

Even more significant is the competition among the small local unions. Under the Indian labor laws, unions do not enjoy the status of exclusive bargaining agents. To foster unionism in the face of adverse circumstances, the government has a complex system of recognizing "representative," "primary," "qualified," and "approved" unions. The strongest status, that of representative union, requires that only 15 per cent of the eligible employees be members. Other types of recognition require even smaller percentages. Since there is no restriction on the number of unions in an establishment, multiple unionism is very common. Commenting on the small size of Indian unions, Kennedy further observes,

> The individual weakness implicit in this situation is intensified by the high proportion of these unions that are rival organizations existing side by side in the same industry and often in the same establishment.[32]

The Communists have an important place in the labor movement. They first acquired strength during the 1920's. Gaining ascendancy in the All-India TUC, they played a leading role in the Bombay textile strike of 1928, which accounted for 22,000,000 man-days of idleness. This was the largest strike in Indian history. The Communists withdrew from the All-India TUC and formed their own Red Trade Union Congress in 1931. The organization was disbanded in the latter years of the decade and the labor movement was temporarily unified in 1940. When the British imprisoned many Congress Party leaders in 1942, however, the Communists were given a clear field, and once more became dominant in the All-India TUC. Although the Communists still retain control of that organization, rival federations emerged in the late 1940's, and rapidly overshadowed the parent group. It is estimated that unions with Communist leadership contain only about 25 per cent of all union members at the present time.

Indian unions have never developed systematic collective bargaining relationships through which labor relations might be stabilized. Ornati points out that until 1947, "the history of the labor movement was the history of nationalism with the union label." [33]   Even at the present time,

> Collective bargaining, as we know it, is almost untried in India.   Trade union-employer relationships are essentially of an *ad hoc* nature.   Where direct and continuing relationships exist between employers and employees' representatives, concentration is on the development of procedure for the settlement of disputes rather than on the discussion of the disputes themselves.[34]

Kennedy agrees with this judgment and states that "systematic collective bargaining is largely unknown outside of a small number of exceptional relationships. . . . Few Indian employers voluntarily grant unions effective bargaining rights and few unions are strong enough to gain this status by economic action." [35]

Under these circumstances most Indian unions do not enjoy any systematic bargaining relationships.   Of those that are relatively well established, many represent only a minority of the employees.   Furthermore, where collective bargaining does occur, it is not customary to execute written agreements.

The resistance of employers combines with the weakness of unions to produce an ineffective bargaining system.   Indian employers have been indifferent to personnel problems and hostile to labor organizations.   Ornati states,

> Traditionally, Indian employers opposed attempts at systematization of working relationships.   As important as their opposition, however, was their lack of interest. . . . Along with a lack of developed employment policies, present day industrial relations in India are plagued by a history of active employer antagonism toward trade unions.   Management identified the trade unionist with the political rebel and employed numerous anti-union tactics—the use of goon squads among others—particularly in times of strikes or when native political groups were on the upsurge as in the 1937–40 period.[36]

In this policy the employers were supported by the British authorities, who rightly feared that trade unions would instill political consciousness and be drawn into the struggle for independence.   Although conditions have changed to some extent since 1945, it cannot be said that there is anything like equality of bargaining power between employers and workers, or that unionism has been accepted in any real sense.   Indian social barriers and traditions reinforce the natural antagonism of employers toward unions.   Workers simply lack the status to negotiate with the employers on a basis of social equality or near-equality.

One of the chief reasons for the high propensity to strike in India is the absence of any systematic procedure for the handling of grievances.

. . . in Indian practice there is no clear concept of grievances as issues distinct from contract issues or of grievance procedure as a daily process of adjustment in the plant apart from negotiations over matters of general interest between the parties. Individual worker complaints are in general accorded no different treatment than are union demands for wage increases or other general changes in conditions.[37]

When workers bring their grievance to the union, the officer may take the matter up with management. If, as often happens, there is no settlement by negotiation, the union has two alternatives. One is to bring the dispute to a government conciliator, who has the power to refer it to a tribunal for compulsory adjudication. The other is strike action. A very large proportion of strikes in India involve disputes which, under American union agreements, would be subject to grievance procedures and private arbitration.

Another explanation for the high ratio between strikers and union members is that non-members often join in strikes. This practice goes back to the civil disobedience protests of the pre-Independence period. It should also be kept in mind, that in the absence of procedures for certifying collective bargaining representatives and enforcing bargaining rights, unions do not have a strong motive to enroll the maximum number of potential members.

Exceptions can be made to all of these statements. There are some well-established unions. Long-standing collective bargaining relationships do exist. Formal written agreements can be found. Effective grievance procedures are not unknown. These are truly exceptions, however, and do not define the general state of affairs.

In our previous chapters we have pointed out that collaboration between the union movement and a strong labor party often exerts a tempering influence on industrial conflict, particularly when the labor party organizes or participates in the government. In India, labor is weak politically as well as industrially. The specifically pro-labor parties—the Socialists, the Praja Socialists, and the Communists—have never come close to attaining political power.

Counteracting influences have set in since independence was achieved, as already noted. The involvement rate has declined sharply during the past decade. This development can be explained by the new relationship between the unions and the government, and by the extraordinary role that the government plays in the settlement of industrial disputes.

The ruling Congress Party is, of course, not a labor party in the Northern European sense. It has reflected all shades of Indian political thought with nationalist inclinations. But as we have noted, the trade unions constituted the labor arm of the independence movement. Since independence, the Congress Party has adopted a mildly Socialist outlook and has represented itself to the urban workers as a worker's party. The Congress Party is firmly in control of the government and has embarked on a program of economic planning through the medium of five-year plans.

Most of the unions of the Indian National TUC have been supplied with "outside leaders," many of whom are long-time members of the Congress Party. These leaders are impressed with the need to reduce losses caused by industrial unrest. Furthermore, the Indian National TUC is the largest federation in the country, and, favored by the government, has been expanding at the expense of the other federations. Thus, an effective link has been welded between the government and the largest group of trade unions in order to secure support for economic programs.

When industrial disputes occur, the government intervenes so actively that, as several scholars have pointed out, terms of employment are basically determined by the employers and the government, rather than by the employers and the unions. As noted above, there is no clear-cut distinction between grievances and basic terms of employment. In either case, it is the task of the "outside leader" in his capacity as worker's representative to secure some action or settlement, and it is his task as a member of the Congress Party to prevent breaches of industrial peace. If, despite his personal prestige, he is unable to reach an agreement with the employer, the matter can be quickly referred to a government conciliator. If the conciliator is not successful in resolving the dispute, he in turn is authorized to refer it to compulsory arbitration. This system of compulsory arbitration has existed in some of the states (for example, Bombay) since the 1930's, and was extended throughout India after independence was gained. In addition, there is a requirement that each factory establish "standing orders" or working rules, which are subject to government approval and can be changed only with the consent of the government.

Although there are no available statistics on the use of the adjudication method, there is no doubt that tremendous reliance is placed upon it. Ornati summarizes the role of the government in the following terms:

The Government has been successful in encouraging the development of trade unions and in reducing strikes. Collective bargaining is essentially tripartite in form; in fact most of the bargaining takes place between the Government and the employers rather than between employers and employees. The development of national legislation and the tendency for disputes to be settled in the higher tribunals have led to an increase in bargaining between national employers' associations and national trade union centers.[38]

In summary, India has a very weak and disunited labor movement. The unions are typically small, and impoverished; membership is often ephemeral. These weaknesses, together with the opposition of employers, have precluded the establishment of a permanent collective bargaining system in which the differences between employers and employees could be settled effectively by their representatives. As a consequence, industrial disputes are largely protests or demonstrations and occur over matters which could have been settled by means of peaceful bargaining, had the requisite procedures and machinery existed. In recent years, however, the active intervention of the Indian government, and its close relations with the largest union federation, have tended to reduce the incidence of disputes.

NOTES TO CHAPTER 9

1. Val R. Lorwin, *The French Labor Movement* (Cambridge: Harvard University Press, 1954), and "France," in Walter Galenson (ed.), *Comparative Labor Movements* (Englewood Cliffs, N. J.: Prentice-Hall, 1952), pp. 313–409; Georges Vidalenc, *The French Trade Union Movement: Past and Present* (Brussels: International Confederation of Free Trade Unions, 1953); Webster Powell, "Activities of French Labor Unions in 1949–51," *Monthly Labor Review,* 72 (June 1951), pp. 642–47; Adolf Sturmthal, "Collective Bargaining in France," *Industrial and Labor Relations Review,* 4 (January 1951), pp. 236–48, and "Collective Bargaining in France," in Adolf Sturmthal (ed.), *Contemporary Collective Bargaining in Seven Countries* (Ithaca: Institute of International Industrial and Labor Relations, Cornell University, 1957); U. S. Bureau of Labor Statistics, *Summary of the Labor Situation in France* (Washington: U. S. Department of Labor, for the International Cooperation Administration, 1956).

2. French union membership statistics are admittedly poor. Doubtless the early postwar figures were quite exaggerated. The estimates cited above appear to be the best available, however. See the Appendix for detailed discussion of statistical problems.

3. There are additional federations, including one representing technical and supervisory employees, Confédération Générale des Cadres (CGC), and the conservative Confédération Générale des Syndicats Indépendants, a small and weak federation with only scattered pockets of local strength.

4. Sturmthal, "France," in *Contemporary Collective Bargaining,* p. 143.

5. Lorwin, "France," in *Comparative Labor Movements,* p. 377.

6. Sturmthal, *Contemporary Collective Bargaining,* p. 144.

7. *Ibid.,* p. 154.

8. *Ibid.,* p. 144.

9. Joseph LaPalombara, *The Italian Labor Movement: Problems and Prospects* (Ithaca: Cornell University Press, 1957); Maurice F. Neufeld, *Labor Unions and National Politics in Italian Industrial Plants* (Ithaca: Institute of International Industrial and Labor Relations, Cornell University, 1954); U. S. Bureau of Labor Statistics, *Summary of the Labor Situation in Italy* (Washington: U. S. Department of Labor, for the International Cooperation Administration, 1955); U. S. Bureau of Labor Statistics, "Labor Practices and Regulations in Italy," (Washington: U. S. Department of Labor, Division of Foreign Labor Conditions, October 1952), mimeo.; Maurice F. Neufeld, "The Italian Labor Movement in 1956: The Structure of Crisis," *The Annals of the American Academy of Political and Social Sciences,* 310 (March 1957), pp. 75–86; Luisa Riva Sanseverino, "Collective Bargaining in Italy," in Sturmthal (ed.), *Contemporary Collective Bargaining,* pp. 210–233; Cesare Vannutelli, "Wage Structure and Cost of Labor in Italy," in Sturmthal (ed.), *Contemporary Collective Bargaining,* pp. 233–52; John Clarke Adams, "Italy," in Galenson (ed.), *Comparative Labor Movements,* pp. 410–79.

10. Italian union membership figures, like those of France, are most unreliable. Actual membership may be 50 per cent lower than the published estimates. Membership claims do indicate the direction of change, however, and, at any rate, no better estimates are available.

11. Claimed membership in 1950: CGIL, 5,000,000; CISL, 1,500,000; and UIL, 400,000. Joseph LaPalombara estimates, for the mid-fifties, that CGIL had perhaps 3,500,000 members, CISL less than 2,000,000, and the UIL perhaps 250,000 or 300,000. LaPalombara, *op. cit.,* pp. 108–10.

12. *Ibid.,* p. 144.

13. *Ibid.,* p. 74.

14. Adams, *op. cit.,* p. 457.

15. LaPalombara, *op. cit.,* p. 36.

16. Neufeld, *op. cit.,* pp. 38–41.

17. *Ibid.,* pp. 45–46.

18. Solomon B. Levine, *Industrial Relations in Postwar Japan* (Urbana: University of Illinois Press, 1958), "Industrial Relations in the New Japan," *Pacific Affairs,* 30 (September 1957), pp. 209–20 and "The Labor Movement and Economic Development in Japan," *Proceedings of the Seventh Annual Meeting, Industrial Relations Research Association, 1954* (Madison, Wisc., 1955), pp. 48–59; Miriam S. Farley, *Aspects of Japan's Labor Problems* (New York: John Day and Co., 1950); Hiroshi Gotoh, *The Industrial Relations in Japan* (Tokyo: Japan Federation of Employers' Associations, 1957); *Labor Movement in Japan* (Tokyo: Japan Federation of Employers' Associations, 1958); *The Labor Union Movement in Postwar Japan* (Tokyo: The Daily Labor Press, 1954); U. S. Bureau of Labor Statistics, *Summary of the Labor Situation in Japan* (Washington: U. S. Department of Labor for the International Cooperation Administration, 1955).

19. Levine, *Industrial Relations in Postwar Japan,* pp. 101–02.

20. *Ibid.,* p. 89.

21. *Ibid.,* pp. 124–25.

22. *Ibid.,* p. 48.

23. Charles A. Myers, *Labor Problems in the Industrialization of India* (Cambridge: Harvard University Press, 1958); Oscar A. Ornati, *Jobs and Workers in India* (Ithaca: Institute of International Industrial and Labor Relations, Cornell University, 1955); Madhurendra Kishore Varma, "Role of Legislation in Regulating Labor-Management Relations in India," *Labor Law Journal,* 8 (April 1957), pp. 257–72; U. S. Bureau of Labor Statistics, *Summary of the Labor Situation in India* (Washington: U. S. Department of Labor, for the International Cooperation Administration, 1956); Ramesh C. Goyal, *Post-war Trends in Industrial Relations in India* (New Delhi; Eastern Economist, 1955); S. D. Punekar, *Industrial Peace in India* (Bombay: Library of Indian Economics, 1952); Van Dusen Kennedy, "The Role of the Union in the Plant in India," *Proceedings of the Eighth Annual Meeting, Industrial Relations Research Association, 1955* (Madison, Wisc., 1956), pp. 249–64, and *Problems of Indian Trade Unionism and Labour Relations* (Bombay: Association of Free Trade Unionists, 1954).

24. Indian statistics are quite unreliable. However, even allowing for underreporting of union membership and restricting the non-agricultural employment base to the "7.93 million employees under conditions approximating industrial employment" [for 1951] as suggested by C. A. Myers, *op. cit.,* p. 8, we estimate the degree of organization at less than 30 per cent. This is still so low that only one country—South Africa—clearly has a lower degree of organization.

25. *Ibid.,* p. 71.

26. Van Dusen Kennedy, "The Role of the Union in the Plant in India," p. 255.

27. Myers, *loc. cit.*

28. Kennedy, "The Role of the Union in the Plant in India," p. 262.

29. Myers, *op. cit.,* p. 75.

30. Kennedy, *Problems of Indian Trade Unionism and Labour Relations,* p. 13.

31. "The threefold classification of Indian unions developed by the Royal Commission on Labour in India in 1931 is nearly as applicable today as it was then. One common type of union is little more than a paper organization with an imaginary membership created and presided over by one or two professionals for the purpose of providing a platform and a name for their own advancement. A second type was called *ad hoc* unions by the Royal Commission because they arose to meet definite and immediate objectives, usually some genuine worker grievance or demand, and relapsed into suspended animation between causes. Some unions have also been termed strike committees. With the intensification of political rivalry in the labor movement after independence, these *ad hoc* unions tended to become perpetuated, at least in nominal form, to bulwark the membership claims of the rival federations. A third type of union is the permanent and regular organization which seeks to maintain a continuing membership and program." Kennedy, "The Role of the Union," p. 256.

32. *Ibid.,* pp. 255–56.

33. Oscar A. Ornati, *op. cit.,* p. 108.

34. *Ibid.,* p. 147.

35. Kennedy, "The Role of the Union," pp. 256–57.

36. Ornati, *op. cit.,* pp. 140, 145.

37. Kennedy, "The Role of the Union," p. 257.

38. Ornati, *op. cit.,* pp. 176–77.

CHAPTER 10

Special Cases

and Mixed Situations

Australia [1]

From surface appearances we would expect to find very little industrial conflict in Australia. The labor force has been highly organized for more than four decades. The Labour Party has been a major factor in politics since 1890, and has organized the government on several occasions. Multi-employer bargaining agreements are typical. The state and federal governments administer a compulsory arbitration system which is the dominant factor in setting wages and employment conditions. A pattern of industrial conflict similar to the English, Danish, or Dutch might be anticipated.

These expectations are not borne out. Instead, Australia is characterized by frequent short strikes along the lines of France, Italy, and Japan. This situation has prevailed since just before World War II. An average of 20 per cent of union members went on strike annually between 1939 and 1941, and this proportion has varied between 20 and 30 per cent ever since. The proportion of non-agricultural employees involved in strikes has been among the highest in the world, ranging from 11 per cent in 1939–41 to 18 per cent in 1951–53. Only France and

Italy have had higher participation rates. Australian strikes were of moderate length until 1938, averaging about ten days. The average duration dropped to five days in 1939–41, and has varied between two days and five days ever since.

Kenneth Walker has developed an interesting table showing in dramatic form the typical brevity of the Australian strike. The proportion of stoppages lasting six days or less was always large, but became particularly great after 1938, never dropping below 84 per cent and rising as high as 98 per cent in 1947. The proportion of stoppages lasting one day or less varied between 55 per cent in 1939 and 71 per cent in 1949.[2] Walker's table does not carry the record beyond 1951, but there is no reason to believe that the trend has reversed itself in subsequent years.

CHART XIV. Australia, Finland, South Africa

Membership Involvement: Workers Involved as a Percentage of
Union Membership

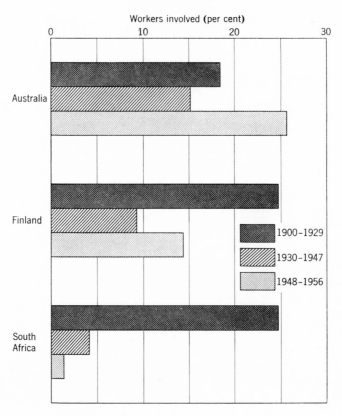

CHART XV. Australia, Finland, South Africa
Duration of Strikes: Working Days Lost per Striker

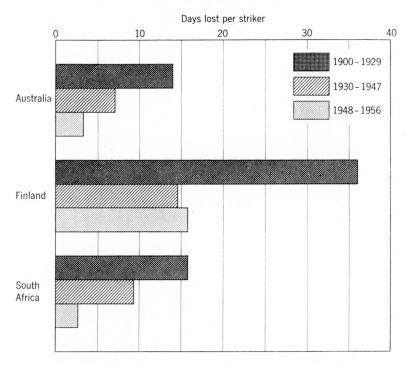

Days lost per striker

Legend:
- 1900 – 1929
- 1930 – 1947
- 1948 – 1956

In the preceding chapters we have tried to show the connection between national patterns of strike activity, on the one hand, and economic and political institutions on the other. That most Australian
strikes are very short is not surprising; the same is true in the United
Kingdom, for example. But as mentioned earlier, the widespread incidence of strikes is not in line with surface indications. High rates of
participation are generally associated with feeble and disunited labor
movements, weak collective bargaining systems, employer hostility
toward unions, and lack of political effectiveness on the part of labor.
If these conditions prevail in Australia, they are certainly not so well
known or obvious as in France, Italy, and Japan. In the case of Australia, therefore, we have a special task of reconciling the apparent con-
tradictions. We believe this can be done without damaging our general
theory of industrial conflict.

Australian workers became strongly unionized at least 15 or 20 years
before those in any other country. By 1916 almost 50 per cent of the

CHART XVI. Australia, Finland, South Africa
Membership Loss Ratio: Working Days Lost per Hundred Union Members

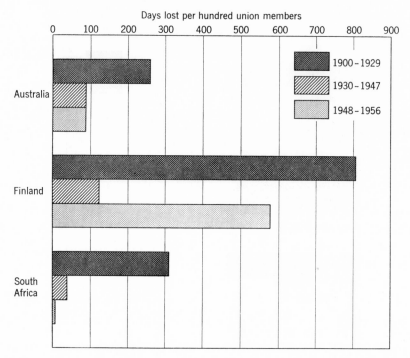

non-agricultural employees had been enrolled in unions. In 1929 about 56 per cent of Australian wage and salary earners were members, compared with 32 per cent in Sweden, the most highly organized of the other countries. The degree of organization fell off somewhat in the 1930's, but increased gradually after 1938 until 65.6 per cent of non-agricultural employees were union members in 1953.

Thus the Australian union movement has been stable, mature, and intensively organized. France and Italy have had higher degrees of organization, but only for brief periods of time. The English, Danish, and Swedish unions have been very stable, but have not organized such large proportions of the labor force as the Australian unions.

Furthermore, the Australian labor movement has been relatively free from extreme rivalries. Since 1927 there has been only one national trade union center, the Australian Council of Trade Unions. Although Communists, Catholics, and other groups have expressed strong opposition to the national leadership from time to time, they have continued to work within the council.

Collective bargaining is a long-established practice and most of the significant terms of employment are covered by the collective agreements. These agreements are usually multi-employer in scope, embracing the whole of the occupation or industry within a state or region. These facts, combined with the strength and influence of the Labour Party since the early years of the present century, would be consistent with a low volume of strike activity.

As we have noted, however, the propensity to strike is very high in Australia. The chief explanations appear to be the following: (1) the concentration of strike activity in the coal and maritime industries, where mature industrial relations have not developed; (2) the absence of centralized control in the labor movement, the employer community, and the collective bargaining system; (3) the prominence of the Communists in the labor movement; (4) the effects of compulsory arbitration; and (5) the constitutional weakness of the Commonwealth government, which has prevented the Labour Party from achieving workers' objectives through political action.

The coal and maritime industries

Although the majority of Australian employers have accepted unionism and collective bargaining, general statements concerning employer policy are of almost no value in understanding industrial conflict in Australia. The reason is that much of the strike activity is localized in two industries. Walker shows that between 1913 and 1953, about 71 per cent of all stoppages were in mining and quarrying, particularly coal mining; and another 7 per cent were in the maritime trades, particularly longshoring. These two industries accounted respectively for 48 per cent and 13 per cent of man-days lost. The metal trades account for another 11 per cent of idleness in strikes.

In 1939, the chief judge of the Federal Arbitration Court stated, "The history of the coal mining industry in Australia from its very inception may be described as an unbridled and unregulated contest between employers and employees, without restraint and actuated only by the rules of the jungle." [3] And about 20 years later, Walker presents essentially the same description:

> Altogether, the coal owners present many parallels with the mine-workers. Intransigent and dogmatic, lacking internal discipline in their associations, they pursue their own interests with the same ruthless application of bargaining power, and with the same incapacity to look beyond their immediate gain to the welfare of the industry as a whole. [4]

The one-day protest stoppage is characteristic of the coal mining industry.

> A steady stream of short local stoppages, many of which last only one day and terminate without any change in the conditions of employment, provide the continuing basis for the industry's record of turbulence. A considerable proportion of these one-day stoppages are in the nature of political protests.[5]

The picture is essentially similar in the stevedoring industry.

> Waterfront employers, particularly those serving coastal shipping, have followed the simple policy of using their bargaining power to the full. The union has represented a threat to unrestricted freedom of action on the employers' part, and has therefore been attacked and circumvented as far as possible . . . The intransigence and apparent instability of union demands are well matched by the attitude of employers.[6]

Like stevedoring unions in many countries, the Waterside Workers' Federation has relied upon "direct action"—a sudden stoppage on the part of a few men—to gain concessions.

Absence of centralized control

As noted above, multi-employer bargaining is generally practiced in Australia. On closer examination, however, we do not find the same consolidated and tightly controlled collective bargaining system that has led to the virtual disappearance of the strike in Northern Europe. The Australian collective bargaining system is not really very centralized. Most collective agreements cover an industry or trade in only one of the six states in Australia. Whereas the minimum wage for unskilled workers, basic hours of employment, and vacations are generally within the jurisdiction of the Federal Arbitration Court, and therefore tend to be covered by industry-wide awards, other terms of employment are established on a narrower basis.

Absence of central control in the bargaining system is matched within the bargaining organizations. Neither in the labor movement nor the employer community is the national leadership in a position to undertake commitments and enforce discipline on subordinate levels. The Australian Council of Trade Unions does not play any significant role in collective bargaining. The state organization, not the national, is the locus of power in Australian unionism. The state organization usually bargains with employers, represents the members in arbitration proceedings, settles grievances, and so forth.[7] Consequently the ACTU is an extremely weak federation. Furthermore, some labor organizations, including the largest in the Commonwealth, the Australian Workers' Union, have remained on the outside. Indicative of the ACTU's weakness is the fact that its staff was limited to a full-time president and secretary until May 1951, when a research director was engaged. Similarly there is no central employers' federation which represents the industrial community as a whole, in the manner of the Dansk Arbejdsgiverforening in Denmark or the Svenska Arbetsgivareföreningen in Sweden.

The Communists

The influence of Communism on Australian strike activity has been subject to much debate, and we do not presume to offer any dogmatic judgment. Certainly we do not entertain "the vulgar belief that industrial conflict in the coal fields is entirely the work of Communists," which Walker labels "patently absurd in the light of the long history of struggle that stretches back generations before the Communist party was formed." [8] Similarly, we can grant that "it would be idle to expect the disappearance of Communist leadership to cause the [Waterside Workers' Federation] to abandon its basic policy of direct action." [9] And it may well be, as Knowles observed with respect to England, that the Communists have been the midwives rather than the begetters of strikes.

Nevertheless, the midwife is entitled to some credit. Without stopping here to review the strike strategy of Communists under various circumstances, we think it significant that in the three industries that account for the bulk of strike activity, the unions are under Communist leadership. These are the Miners' Federation in the coal industry, the Waterside Workers' Federation in longshoring, and the Iron Workers' Association in the metal trades, which has been Communist-led during most of its brief history. [10]

The peak of Communist influence in the Australian labor movement was reached during World War II and in the first few postwar years. For some time the leadership of the Labour Party and the ACTU were ambivalent in their attitude toward Communists, recognizing the dangers of association but still desiring their support. As in many other countries, the parting of the ways was reached in 1948–49. Since then the Communists have lost considerable strength in the ACTU and in the Labour Party. They are still firmly in control of the Miners' Federation and the Waterside Workers' Federation, however, and represent an influential bloc in the Iron Workers' Association, although the exact situation in that union is not clear.

Mark Perlman points out that as political "outcasts" the Communists do not have direct access to decision-making power in the compulsory arbitration scheme.[11] Furthermore, the ACTU has no power over Communist-controlled unions and no influence on their strike policies. Therefore, arbitration awards which are acceptable to the higher leadership of Australian labor may nevertheless be subject to protest strike.

Compulsory arbitration

The Australian compulsory arbitration system has been evolving continuously since the beginning of the century and has become quite complicated. Briefly, each state has a court of arbitration empowered to deal with wages and industrial disputes within its territorial jurisdiction. In addition there is a Commonwealth or Federal Court of Arbitration, which handles interstate disputes and defines the basic or minimum wage and standard hours of work in particular industries on a nation-wide basis. Cases are presented in a highly legalistic atmosphere. In some instances the parties agree on terms of employment, whereupon the agreement is recorded with the appropriate court. Otherwise, an arbitration award is issued.

The term *compulsory arbitration* is misleading to some extent. Except in certain essential public services, unions generally have the right to strike unless they register with the government. Registration subjects a union to a number of regulations of its internal government and requires it to use a court of arbitration for most disputes. Unions that prefer not to register may strike at any time, unless employees of government or other essential services are involved. Furthermore, the penalty for striking against an arbitration award is rather light, usually amounting to little more than deregistration and the consequent loss of access to the arbitration court.

In appraising the effect of the arbitration system on industrial conflict, we should begin by emphasizing the importance of the collective bargaining structure. Government intervention is most effective when it serves as an auxiliary mechanism supporting a centralized bargaining system and giving status and authority to the decisions of the top labor and employer representatives. The success of government intervention in the United Kingdom, Denmark, and the Netherlands can be explained in these terms. The Indian government has been able to bring about a substantial reduction in strike activity, even in the absence of an effective collective bargaining system, by taking the most important group of unions in tutelage and by exerting powerful pressure on employers in the interests of achieving the objectives of the Five-Year

Plans. The case of Finland, which has unsuccessfully resorted to compulsory arbitration on various occasions, demonstrates that government intervention in itself will not necessarily mitigate industrial conflict.

It follows from what has been said that the effects of compulsory arbitration will depend largely on the underlying labor-management relationships. Walker has made a detailed analysis in his book and makes this comment in a letter:

> It would be tempting to attach all the blame to the compulsory arbitration system for taking the responsibility of reaching agreement from the parties, but . . . in some industries arbitration fostered peace and in others it did the opposite. I draw the conclusion that in a "naturally" strike-prone industry arbitration made matters worse but in a peaceful one it helped to stabilize matters.[12]

Attempts have been made to penalize striking unionists from time to time, but except where the entire community has been aroused, punishment has not been an effective sanction. Every government that has endeavored to apply severe penalties has suffered political defeat except on one occasion in which a Labour government avoided this fate.

J. E. Isaac, Senior Lecturer in Industrial Relations at the University of Melbourne, gives somewhat more credit to the compulsory arbitration system for eliminating long strikes and encouraging frequent short stoppages. He states in a letter:

> I believe that the system of compulsory arbitration, in spite of its many failings and its impotence to apply sanctions on a large scale, has been responsible for mitigating the "trial by strength" feature of collective bargaining in the determination of the terms of employment. The development of centralized wage determination with nation-wide application of key wage elements has discouraged the use of the strike weapon in the process of wage determination.
>
> However, compulsory arbitration has not prevented other types of strikes. These are more in the nature of protests against arbitration awards regarded as unacceptable by sections of workers; protests against unsettled or unattended grievances; and protests of a political (non-industrial) nature, e.g., the enactment by the government of an anti-communist bill; foreign policy, etc. The first two types of protests may well be aggravated by compulsory arbitration itself. The third type may be accentuated by communist leadership.
>
> These protests have one thing in common—they are short in duration. Thus it is arguable that the system of compulsory arbitration has tended to modify strike action in the direction of abundant but short-lived protests. Non-industrial issues have added to these protests. And the period of full employment has provided a favourable environment for the full release of these forces of protest.[13]

Constitutional weakness of commonwealth government

It has been shown previously that a strong labor party generally has a restraining effect on overt expressions of industrial unrest. Why has not the Labour Party in Australia exercised the usual disciplinary influence on the labor force? One of the principal reasons is that the Labour Party has had rather poor success in achieving its objectives while in power. In the brief Labour government of 1929–30, the party had a majority only in the lower legislative house. In the 1942–49 period, Labour had a majority in both houses, but its efforts were frustrated by the limitations of the Australian constitution. The constitutional powers of the federal government are quite weak, much authority being reserved to the states. The Labour government was blocked in 1942 when it endeavored to adopt price control and similar measures to cope with the wartime emergency. In 1946 the Labour government sought three constitutional amendments, by the referendum method, to give the federal government "direct powers over employment, organized marketing of primary products and a wide field of social and health services and benefits." [14]   Only the amendment pertaining to social and health benefits carried. A subsequent attempt in 1948 to obtain constitutional power to control prices and rents also failed. Efforts to carry out a program of limited reform without constitutional changes were thwarted from time to time by court action. For example, Labour's attempts to nationalize the airlines and private banks during this period were set aside by the High Court and the Judicial Committee of the Privy Council as unconstitutional.[15]

Thus the Labour Party, although it achieved political power, was not only incapable of achieving any of its socialist objectives but also lacked constitutional power to execute more conservative economic policies designed to produce price stability and full employment. Crisp observes,

> With the better understanding of the problems of managing the economy which Keynesian and post-Keynesian writings brought, this continued failure to widen the economic ambit of Commonwealth powers was becoming more serious every year. Federalism became a greater obstacle to coherent economic policy and to a sense of economic responsibility on the part of all governments.[16]

Finally, a Labour Party can discipline the trade unions only in cooperation with the federation with which the important unions are affiliated and which possesses strong central powers. The ACTU does not possess such powers, and, in particular, is not in a position to control the strike policies of the Communist-led unions.

The Australian pattern of strike behavior, then, does not really contradict our theory but is generally consistent with it. There is a lack of centralized control in both the employer and labor organizations. The collective bargaining system is not consolidated along Northern European lines. Although Australian labor achieved political power, the government was unable to take the strong steps deemed desirable to accomplish social and economic reform.[17] As we have pointed out in preceding chapters, massive intervention in labor disputes does not necessarily eliminate industrial conflict. The impact of government policies on the workings of the collective bargaining system is the determining factor. In Australia, compulsory arbitration has probably shortened the length of strikes, but has not reduced their frequency.

Finland [18]

Finland has a pattern of strike activity which does not fit easily into any of our classifications. The rates of participation are much higher than those of the other Northern European countries. The number of workers involved in strikes averaged 27 per cent of union membership during the 1945–1956 decade. This figure resembles Japan's 20.7 per cent and Australia's 25.5 per cent more than it does Sweden's 1.8 per cent and Norway's 1.2 per cent. On the other hand, the duration of strikes in Finland is similar to the duration of strikes in the Scandinavian countries and much greater than in other countries—Australia and the Mediterranean-Asian group—where industrial conflict has widespread incidence. Loss of working time per striker in Finland was 13.7 days between 1945 and 1956, only slightly below Norway's 14.3 days and Sweden's 24.5 days. What with a high propensity to strike and relatively long stoppages, Finland has had the highest lost-time ratios, during the postwar period, of any country studied.

There have been wide fluctuations from year to year in the volume of industrial disputes. Three postwar years—1949, 1950, and 1956—were marked by large-scale strikes; strike activity was moderate in the remaining years. It must be kept in mind, therefore, that the averages are strongly affected by these periods of widespread conflict.

As these facts would suggest, the institutional setting of industrial relations in Finland is peculiar. The labor movement is half a century old; there is a centralized collective bargaining system and a fairly strong Social Democratic Party. In most other material respects, however, Finland resembles the Mediterranean-Asian countries. Thus the labor movement is weak and divided, employers have resisted unionism, there is an important Communist faction, the economic situation has been most difficult, and government policies have not been effective.

Although the Finnish labor movement is an old one, the workers have never been solidly affiliated. There was substantial organization prior to World War I, with 160,000 members enrolled as of 1917. Membership declined as the unions were weakened by the civil war of 1918, by employer hostility, by a succession of conservative governments, and by struggles between Social Democrats and Communists. The suppression of the Labor Federation by the government in 1930 further reduced union membership to its lowest point of 15,000 members, representing only about 5 per cent of non-agricultural employees. Until World War II, the degree of organization was the least of any country included in this study. Large-scale organization was not achieved until 1944 and 1945; but after reaching a peak of 342,000 in 1947, membership again declined. Thus, Finnish unions have never had the assured working-class loyalty which has been characteristic of the other Northern European labor movements. The intensity of organization was about 19 per cent in 1927–29, 5 per cent in the early 1930's, 13 per cent in 1939–41, 45 per cent in 1945–47, and only 28 per cent in 1954–56.

The Finnish labor movement has been disunited as well as unstable, another point of similarity with such countries as France and Italy. Rivalry between Communists and Social Democrats in the unions was strong during the 1920's, and at the end of the decade the Social Democratic unions withdrew from the Labor Federation, leaving it in Communist hands. Within a few months the federation was suppressed by the government, and the Social Democrats held sway in a field much reduced in size. The Communists began their recovery slowly in the late 1930's, and picked up speed during World War II. At that time they gained sufficient support to dominate many of the country's largest unions. By 1947, their control extended to nearly half the votes on the Executive Board of the Federation of Labor itself.

Although the Communist and non-Communist factions have not established separate federations in Finland as they have in Italy, France, and elsewhere, the effect of their rivalry on industrial conflict is clear. Capitalizing on rank-and-file discontent over economic austerity, price inflation, and declining real wages, the Communists led repeated waves of strikes during the postwar period. There was bitter controversy over these strikes, many of which had not been sanctioned by the Federation of Labor. The upshot was that in 1949 the federation expelled some of the offending Communist unions and, along with central labor bodies in the United States and various other countries, withdrew from the

World Federation of Trade Unions. Despite their expulsion from the Labor Federation and serious membership losses, the Communists still control some of the largest and strongest unions in Finland.

Collective bargaining has not been an established institution for any long period of time. Company towns, paternalistic policies, and general hostility to unions appear to have been characteristic of prewar Finland. Some rudimentary collective bargaining relationships were initiated in 1940, when labor and employer federations signed an agreement providing for mutual recognition. This development was cut off by stringent government controls, including a prohibition of strikes, during World War II. Consequently, when collective bargaining was reinstated in 1946, a tradition of mutual acceptance and respect, which might have mitigated industrial conflict under the difficult conditions that ensued, did not exist.

It is true that, like the Scandinavian countries, Germany, and the Netherlands, Finland has a rather centralized bargaining structure. As noted above, the peak organizations of labor and management negotiated a general agreement, in the nature of an armistice, in 1940. There was a more detailed master agreement of 1946 reaffirming mutual recognition, establishing procedures for negotiations, defining the forms of worker representation in the shop, and containing other institutional provisions. Specific terms of employment were then negotiated at the industry level. This combination of economy-wide and supplemental industry-wide negotiations still prevails, but peaceful and stable labor-management relations have not developed.

A further reason is that Finland's economic position has been unusually irksome and precarious. It has been necessary to create a metal-working and shipbuilding industry, and to change the composition of the economy in other ways, in order to carry the heavy reparations load imposed by the Russians. Furthermore, the Finns have had to relocate large numbers of refugees dispossessed by the cession of eastern lands to the Russians, and to repair extensive war damage in the north caused by the Germans. All these tasks have had to be carried out by a relatively poor country cut off from any large-scale foreign aid. It is understandable that the strain on a newly established collective bargaining system would be great.

Government intervention in the labor market has been frequent and sometimes oppressive, but not sufficiently consistent or effective to provide the basis for stable industrial relations. In the 1930's, the governments were either indifferent or hostile to unionism. Then came a period of strict wartime controls, including a prohibition of strikes.

Since the war Finland has made a succession of improvised attempts to deal with inflation and wage pressure. Wage freezes have been imposed; permissible cost-of-living increases have been defined; there was a brief experiment with compulsory arbitration of primary disputes during 1951. During the same year the speaker of the Diet, who was the head of the Social Democratic Party, participated in negotiations between the labor and employer federations to obtain acceptance of specific cost-of-living escalation formulas.

The government participates in other and more conventional ways as well. There is a Labor Court for secondary disputes, and a compulsory mediation system. The law provides for paid vacations and family allowances, in addition to an eight-hour working day and comprehensive social insurance. But these activities have been overshadowed by the spasmodic and unsuccessful attempts of the government to deal with the problem of inflation. The Finnish experience demonstrates that government intervention can eliminate industrial conflict only when it serves to support the collective bargaining system or provides a workable substitute.

Turning to labor's role in politics, we may note that, again like the other Scandinavian countries, Finland has had a labor-oriented political party for over fifty years. The Social Democratic Party has existed continuously since 1903, when it succeeded the Finnish Labor Party, and has been the largest single political party practically all of the time since 1907. The Social Democrats have governed in coalition with the Agrarians since the end of World War II, with the exception of about a year in 1950–51 when they were out of power. There has always been close cooperation between the Social Democrats in the unions and in the party.

As we have seen, cooperation between union leaders and an influential labor party often results in the waning of industrial conflicts. That this result has not occurred in Finland can be explained by the unstable position of the Social Democrats both in the labor movement and in political life.

Unlike their counterparts in neighboring Northern European countries, the Social Democrats in Finland have not been able to exercise real hegemony in political life. There are three major parties of approximately equal strength—the Social Democrats, the Agrarians, and the Communists—as well as several smaller parties. The Social Democrats have never had a majority in Parliament; in fact, in the 1958 elections no two parties had a majority. Thus, governments have been uneasy coalitions of Agrarians, Social Democrats, and one or more splinter parties. Hampered by ideological differences among the participants, Finnish governments have been unable to formulate or execute vigorous policies to cope with the country's economic problems.

The Communists contribute to the political weakness of the government and the Social Democratic Party. Rising from a very small minority in the prewar years, the Communists rapidly gained strength after the war. Their influence waned to some extent in the early part of the fifties, but subsequently their strength increased in electoral contests. They emerged from the 1958 elections holding one more seat than the Social Democrats. As a major party, the Communists not only draw labor support which would otherwise go to the Social Democrats, but, as in France, their presence as a large non-parliamentary bloc frustrates the formation of strong and stable parliamentary governments.

In brief, the role and experience of Finnish labor in government is quite different from that of other Northern European labor movements. The unions have not felt the same impulse to cooperate with the government that Scandinavian unions have experienced. It is not clearly "their" government, being at best a partnership between Social Democrats and the conservative Agrarians. As a result of parliamentary weakness, the government has not been in a position to adopt policies advocated by the unions and favorable to the urban workers.

In summary, Finland resembles the Mediterranean and Asian nations in many ways. The important and disruptive role of the Communists in politics and in the unions, the absence of any long tradition of collective bargaining, the instability and weakness of unionism, the governments which are either ineffective or unsympathetic to labor, and the difficult economic conditions are points of similarity. On the other hand, Finland differs from these countries in several important aspects. The Social Democrats are much stronger than the corresponding labor parties in the Mediterranean and Asian countries. The collective bargaining system is more significant and somewhat more centralized. Finally, Finland is less subject to population pressures and extreme poverty.

Thus, it may be that Finland is moving along the same path followed by her Northern European neighbors a few decades ago. Certainly the resemblance between the Finland of the past decade and the Norway or Sweden of the post-World War I era is strikingly close. The pattern of industrial unrest in Finland may be that of a country in transition. Relations with Soviet Russia and the future role of the Communists will doubtless tell the tale.

South Africa [19]

South Africa has almost no strikes; those which do occur take very little time. Thus, from a behavioristic standpoint, South Africa strongly resembles Denmark or the Netherlands. The explanations are very different, however.

South Africa is a special case in a different sense from Australia and Finland. These two countries could not easily be placed in any of our categories. Nevertheless, we found it possible to analyze their patterns of industrial conflict in the light of causes that had proved generally significant in other countries studied.

Try as we might, we cannot explain South African industrial relations in terms of our usual criteria: the strength and stability of unionism, labor's role in politics, centralization of the collective bargaining system, the policies of government, employer reactions to unionism, and so on. We include South Africa primarily to emphasize the fact that our theory of industrial conflict assumes economic freedom in the labor market. Inclusion of Spain or Czechoslovakia would satisfy the same purpose.

Although unionism and collective bargaining, as we know them, are limited to persons of European descent, race is nonetheless the dominant fact of industrial relations in South Africa. The presence of the non-whites, and the peculiar institutions of control which have been developed, have had a crucial impact on the white unions and on labor politics.

The non-whites—Asiatics from India, "coloreds" of mixed ancestry, and especially the African Negroes—are the overwhelming majority of the population in South Africa. Not only do they constitute most of the agricultural labor force, including subsistence farmers on the tribal reserves, but also more than 70 per cent of the non-agricultural workers. The proportion of non-whites varies from just over 50 per cent to almost 90 per cent in every major industrial classification except transport and communications. The non-whites typically fill the unskilled and semi-skilled labor positions in private industry. To the whites are reserved nearly all the jobs in government, which administers telecommunications, the railroads, and other public utilities, as well as the more usual public functions. Also reserved for the whites are the skilled, supervisory, managerial, and technical jobs throughout the economy. Thus, South Africa has a single society and economy with two horizontal layers, rather than two vertically organized racial groups coexisting separately.

In most countries, the degree of worker organization, the stability of unions, and the extent of rivalry and factionalism in the labor movement have had a rather conventional and predictable effect on labor relations. Industrial peace has been generally associated with strong, stable, and unified union movements. Weakly organized unions with ephemeral membership and numerous rival factions have been correlated with a high propensity to strike. This relationship breaks down in South Africa. Only whites may belong to registered unions. The white workers have been organized to a significant extent since about 1920. But when union membership is compared with the entire non-agricultural labor force, the degree of organization appears very low indeed. Furthermore, whereas most national labor movements were disunited at the outset and eventually achieved unity, the contrary movement has taken place in South Africa. For many years there was one trade union center, which has broken apart during the past decade. The reasons for the schism are also unusual. In most countries, internal labor-movement conflict has been jurisdictional and ideological—strivings for power and struggles between pragmatic, religious, socialist, syndicalist, and communist points of view. In South Africa, the disagreements have turned mainly on the proper amount of repression of non-whites. Further confusing the picture is the fact that South African unions are predominantly composed of government employees, white-collar workers, skilled technicians, and foremen.

In many countries the role of the labor or social democratic party has been significant in the evolution of union-management relations. In South Africa, again, this influence has broken down. Although the Labour Party has existed for many years, and even participated in the government as a junior partner from 1924 to 1933, it has crumbled under pressure of the controversy over racial policies, which is the dominant theme of South African politics. The division of the white population into Afrikaans and English-speaking groups, and the complete untouchability of the non-whites and particularly the Negroes, have deprived the Labour Party of a broad basis of support. Furthermore, by restricting its appeal to the white workers, the Labour Party has given up significant issues.

As in other countries, the method for determining conditions of work, and the role of the government in particular, are important to the understanding of industrial unrest. In South Africa, collective bargaining, like unionism, does not exist for the bulk of the labor force. Terms of employment for the non-whites are in effect set by the government. Local and regional Native Labour Committees, with government-appointed Negro members and a white chairman, have jurisdiction together with the central Native Labour Board to fix the wages and other conditions of work. For many years there has been legislation prohibiting various racial groups from entering certain industries and occupations, and regulating the ratio between the pay of white workers and that of Africans in other occupations. More recently the minister of labour was given broad power to set aside specific types of employment for exclusive occupancy by particular racial groups. The gold mines, South Africa's most important industry, are closely regulated under separate legislation.

Thus nearly three-quarters of the non-agricultural work force, consisting of non-white workers, are without voice in determining their wages and working conditions. They are barred from expressing their discontent by governmental contraints which hinder the formation of organizations (such as the Suppression of Communism Act of 1950), impede the geographical movement of non-whites, impose the penalty of imprisonment for minor offenses, and so on.

Workers of European descent, who make up the remainder of the labor force, are also restricted to a considerable extent. As already pointed out, nearly all the employees of the regular government departments, the railways, the telephone and telegraph industries, the public utilities, and the publicly owned iron and steel works, are white. These groups also include a large proportion of the unionists. Their conditions of work as public employees are determined by the government and they, too, are denied the right to strike. Many of the remaining white wage and salary earners are white-collar, technical, and supervisory personnel. Although these latter groups are covered by collective bargaining contracts, they are also the groups that are usually disinclined to strike.

There is reason to think that the general repression of the non-whites may have the added effect of inhibiting aggressiveness in white unions. Most of the major strikes in the past were on the part of white workers, protesting inroads into "white jobs" by the Africans. This source of discontent has been removed by Apartheid policies, but the possibility that Africans could be used against the white workers should they displease the government and the employers may have reduced strike activity greatly. The mine owners have repeatedly asserted that Africans could do many jobs now barred to them; the Africans have worked successfully in semiskilled manufacturing jobs; and the government wishes to develop industries near the native reserves which will use native labor exclusively. All these developments work to keep alive the threat of white labor displacement. In addition, although prosecution under the Suppression of Communism Act is most likely to be directed against non-white union activity, the broad powers conferred on administrative officers may well be considered threatening to the white unions.

In summary, we might expect widespread industrial conflict in South Africa, but find very little. In other countries with weak and divided unionism, relatively little collective bargaining, and governments hostile or indifferent to labor, rates of strike activity are high. It appears that the opposite situation in South Africa is explained largely by the thoroughgoing repression of the non-white majority practiced by nearly all white groups, and particularly by the government. With the large majority of workers in mining, manufacturing, and other unskilled and semiskilled jobs forbidden to join unions or express discontent, it is not surprising then that South Africa has so few industrial disputes. Furthermore, the white unions seem to be rendered less militant by their occupational composition, the threat of displacement, and the possibility of government repression.

NOTES TO CHAPTER 10

1. Kenneth F. Walker, *Industrial Relations in Australia* (Cambridge: Harvard University Press, 1956), and "Australia," in Walter Galenson (ed.), *Comparative Labor Movements* (Englewood Cliffs, N. J.: Prentice-Hall, 1952), pp. 173–242; Mark Perlman, *Judges in Industry, A Study of Labour Arbitration in Australia* (Melbourne: Melbourne University Press, 1954); L. F. Crisp, *The Australian Federal Labour Party, 1901–1951* (London: Longmans, Green and Co., 1955); D. W. Oxnam, "Some Economic and Social Consequences of the Australian System of Wage Regulation," The Australian Institute of Political Science Winter Forum, Canberra, 1952 (mimeo.); James W. Kuhn, "Grievance Machinery and Strikes in Australia," *Industrial and Labor Relations Review*, 8 (January 1955), pp. 169–76.

2. Walker, *Industrial Relations in Australia*, p. 357.

3. *Ibid.*, p. 201.

4. *Ibid.*, p. 248.

5. *Ibid.*, p. 201.

6. *Ibid.*, p. 288.

7. The concentration of power at the state level may affect the nature of Australian strikes by the weakening of the union functions at the local level as well. James W. Kuhn argues that the interest in politics and the arbitration system of the higher union officers has led to lack of a well-developed grievance procedure and, consequently, to protest strikes. See Kuhn, *op. cit.*, pp. 169–76.

8. Walker, *Industrial Relations in Australia*, p. 248.

9. *Ibid.*, pp. 286–87.

10. The ironworkers' association is not the only union in the metal trades, but

it has been particularly successful in organizing unskilled and semiskilled workers. Walker shows that between 1913 and 1953, about 71 per cent of all stoppages were in the mining and quarrying industry, particularly coal mining; another 7 per cent were in the maritime trades, particularly longshoring; and 6 per cent in the metal trades. These three industries accounted for 48 per cent, 13 per cent, and 11 per cent, respectively, of man-days lost. Thus, five-sixths of all stoppages and three-fourths of all idleness have occurred in these relatively small sectors of the economy, in which no more than about one-sixth of the non-agricultural labor force is employed. See *Ibid.*, p. 345.

11. Letter to A. M. Ross, dated September 23, 1958.

12. Letter to A. M. Ross dated August 19, 1958.

13. Letter to A. M. Ross dated August 27, 1958.

14. Crisp, *op. cit.*, p. 255.

15. *Ibid.*, p. 290.

16. *Ibid.*, p. 255.

17. Crisp speaks of the various attempts at greater government control in the social and economic affairs as "steps towards the realization of what the average Australian worker expects of his Labour Party." *Ibid.*, p. 290.

18. J. Hampton Jackson, *Finland* (London: Unwin, 1938); Elizabeth Elfvengren, "The Finnish Labour Force," *International Labour Review,* 73 (April 1956), pp. 358–76; Niilo A. Mannio, "Recent Social Developments in Finland," *International Labour Review,* 57 (January–February 1948), pp. 1–14; Anna-Stina Ericson, "Labour Situation in Finland, 1949–51," *Monthly Labor Review,* 73 (August 1951), pp. 144–47.

19. Muriel Horrell, *South Africa's Non-White Workers* (Johannesburg: South African Institute of Race Relations, 1956); Lewis Sowden, *The Union of South Africa* (New York: Doubleday, 1943); Sir Tom O'Brien, "In the Land of Baas and Servant," *Free Labour World,* 90 (December 1957), pp. 5–14; "The Free Trade Unions of South Africa Fight for Existence," *Free Labour World,* 68 (February 1956), pp. 20–24; "Conditions of African Employment on the Rand Gold Mines," *International Labour Review,* 41 (January 1945), pp. 56–65; Ernest Gitsham, *Labour Organization in South Africa* (Durban: E. P. and Commercial Printing Co., 1926).

CHAPTER 11

North American Pattern:

United States and Canada[1]

Thus far we have described and endeavored to explain three patterns of strike activity. The North European pattern, first variant, is characterized by infrequent stoppages of very brief duration. Industrial conflict has been reduced to a nominal quantity in Denmark, the Netherlands, United Kingdom, and Germany. The North European pattern, second variant, is found in Norway and Sweden. Strikes are seldom called, but those that do occur tend to be real trials of economic strength. The distinguishing feature of the Mediterranean-Asian pattern is the short, massive protest or demonstration strike. Rates of participation are high but duration of stoppages very low in France, Italy, Japan, and India. Then we dealt with three countries, Australia, Finland, and South Africa, which do not easily fall into any of these classifications.

With the United States and Canada we come to the fourth pattern. Stoppages are fairly frequent and unusually long. Strike participation rates are higher than in the Northern European countries, and at the same time lower than in the Mediterranean-Asian group. Between 1948 and 1956, the number of strikers averaged 15.4 per cent of union membership in the United States each year, and 6.3 per cent in Canada.

161

The corresponding proportions varied between 1.3 and 5.9 per cent in the Northern European nations, and between 21.5 and 62.4 per cent in the Mediterranean-Asian countries. In recent years, strikes in the United States and Canada have been the longest in the world with the exception of those in Sweden. During the 1948–56 period, approximately twenty-three working days were lost for strikers in Sweden, nineteen in Canada, and fifteen in the United States.

It seems sensible to regard the United States and Canada as having one system of industrial relations. This is so not merely because most Canadians live within fifty miles of the American border, and not merely because the two countries have the same economic, social, and political institutions. After all, Norway and Sweden have similar institutions and are geographically contiguous, but it would be oversimplifying to lump them together in a study of this kind. The same can be said of France and Italy. The reason for discussing the United States and Canada jointly is that we are dealing with largely the same unions and major employers in both countries. Speaking of the "Americanization" of Canadian life, Stuart Jamieson observes,

> Trade unionism and industrial relations reflect this growing dominance of the United States in the general trend of economic and cultural change. By far the majority of all unionized workers in Canada belong to organizations that are branches of the so-called international unions, the membership, headquarters and executive personnel of which are over-whelmingly American. Union organizational structures, governmental systems, policies, and objectives in Canada, therefore, tend to reflect to a considerable degree those of American parent bodies in their respective industry or trade jurisdictions.
>
> American policies and personnel are likewise heavily represented on the employer side. While no exact statistical estimate has been made of this question, it is safe to say that a large fraction of the organized wage earners in Canada are employed in the 3500-odd enterprises that are branch plants or subsidiaries of U. S. corporations. These include some of the largest, the most widely known and influential firms on the continent, such as Ford and General Motors, Westinghouse and General Electric, Dow Chemicals and Crown-Zellerbach.[2]

There are some differences in strike activity between the United States and Canada, however. The first is that membership involvement rates have always been higher in the United States. Some 33.2 per cent of union members in the United States went on strike annually from 1900 to 1929, compared with 14.7 per cent in Canada. For the period 1930–47, the average for the United States was 20.3 per cent, and for Canada 13.3 per cent. For 1948–56, the United States average was 15.4 per cent and the Canadian 6.3 per cent. On the other hand, strikes have been lengthening in Canada since the late 1920's, but have been growing shorter in the United States. Since the end of World War II Canadian strikes have been more than twice as long as in the 1920's and 1930's, and considerably longer than in the United States.

Nevertheless, the similarities are greater than the differences and should be given primary emphasis. It appears that five principal features of industrial life in the United States and Canada are associated with the moderately high rates of participation and extremely high duration of strikes which define the North American pattern. First, mass unionization is fairly recent and mature labor-management relations are still in the course of development in a number of major industries. Second, organizational and leadership rivalries have been very prominent in the labor movements and have been prosecuted in exuberant fashion. Third, the structure of collective bargaining is very decentralized. Fourth, neither country has a strong or dominant labor party. Finally, both countries generally permit collective bargaining controversies to be settled by trials of economic strength, although in Canada a compulsory mediation procedure must be utilized first.

Unionism had early beginnings in North America, but never won the allegiance of the mass of industrial workers until recently. Union membership in the United States increased four-fold between 1900 and 1930, but only covered about 11 per cent of non-agricultural wage and salary earners by the latter date. In the same time span, membership expanded thirty times in Norway, and nine times in Sweden, to include 21 per cent and 35 per cent of the non-agricultural workers in these two nations. Prior to 1935, the only countries having a lesser degree of organization than the United States and Canada were those where industrial development was still rudimentary, for example, India; or where union activity was circumscribed by hostile governments, for example, South Africa, Japan, and Finland.

Furthermore, the unions did not enjoy stability of membership prior to the 1930's. As is well known, a rapid attrition took place subsequent to World War I, and a further shrinkage lasted into the New Deal period. The historical dangers of membership apathy, employer enmity, and government hostility undoubtedly help to explain the strength of the union security demand in the United States and Canada.

Beginning in 1935, however, there followed about a dozen years of rapid union growth to a point where, by 1947, approximately one-third of the non-agricultural workers had been organized in each of the two countries. Thus, there has been little more than a decade free from sharp fluctuations in the relative strength of organization. Since periods of rapid membership change are usually marked by frequent strikes, it is not surprising that the propensity to strike in both countries has been consistently lower since World War II than in the prewar decades.

Leadership and organizational rivalries have been endemic in both countries. In the United States there has been rivalry between craft and industrial unions, between left-wing and right-wing unions, between AFL unions and CIO unions; but most frequently these rivalries have been based not on structural or political differences but on a vigorous pursuit of elastic, opportunistic, and overlapping jurisdictional claims. Canada has had all these conflicts and others. Among the groups not found in the United States are some exclusively Canadian and rather nationalistic unions, such as the Canadian Brotherhood of Railway Employees and the Catholic unions of eastern Canada.

For a number of years the Communists had considerable prominence in labor. It is true that the Communists in the United States and Canada, unlike those in Europe and Asia, adopted the practice of business unionism and never used the mass demonstration strike to any extent. But the competition between right-wing and left-wing unions in the electrical, maritime, longshoring, non-ferrous metals, and other industries clearly had an unsettling influence on industrial relations while it lasted. The same can be said of competition between right-wing and left-wing factions in such unions as the United Auto Workers and the International Woodworkers of America. As in most countries of the Western world, Communist influence reached its peak in the United States and Canada during and just after World War II. The crisis came with the expulsion of left-wing unions from the CIO in the late 1940's. In subsequent years Communist strength has been greatly reduced, localized, and sealed off from the rest of the labor movement.

One of the important causes of the declining propensity to strike in both countries has been the abatement of rivalry within the union movement. In Canada the Catholic unions have moved toward closer working relations with the AFL–CIO unions. In both countries the Communists have dwindled to relative insignificance. Beginning about 1950, relations between the AFL and the CIO entered a period of change. First, the two federations cooperated closely on issues of government policy during the Korean War. Next they worked together, although not with success, in the 1952 election campaign. Then came the development of no-raid agreements and internal disputes arbitration machinery; and the culminating step was the organic merger between the two federations in 1956. Although there have been no significant mergers of dual national or international unions, de facto jurisdiction has been increasingly respected, on the theory that "raiding doesn't pay." It seems clear that the abatement of organizational rivalry must be counted among the causes of declining participation rates in the United States and Canada during the past decade.

Turning now to employer policies as they affect strike activity, the strength of antiunionism in the United States until recent years is so well known to readers of this monograph that there would be no purpose in belaboring it unduly. Suffice it to note that resistance remained undiminished for the first third of the present century, during which employers and unions were able to reach a basic accommodation in many European countries. Aside from company unionism, the yellow-dog contract, the injunction, and other specific devices of the "open shop" movement, the development of personnel administration and "welfare capitalism" inhibited the growth of labor organizations. In the words of Millis and Montgomery,

> The impact of management's new and "enlightened" labor policies was upsetting to the kind of unionism that had enjoyed such good health and rapid growth during the war years. . . . Employer labor policies, combined with . . . anti-union weapons . . . proved to be powerful barriers to outside unions.[3]

Canadian employers have traditionally been even more reluctant to recognize unions and offer concessions. But they have also been in a better position to resist union demands. As Jamieson points out,

> Canadian workers have been less willing or able than American workers to organize and strike for their objectives.

Under these circumstances the spectacular and violent organizational conflicts of the United States have not been repeated in Canada.

> The use of professional strike-breakers, labor spies, "goon squads," "vigilante" groups, armed militia and other spectacular features of industrial warfare in the United States in previous decades have [sic] been absent from the Canadian scene . . . with several notable exceptions.[4]

The achievement of stable union-management relations in leading American industries, such as automobiles and rubber, which were the scene of violent organizing conflicts only two decades ago, is likewise too well known for extended comment. In Chapter 5 we noted that employer attitudes toward workers have changed so profoundly that a "metamorphosis of the employment relationship" or "revolution in industrial employment" is said to have occurred. We observed also that building friendly relations with the unions is generally considered one of the central responsibilities of management in the United States.

The same evolution has been taking place in Canada. "Employers in most industries and enterprises of major importance," we are told, "whether from necessity or choice, have become resigned to the prospect of having to deal with unions as a necessary and integral factor in the industrial scene." [5]

Although collective bargaining is now firmly established in the United States, the structure of bargaining is perhaps the most decentralized in the world. In the United States there are only a handful of national collective agreements, such as those in the bituminous coal, men's clothing, and wallpaper industries. The number of regional agreements is somewhat larger, and includes the maritime, West Coast longshoring, pulp and paper, and Pacific Northwest lumber industries. There are numerous multi-employer contracts in local market industries such as construction, printing, retail trade, hotels, and cemeteries. When all is said and done, however, we have nothing like the consolidated bargaining structure of England, Norway, or Sweden. In the United States, about five-sixths of the labor contracts are negotiated in single-firm units, and these cover two-thirds of all workers under collective agreements. Some 68 per cent of the contracts are in single-plant units. [6] In Sweden more than half the labor force is covered by nation-wide agreements. [7]

Canada's bargaining system is almost a carbon copy of that in the United States. There is some multi-employer bargaining, almost no industry-wide bargaining, except where one firm constitutes the industry; and the great majority of contracts cover the employees of single firms.

The most telling distinction between Northern European and North American collective bargaining is in the part played by central organizations of unions and employers. Although the AFL–CIO has been moving aggressively in the matter of corrupt practices and political endorsements, it has not sought to play any significant role in collective bargaining. Its participation is limited to research studies of various issues, generalized arguments that higher wages are necessary in order to provide sufficient purchasing power, etc. Similarly, the National Association of Manufacturers and the U. S. Chamber of Commerce represent industry in the political world and can be counted on to warn against the inflationary consequences of wage increases, but they do not take any important part in bargaining decisions.

Collective bargaining structure in the United States and Canada is perhaps not quite so decentralized as the foregoing description might imply. Up to a certain point "pattern bargaining" or "wage leadership" accomplishes the same results as multi-employer bargaining. As Chamberlain says,

> If the United States is characterized by a relatively low incidence of multi-employer and particularly industry-wide bargaining, the consequence is not . . . a myriad of isolated, unrelated wage bargains.[8]

But the similarity between industry-wide bargaining and key bargaining should not be exaggerated. In the first place, the dominant influence of the pattern diminishes when we move from the center of the industry into peripheral sectors, such as fabricating firms in the iron and steel industry.[9] In the second place, whereas general wage adjustments and certain major fringe benefits may be subject to pattern bargaining, other issues will arise within the individual firms of the industry. For instance, one of the most prolonged major strikes in recent American history, the Westinghouse strike of 1955, turned on production standards for skilled employees and was not prevented by the existence of a wage pattern in the electrical industry. In the third place, the pattern that ultimately is extended throughout an industry may be determined initially in bargaining between the union and only one of the major companies.

In any event, however these informal influences may be evaluated, there is no dispute that the bargaining system of the United States and Canada is much less centralized than it is in the Northern European countries.

There is reason to think that employers in the major industries are beginning to collaborate more closely than they have done in the past. The united front maintained by employers in the airframe and automobile industries in 1958 was effective in paring down union demands without recourse to a work stoppage. Another interesting development is the plan of co-insurance against strike losses adopted by the airlines.

In order to improve their relative position, employers can take one of two paths: they can endeavor to weaken the unions or to strengthen themselves. The former is a beguiling objective to many but the prospects of achieving the objective are not good. The latter requires more effective organization, a willingness to make demands upon the union, and consideration of additional techniques such as the lockout for bargaining purposes. It would not be surprising to witness these changes in employer organization and policies during the next decade or two. Although a highly consolidated bargaining structure of the Northern European variety is not likely, further centralization within major industries would probably tend to lessen the volume of strike activity.

Among all the labor movements in the world, the American and

Canadian have probably had the least political involvement. Political experiments were made as early as the 1830's, but these were confined to state and local arenas, and were not carried into the orthodox tradition. The main elements of the tradition were defined during the long tenure of Samuel Gompers. "Voluntarism," or primary reliance on industrial action, had a prominent place. Dependence on social legislation, establishment of a labor party, and sustained association with any political party were discountenanced.

Obviously the situation is changed—but not fundamentally so. Much emphasis is laid on social legislation, but even more on contract negotiations. Political action is stressed, but is still a relatively peripheral function. The American union is a business union, and its chief business is still collective bargaining. Organized labor is close to the Democratic Party, but on a pragmatic rather than ideological basis. The association does not conflict with the traditional policy of "rewarding our friends" and is not so close as to inhibit the use of the strike weapon.

With respect to the political role of organized labor, there is one difference between the United States and Canada, but this is not sufficient to affect strike activity. Whereas there has never been a labor party in the United States, the Canadian Cooperative Commonwealth Federation can be regarded as something of a labor party. Founded in 1932, the CCF has a mildly socialist outlook and has bid strongly for the support of unions as well as discontented agrarian groups. Although the Trades and Labour Congress, which consisted of AFL unions prior to the merger between the AFL and CIO, never officially endorsed the CCF, many leaders of constituent unions did support it. The Canadian Congress of Labour, comprising CIO affiliates in the Dominion, formally supported the CCF in 1943, and continued its advocacy until the merger of the two labor groups in 1956. The new Canadian Labour Congress has given qualified support to the CCF.

Although the CCF has been sufficiently close to the labor unions to constitute a labor party, it has not come sufficiently close to political power so that collective bargaining and strike policy have been affected. Only in the province of Saskatchewan has the CCF formed a majority government. In Ontario and British Columbia, it has furnished strong opposition to the leading party. In the Dominion Parliament, however, it has always run third to the Progressive Conservative Party and the Liberal Party; and its fortunes have been at a low ebb in recent years.

Thus far we have been discussing the fact that participation in strikes is relatively common in the United States and Canada, although it has diminished considerably since the 1930's and 1940's. It remains to comment on the long duration of strikes in these two countries.   The basic explanation, of course, is that resort to economic strength is still an important feature of the industrial relations system.   Unlike the Mediterranean-Asian countries, terms of employment in the organized sector of the economy are defined in collective bargaining agreements rather than by unilateral employer decision or by government action. These agreements have penetrated into every nook and cranny of the employment relationship and regulate it intensively.   Thus matters of real substance are involved in labor-management negotiations.   At the same time, the governments of the United States and Canada have generally been willing to permit labor and management to resolve their disputes by tests of staying power.   In the usual type of dispute, alternative methods of settlement have not been imposed.

In fact, the governments play a modest role in all respects: in conducting public enterprise, in regulating terms of employment, and in pressing for the settlement of industrial controversies.   Although the railway, telephone, telegraph, radio broadcasting, and similar industries are publicly owned in numerous countries, in the United States they remain in private hands, along with the bulk of the electric power industry.   The Canadian National Railway and the Canadian Broadcasting Corporation are owned by the Dominion, but otherwise private ownership remains dominant.

Both countries have approximately the same kinds of social legislation. There are minimum wage and maximum hour laws, unemployment insurance, workmen's compensation, and retirement benefits.   Other problems handled by legislation in many European and Asian countries, including paid holidays, paid vacations, and health insurance, are left in private hands.

The federal and state governments in the United States have attempted to eliminate certain kinds of stoppages.   Under the Railway Labor Act and the Taft-Hartley Act, cooling-off periods can be invoked in so-called emergency disputes.   The latter statute makes jurisdictional strikes and secondary boycotts illegal and offers a peaceful procedure for resolving representation disputes.   In a few states, public utility strikes have been made illegal.   In the great bulk of disputes, however—those relating to conditions of employment and not considered emergency cases—intervention is limited to the provision of mediation services.   Employers and union officials are almost unanimous in opposing stronger forms of intervention in peacetime, and the informed public appears generally willing to countenance a considerable volume of strike activity as an incidental cost of a free-enterprise system.

Dominion and provincial governments in Canada have recently established elaborate conciliation procedures, generally involving delay periods, compulsory mediation, and recommendations by conciliation boards. Jamieson criticizes these procedures on the ground that they are used too indiscriminately, occasion too much delay, and interfere unduly with the collective bargaining process. He suggests that the mediation statutes may serve to explain the fact that strikes in Canada are less frequent and longer than those in the United States.

> The elaborate conciliation procedures required under most of the new legislation have undoubtedly been of some effect in [economic disputes], in preventing a number of strikes that might otherwise have occurred. To this extent, therefore, the new post-war labor legislation may claim at least some credit for the fact that the number of strikes, and of man-days of employment lost in strikes, has not increased in proportion to total union membership and non-agricultural employment since the war. . . .
> But the very features of Canadian legislation that have been effective in preventing numerous strikes from occurring may also have rendered strikes more difficult to settle once they did develop. This may be one of the major reasons that, in contrast to trends in the United States and elsewhere, the average duration of strikes in Canada has risen since the pre-war period and has remained considerably above that in the United States.[10]

In the next chapter we shall comment on the probable future of strike activity in the United States. These comments will apply generally to Canada also.

NOTES TO CHAPTER 11

1. Lewis L. Lorwin, *The American Federation of Labor* (Washington: The Brookings Institution, 1933); Harry A. Millis and Royal E. Montgomery, *Organized Labor* (New York: McGraw-Hill Book Co., 1945); Philip Taft, *The A.F.L. in the Time of Gompers* (New York: Harper and Brothers, 1957), and *The A.F.L. from the Death of Gompers to the Merger* (New York: Harper and Brothers, 1959); Neil W. Chamberlain, *Collective Bargaining* (New York: McGraw-Hill Book Co., 1951), and "Collective Bargaining in the United States," in Adolf Sturmthal (ed.), *Contemporary Collective Bargaining in Seven Countries* (Ithaca: Institute of International Industrial and Labor Relations, Cornell University, 1957), pp. 252–307; Lloyd Ulman, *The Rise of the National Trade Union* (Cambridge: Harvard University Press, 1955); Arthur Kornhauser, Robert Dubin and Arthur M. Ross (eds.), *Industrial Conflict* (New York: McGraw-Hill Book Co., 1954); John I. Griffin, *Strikes* (New York: Columbia University Press, 1939); H. A. Logan, *Trade Unions in Canada* (Toronto: The Macmillan Co., 1948); Stuart Jamieson, *Industrial Relations in Canada* (Ithaca: Cornell University Press, 1957).

2. Jamieson, *op. cit.,* pp. 5–6.

3. Millis and Montgomery, *op. cit.,* p. 160.

4. Jamieson, *op. cit.*, pp. 6–7.

5. *Ibid.*, p. 27.

6. Neil W. Chamberlain, "Collective Bargaining in the United States," *op. cit.*, pp. 259–60.

7. *Perspective on Labor Conditions in Sweden* (Stockholm: Swedish Employers Confederation, 1954), p. 38.

8. Chamberlain, *op. cit.*, p. 263. See also Arthur M. Ross, *Trade Union Wage Policy* (Berkeley: University of California Press, 1948), Chapter III.

9. See George Seltzer, "Pattern Bargaining and the United Steelworkers," *Journal of Political Economy*, 59 (August 1951), pp. 319–31.

10. Jamieson, *op. cit.*, pp. 117–18.

CHAPTER 12

Conclusion

One of the hazards of authorship is that one's classifications will be taken more seriously than was ever intended and will be put to uses for which they were never designed. In this book we have found it helpful to classify most of the countries into four groups. Our "patterns" should be regarded as useful pedagogical devices, however, and nothing more. We are not suggesting that all the countries within a group are identical with respect to the condition of the labor movement, the structure of collective bargaining, the role of government, and other aspects of their collective bargaining systems. We merely state that they have a good deal in common. The patterns are meant to fit loosely, although not so loosely as to constitute intellectual Mother Hubbards. Thus the collective bargaining structure in Denmark and the Netherlands is more centralized than in the United Kingdom. The Communists had more strength in Norway than in Sweden during the early postwar period. More of the terms of employment have been legislated in France than in Italy. The Canadian government intervenes more frequently in labor disputes than does the government of the United States. We are satisfied, however, that the nations in a given group have more in common with each other than with those in the other groups.

We do not wish to claim too much for our four-way classification. It does not exist in a state of nature but is the kind of organizing concept that is essential in simplifying the chaotic variety of raw experience.

Most of the countries we have studied fit into these categories. Probably others could be slotted into them. Australia, South Africa, and Finland did not fit; undoubtedly certain other nations would be difficult to classify. If industrial conflict in the rest of the world were analyzed, additional groupings would emerge. As we observed in Chapter 4, for example, an "Economic Development Pattern" might be described with reference to Israel, Egypt, and other nations where the themes of nationalism, anticolonialism, and central planning are combined in aggressive development programs. Totalitarian societies would constitute still another group. Furthermore, the classification of any given country is not necessarily permanent. India, for example, may shift out of the Mediterranean-Asian pattern if the Congress Party program comes off successfully. The distinction between Norway and Sweden and the remaining Northern European countries may ultimately disappear.

We have chosen to pitch the research at a rather technical industrial-relations level. In searching out the influences on strike activity in particular countries, we have therefore emphasized certain principal aspects of their industrial relations systems.[1] It goes without saying that these cannot be regarded as the original or ultimate or most fundamental causes. As Adolf Sturmthal remarked in a comment on "Strike Experience in Five Countries,"

> It seems plausible to expect that much more permanent elements are at the root of the . . . explanations proposed by Ross and Irwin. . . . The answer might be in some more fundamental behavior patterns of the different nations.[2]

Indeed it might. And once the "fundamental behavior patterns" had been described, we would then have the problem of explaining them. Every cause has its antecedent causes; and one of the classical definitions of science is "the certain and evident knowledge of things by their causes." Yet for some purposes the search for more ultimate causes is not so important as an understanding of the character or configuration of a phenomenon.

We shall return to this thought in a moment. But first we can certainly agree that the industrial-relations system in any country is part of a larger social context. Take the matter of national wealth, for example. Our Mediterranean-Asian countries are relatively poor, with the exception of France. In 1952–54 the annual per-capita national product averaged $60 in India, $190 in Japan, and $310 in Italy.[3] National poverty is certainly related to the weakness of unionism and the ineffectiveness of collective bargaining. At the other extreme, per-capita product averaged $1,310 in Canada and $1,870 in the United States. It is probably no coincidence that a relatively large amount of industrial conflict is tolerated in these two countries with no great discomfiture. (The Northern European nations are in between; per-capita product ranged from $500 in the Netherlands to $950 in Sweden.)

We have noted unity and centralization in the labor movements of Norway, Sweden, and the United Kingdom; rivalry and disorganization in those of France and Italy. Here again pertinent differences in national "style" and culture are not hard to find. The stock portrayal of the stolid, practical Englishman or Scandinavian and the excitable, individualistic Frenchman or Italian, and the contrast between parliamentary politics in these Northern and Southern European countries, will suffice. Instability in French and Italian political life is undoubtedly a larger expression of the same cultural forces which produce instability in the labor movement.

Likewise there are evident national differences in the ability to develop viable compromises. Compromise is the essence of collective bargaining, not merely in the sense that particular bargaining issues are compromised, but in the more fundamental sense that the bargaining system itself represents a settlement of the basic power issues between Labor and Capital. It is a well-established fact that collective bargaining does not thrive on a diet of principles. In fact, one of the great virtues of collective bargaining is that it permits the formulation of limited issues which are amenable to resolution and blurs over large differences of principle which can never really be settled. Without indulging further in the dubious science of speculative anthropology, we may confidently state that the willingness to "muddle through" is unevenly distributed over the globe. For example, the graceful retreat of the English from India and Burma may be contrasted with the debacles suffered by the French in Indochina and Algeria.

We might go on at length, but enough has been said to illustrate the point that a country's industrial relations system is only a small part of a much larger context.

Let us return, then, to the level of industrial-relations institutions and practices. In Chapters 6–11 of this book we have dealt at length with a group of influences on relative strike activity—the condition of the labor movement, the collective bargaining structure, the role of the state, labor's political program, and so on. We must emphasize, however, that their influence is exerted jointly rather than severally, as a configuration rather than as a group of independent variables. By *configuration* we mean a whole which is more than the sum of its parts.

The central concepts in every one of our disciplines, sciences and arts are patterns and configurations. . . . These configurations can never be reached by starting with the parts—just as the ear will never hear a melody by hearing individual sounds. Indeed, the parts in any pattern or configuration exist only, and can only be identified, in contemplation of the whole and from understanding of the whole.[4]

If this be true, a nation's industrial-relations system cannot be thought as the product of various independent "causes," but can only be comprehended as a whole.

When we say that a certain factor is conducive to industrial peace or to industrial conflict, we mean that it has this effect *in combination with other influences with which it is characteristically conjoined.* The context is crucially important. Disunity and factionalism in the labor movement evidently increase the propensity to strike in the Mediterranean-Asian countries, but they work in combination with other factors, such as the weakness of collective bargaining. In the Netherlands the labor movement is divided into Socialist, Protestant, and Catholic federations; but in a context of centralized bargaining, labor political activity, etc., divisive tendencies have been held in check. Government techniques of disputes settlement have contributed to the elimination of strikes in those countries where they support the collective bargaining system or provide a workable substitute. Where they obstruct and impede collective bargaining, as in Finland and Canada, they probably increase the amount of conflict. In most of the Northern European countries, a successful labor party is part of the total configuration in which strike activity has been reduced almost to the vanishing point. Here Australia stands as the exceptional case. The Labour Party has been a major factor in politics since 1890, but some of the other elements of the North European pattern are missing; so that the membership involvement rate is among the highest in the world.

It follows also that a desired condition of labor relations cannot be produced in a given country merely by grafting or transplanting certain arrangements which have succeeded elsewhere. American experience in occupying defeated nations, encouraging European recovery, and administering foreign aid programs will testify to the truth of this proposition. It soon developed that enacting a reasonable facsimile of the Taft-Hartley Act and creating a rough equivalent of the International Association of Machinists were not sufficient to solve all labor problems in every foreign clime!

To conclude this book with a chapter on "The Future of Industrial Conflict" would be an engaging flourish. The easiest method would be to project recent trends. Projection is the poor man's prophecy. Since there is a great deal of momentum in human history, distinguished reputations are often acquired with the use of this technique. The recent trends in strike activity have been made sufficiently clear in previous chapters, and the reader may project them, if he chooses, without further assistance.

Difficulties are involved in making more subjective predictions. Even if we could foretell the practices and institutions in each country twenty-five or fifty years from now, we would know them only as separate elements rather than as a total system. And, of course, we cannot know what strains these systems will be subjected to as a result of political upheavals, economic changes, and military events.

A few general expectations may be stated notwithstanding these difficulties.

We do not see any substantial evidence of any impending revival of strike activity in the Northern European countries. To use the words of Reinhard Bendix, the "civic reintegration of the industrial work force" [5] has been accomplished in these countries, and there is no compelling reason to think it will be undone.

As Bendix points out, "civic reintegration," which is associated with a decline in political radicalism, depends on "the willingness of the entrepreneurial classes to compromise" and the restoration to the workers of "the rights of equal citizenship." [6]   Just as the survival of limited monarchy in Northern Europe has required a basic compromise between royalty and commonalty, likewise the stabilization of class relations has required a *modus vivendi* between entrepreneurs and workers, based on the institutions of unionism and collective bargaining. After the struggles for organization and recognition had concluded, strikes became trials of economic strength in disputes over the terms of employment. But strike activity has tended to disappear as the labor market has been more tightly organized, union-management relations have become more solidaristic, and labor has directed its energies into the political sphere.

It has often been noted that the principles of the French Revolution are still controversial in France, and it cannot be said that political democracy has become firmly rooted in Italy or Japan. By the same token and for some of the same reasons, neither can it be said that a *modus vivendi* has developed there between labor and management. In the absence of an effective collective bargaining system, the strike has not come into its own as a trial of economic strength. Instead the strike takes the form of a brief, massive gesture of protest and expression of political radicalism. We Americans have hoped that we could transplant our own industrial-relations practices into these countries, but the soil has not been receptive. Although no one can say what will happen in twenty-five or fifty years, so far there is no clear indication that the necessary basic compromise is being made; and as we have already observed, the larger social and economic environment is unfavorable. The only recent change affecting strike activity in France, Italy, and Japan is the decline in union membership.

The requisites for a viable system of private collective bargaining are not found in India, but the government is moving in to fill the breach. As we observed in Chapter 4, there is no reason to believe that the newer countries now attempting to industrialize under forced draft will rehearse the historical Western cycle of industrial conflict. The strong probability is that governments will dominate labor-management relations in such countries for the indefinite future, either in close collaboration with the unions or by suppressing them or by taking them over. Conceivably unions and employers will eventually demand rights of self-determination, but as to this we can only speculate.

What about the United States? Here at home strike activity has been on the wane since the end of World War II. The membership involvement rate dropped off steadily from 26.0 per cent in 1945–47 to 10.1 per cent in 1954–56. The average duration fell from 17.4 to 14.3 days, but a long-run decline is not evident. We must reiterate that it is hazardous to prophecy the effect of particular institutional changes, apart from the total context in which they will operate. However, American authors discussing the future of industrial conflict in the United States can claim to be sufficiently familiar with the total context that the danger of going astray is not so great.

The prospects for strike activity in the United States are difficult to read because the tendencies are mixed. There are persistent influences tending to reduce the frequency and duration of strikes, but also there are more recent developments having the opposite effect.

The intensity of organization has been relatively stable for about fifteen years. Changes in occupational structure have been working against the unions, and organizing campaigns have had limited success. Any future expansion of the labor movement will be concentrated, to a considerable extent at least, in the white-collar and professional fields, where employees are reluctant to strike.

The strength of interunion rivalries in the foreseeable future is not clear. On the one hand, the no-raid agreements have been in effect several years. Arbitration awards enforcing these agreements are generally observed and are beginning to be honored by the courts. AFL and CIO have been merged since 1956. Although opportunism is still the primary basis of jurisdictional claims in the American labor movement, *de facto* rights have become more solid and deeply entrenched with the passage of time. On the other hand, rapid technological change may be reopening some old conflicts between the building trades and the industrial unions. The AFL–CIO has been striving to develop procedures for resolving disputes over installation and maintenance work, and in 1959 it adopted a vaguely worded statement of principle endorsing the use of arbitration for this purpose. There is also some possibility, although not a great deal, of intensified jurisdictional warfare between unions inside the AFL–CIO and those on the outside, particularly the Teamsters. On balance the stabilizing forces appear stronger than the unstabilizing.

In addition, internal (intraunion) leadership conflicts are continuing to diminish. Temporarily the Landrum-Griffin Act will stimulate political activity within local unions, and will make it more difficult to secure ratification of negotiated agreements in many instances. Eventually, however, local unions will simmer down again. Furthermore, the act is unlikely to have even a temporary effect in the political life of the national unions. Despite current emphasis on union democracy, the "one-party" government is clearly the standard model for a specialized interest group such as a labor organization.

(These observations concerning the Landrum-Griffin Act are not intended as an expression of disapproval. Many of the provisions are desirable. In the long run, however, the provisions implementing the fiduciary concept of union leadership will be more significant than those encouraging internal political activity.)

There is no reason to think that a successful labor party will be organized in the foreseeable future. Without analyzing this question in detail, we might point out that in every country where a labor party has achieved political success, at least 45 per cent of non-agricultural employees have been union members. In the United States only about 33 per cent have been organized.

Looking now at the employer community, we may note the tendency toward industry-wide bargaining strategy in some of our key industries. Informal collaboration among major producers is being used rather than the formal employer associations, with power of attorney, which are essential where numerous small businesses are involved. Evidence of industry-wide bargaining strategy is found in the 1958 and 1959 airplane, automobile, and steel negotiations. The united front maintained by employers in the airplane and automobile industries in 1958 and 1959 was effective in paring down union demands without work stoppages. Industry-wide bargaining in steel did not produce a peaceful settlement in 1959, it is true. The extraordinary length of the steel dispute did not result from changes in bargaining structure, however, but rather from the stickiness of the issues and the employers' strategy of seeking "too much too soon."

We are satisfied that industry-wide bargaining will become more widespread in major industries, even though the steel companies did not employ it as wisely as would have been desired; and that this development will lessen the volume of strike activity in the long run, even though there may be transitional frictions. But the advanced type of consolidated bargaining structure, in which key decisions are made by central federations of employers and unions, is most unlikely. The very size of the country and the heterogeneity among unions and employers, as well as economic custom and philosophy, militate against this possibility.

As we enter a new decade of the 1960's, we find labor-management relations somewhat mixed. Certainly these relations have been growing more accommodative or corporative in the long run. Scholars have long been aware that employers and unions have a significant mutual interest in doing business effectively. Now the point is becoming clearer to journalists who write for a wider public. In *Harper's Magazine* Bernard D. Nossiter writes melodramatically of "The Hidden Affair between Big Business and Big Labor." He reveals that "the tacit collaboration between management and union officers has been thriving all through the period of postwar prosperity, and is still spreading." He then continues:

> The trucking industry has rushed to defend both Beck and Hoffa. In coal, the incorruptible Lewis will be memorialized by both unions and operators. New York's garment manufacturers have learned to love David Dubinsky . . . On the Pacific Coast, Harry Bridges has no bigger booster than the Pacific Maritime Association unless it is his ILWU stevedores.[7]

Although the 1959 steel strike was the longest major stoppage in our national history, it would be erroneous to draw too many ominous conclusions with respect to collective bargaining generally. The fact is that collective bargaining has never been successfully stabilized in the steel industry. There have been seven industry-wide strikes since the end of World War II; the government has intervened with fact-finding boards in 1946 and 1949, seizure of the industry in 1952, and a Taft-Hartley injunction in 1959. Other industries such as coal mining, automobiles, and West Coast longshoring have worked out accommodative patterns after lengthy periods of conflict; presumably steel will do so eventually.

As the new decade begins, management's more aggressive role in contract negotiations is ruffling the surface of the collective bargaining system, which has been generally smooth and placid during the 1950's. It was to be expected that employers would eventually take the initiative in making demands on the unions in addition to collaborating more closely among each other through joint bargaining committees, strike insurance, etc. Although management's specific demands may or may not be reasonable, there is nothing immoral or unethical in making them, and no reason why collective bargaining must be a one-way street. Nevertheless, if such demands become at all widespread, several years will probably pass before unions and union members have adjusted to the change and before employers have learned to avoid romanticism and to settle for what is attainable.

In several industries, management has adopted this more ambitious strategy in an effort to revise work rules and practices. This issue is coming to a head particularly in industries where employment is shrinking. (The number of production workers has steadily declined in basic steel, railroads, automobiles, tires, meat packing, sawmills, shipping, longshoring and motion picture production.) One purpose of work rules is to conserve job opportunities, a purpose that gains greater force where employment has ceased to grow or is falling. Management, on the other hand, will seek to preserve maximum autonomy and flexibility. Thus the need is created to strike a proper balance between the employer's interest in economy and efficiency and the worker's interest in security and stability; to distinguish between those rules and practices that are still viable and those that have become insupportable; and to meet the transitional problems that will emerge if workers are displaced and dislocated. At the moment both unions and employers appear reluctant to submit the issues to the collective bargaining process. The unions are denying that there is any real problem, aside from management's desire to undermine labor's hard-won gains. The employers are addressing their arguments to newspaper readers, rather than to the union officials, and demanding "sole authority" to reconstitute working practices.

Collective bargaining has shown a great potential for the constructive handling of new issues in the United States. Principles of scientific management, rules of industrial discipline, intricate systems of job evaluation and incentive pay, and complex programs of economic security have all been reconciled with the imperatives of union-management relations. Certainly history teaches that collective bargaining is compatible with economic progress and technological change. Therefore, we can assume that the working-rule issue will be handled successfully also. Detailed substantive questions must be defined. Employees must understand the reasons why changes are necessary. The effects of change must be projected, and the transitional problems identified. Measures must be adopted to meet these transitional problems. The essence of the strategy will be for management to obtain greater flexibility in return for compatible protection of the employees. Obviously this process will take time, but there is little reason to doubt that it will eventually be consummated.

Thus the current influences on strike activity are somewhat mixed. Our present judgment is this: (a) The volume of industrial conflict may well increase in the short run. (b) It will continue to diminish over a longer period of time. (c) However, the strike will not wither away in the United States as it has done in Northern Europe.

Is the decline of the strike good or bad? It seems impossible to answer this question in any significant way, for the reason that society is constantly redefining its problems. Generally the solution to any problem becomes a problem in itself. After struggling to eliminate economic insecurity, we now wonder what happens to men when their every need is provided for. After striving to abolish human want, we are worried about obesity, alcoholism, excessive smoking, and too much chromium. Now that people have more leisure, the problem is boredom and loss of meaning. Now that Victorian sexual mores have been overrun, some unlovely consequences are evident. Now that labor turnover has been reduced, a new industrial feudalism is feared; and as the long-standing objective of industrial peace is increasingly achieved, some of the values of conflict will undoubtedly be missed. In this interim period, opinions regarding the trend will be highly subjective, so that probably it is best for each reader to answer the question himself.

NOTES TO CHAPTER 12

1. This concept is developed, in somewhat different terms, in John T. Dunlop, *Industrial Relations Systems* (New York: Henry Holt, 1959).

2. Adolf Sturmthal, "The Labor Movement Abroad," in Chamberlain, Pierson, and Wolfson (eds.), *A Decade of Industrial Relations Research, 1946–1956* (New York: Harper and Brothers, 1958), p. 189.

3. National Industrial Conference Board, *Economic Almanac 1958* (New York: Crowell, 1958), p. 488.

4. Peter F. Drucker, *Landmarks of Tomorrow* (New York: Harper and Brothers, 1958), p. 5.

5. Reinhard Bendix, *Work and Authority in Industry* (New York: John Wiley and Sons, 1956), p. 434.

6. *Ibid.,* p. 438.

7. Bernard D. Nossiter, "The Hidden Affair Between Big Business and Big Labor," *Harper's Magazine,* 219 (July 1959), pp. 29, 31.

Statistical Sources

and Limitations

The Appendix tables present annual data for each of the fifteen countries covered by this study. In Tables A-1 through A-5 are found the basic statistics on the number of industrial disputes, workers involved, man-days of idleness, union members, and non-agricultural employees in each country. All the remaining statistical data in the book are derived from Tables A-1 through A-5. Table A-6 shows the degree of organization, beginning with 1927. Our five comparative measures of strike activity are set forth in Tables A-7 through A-11.

The text tables in Chapter 3 are condensed versions of Tables A-6 through A-11, using annual averages for three-year periods.

At this point we shall indicate the sources and discuss the limitations of our basic statistics. Where projections, interpolations, and estimates have been made, we shall describe the methods which were used. As we have previously remarked, we must often deal with imperfect data in analyzing social phenomena. To ignore the imperfections would be unfair to the reader. To ignore the data might unnecessarily impede the pursuit of knowledge. In our opinion the best procedure is to make an informed decision as to whether the data are useful notwithstanding their limitations.

Strike and Lockout Statistics

The material in Tables A-1, A-2, and A-3 consists of strike and lock-out statistics collected and reported by the national governments. Published sources include the official publications of the ministries of labor and the statistical abstracts or yearbooks of the various countries. For the years since 1927, the *Yearbook of Labor Statistics* of the International Labor Office at Geneva is the most convenient source.

In general, the reported figures—number of disputes, number of workers involved, and working days lost—are simple summations for the given year. The figures relate to actual work stoppages, excluding threats of strikes and lockouts, slowdowns, sabotage, and the like. Political strikes are excluded where the reported figures furnish a sound basis for exclusion.[1] Strikes and lockouts are combined in those instances where the countries have reported them separately.

There are certain ambiguities in the strike and lockout data. All governments exclude disputes below a certain nominal size. Constructing statistics on workers involved requires that a line be drawn between those "directly" and "indirectly" involved. The latter are the employees rendered idle by the work stoppage although not actively participating in it. Estimates of working days lost are affected by varying practices as to the length of the work week, paid holidays and vacations, and so forth. Some countries do not report lockouts; it may be that the lockout is not practiced in such countries, but the point is not entirely clear.[2]

Under these circumstances, international comparisons must necessarily be somewhat imprecise. Political strikes in economic disguise are more significant in some countries than in others. Many countries exclude workers indirectly affected; a few do not. Where workers indirectly affected are included, definitions vary to some extent from one country to another. There are similar variations in the minimum size of stoppage that is subject to reporting. The United States, for example, excludes disputes involving fewer than six workers or lasting less than a full day or workshift. In Denmark the test is whether at least one hundred working days have been lost. In the United Kingdom, disputes involving fewer than ten workers or lasting less than one day are not counted unless they result in a loss of more than one hundred working days. Finally, there are variations in the industrial coverage of strike statistics. All sectors of the non-agricultural economy may be covered in one country, whereas only disputes occurring in mining, manufacturing, construction, and transportation are covered in another.[3]

Despite these difficulties, we think the strike and lockout statistics are usable. When all is said, the dissimilarities in methods and definitions are not very great. Furthermore, the conclusions reached in this study do not require a high degree of precision in the basic data. The recorded differences in experience among the several groups of countries are so great as to outweigh the relatively minor inaccuracies and ambiguities in the statistics.

The following pertinent comments are made in the national reports on industrial disputes:

Denmark. Only disputes involving enterprises affiliated with the national Employers' Federation are counted. Practically all the larger employers belong in the federation. Disputes in which less than one hundred working days were lost are omitted. The *Statistisk Årbog* (Copenhagen: Danmarks Statistiske Departement), annual issues, includes strike data for the years since 1900.

Netherlands. Strike and lockout data, reported separately since 1913 in the *Jaarcijfers voor Nederland* (The Hague: Centraal Bureau voor de Statistiek), annual issues, were combined in our table. Only the first half of 1940 and the last half of 1945 are included.

United Kingdom. Disputes not connected with terms of employment are eliminated. Those involving fewer than ten workers or lasting less than one day are excluded unless more than one hundred working days are lost. The figures are published in the *Annual Abstract of Statistics* (London: Central Statistical Office), for the years from 1911 to date. The 1,580,000 workers and approximately 15,000,000 man-days of idleness, involved in the 1926 General Strike are not counted.

Germany. Strikes lasting less than one day are excluded unless more than one hundred working days were lost. Data are not available for 1933 through 1948. Strike and lockout statistics are published in the *Statistiches Jahrbuch für das Deutsche Reich,* annual issues, for the years prior to 1933. Political strikes were reported for the years 1919–23, and were excluded from our tables. The *Statistiches Jahrbuch* did not report working days lost prior to 1915; therefore the estimates of S. Nestriepke, *Die Gewerkschaftsbewegung* (Leipzig: 1921–23), p. 394, were used.

Norway. Disputes lasting less than one day are not counted. Workers indirectly affected are excluded. Strike and lockout data are available for the years since 1903 in the *Statistisk Årbok for Norge* (Oslo: Statistisk Sentralbyrå), annual issues.

Sweden. Statistics for the period since 1903 are found in the *Statistisk Årsbok för Sverige* (Stockholm: Statistiske Centralbyrån).

France. The figures on strike and lockout activity in France are published for the years since 1890 in the *Annuaire Statistique* (Paris: Imprimerie Nationale), various issues.

Italy. Workers indirectly affected and disputes lasting less than one day are not taken into account. Information for the years between 1924 and 1949 is not available. (Strikes and lockouts were prohibited during the Fascist regime.)

Japan. Workers indirectly affected and disputes lasting less than four hours are excluded. Industrial conflict data for the prewar period are published in the *Résumé Statistique de L'Empire du Japon* (Tokyo: Bureau de la Statistique Générale au Cabinet Impérial), various issues. For the period 1920–28, there are no figures on man-days of idleness which are comparable with those for later periods and for other countries.

India. The figures include only disputes involving ten or more workers. Political strikes are omitted. Data are not available for years prior to 1921.

Australia. Information for the years since 1913 is published in the *Official Yearbook of the Commonwealth of Australia* (Canberra: Commonwealth Bureau of Census and Statistics), annual issues. Workers indirectly involved are included.

Finland. Political strikes are eliminated. Workers indirectly affected are omitted, but the working-days lost by such workers are included. Industrial dispute data for the period since 1907 are published in the *Suomen Tilastollinen Vuosikirja / Statistical Yearbook of Finland* (Helsinki: Central Statistical Office), annual issues.

South Africa. Data are published in the *Official Yearbook of the Union of South Africa* (Pretoria: Bureau of Census and Statistics), annual issues, since 1906.

Canada. Disputes involving fewer than six workers and those lasting less than one day are excluded, unless ten or more working days were lost. Workers indirectly affected are not counted. The industrial conflict statistics are published in the *Canada Yearbook* (Ottowa: Dominion Bureau of Statistics), annual issues, for the years since 1901.

United States. Disputes involving fewer than six workers and those lasting less than a full day or shift are omitted. Industrial conflict figures for the earlier years are available in Florence Peterson, *Strikes in the United States, 1880–1936* (Washington: U. S. Department of Labor, Bureau of Labor Statistics, 1938), and *Handbook of Labor Statistics, 1950 Edition* (Washington: U. S. Department of Labor, Bureau of

Labor Statistics, 1951), p. 142. Recent data are available in the *Monthly Labor Review,* various issues.

Union Membership Statistics

Most of the membership figures used in this study were published by the governments of the respective countries. Problems of international comparison are more serious than in the case of strike statistics. Some adjustments have been made in order to rectify discrepancies in methods and definitions, but the resulting data are still not closely comparable from one country to another. Estimates by scholars and historians of the national labor movements have been used in some cases where government reports are not available, or are known to be highly inaccurate.

The most common deficiencies of union membership statistics include inflated membership claims on the part of some unions, incomplete coverage of labor organizations in the reports of some governments, gaps in certain time series, and inconsistent definitions of union membership. In most cases, the deficiencies are simply noted; and if no better estimates by students of the national labor movement are available, corrections have not been attempted. It is also worth repeating that union membership has a very different meaning in a country like the United States, where there are substantial initiation fees and dues, than it does in Japan or India, where members do not contribute systematically.

Denmark. Membership of the national federation was added to that of "all other unions." These figures are published in the *Statistisk Årbog.*

Netherlands. Total union membership reported by all federations is published in *Jaarcijfers voor Nederland.*

United Kingdom. Total union membership as published in the *Annual Abstract of Statistics,* annual editions, was used.

Germany. For the years 1903 through 1931, the reported memberships of the ADGB, the Catholic unions, and the Hirsch-Dunker unions were added together. The *Statistiches Jahrbuch für das Deutsche Reich* was used for these years. For 1950 through 1955, the membership totals of the DBG and the DAG, published in the *Statistiches Jahrbuch für die Bundesrepublik Deutschland,* were combined.

Norway. Only the reported membership of the national federation was readily available, in the *Statistisk Årbok for Norge,* various issues. Although a very high proportion of Norweigian unionists are affiliated with federation, Table A-4 does understate total membership to some extent.

Sweden. For 1900–24, we used total union membership as reported by Sigfrid Hansson, *Den Svenska Fackföreningsrörelsen* (Stockholm: Tidens Förlag, 1923), pp. 144–45. For 1925 through 1947, only the membership of the national federation (LO) reported in *Statistisk Årsbok för Sverige,* was readily available. Membership of the salaried workers' federation (the TCO), reported in the *Statistisk Årsbok* since 1948, was added to that of the LO for 1948 through 1956.

France. French union membership statistics are particularly weak. The concept of membership is vague, union claims are inflated, and there are significant gaps in the data. Under these circumstances the figures should be regarded as rather crude approximations. The data for 1900 through 1914 are those reported to the government and published in the *Annuaire Statistique.* For the years 1920 through 1955, estimates are available for scattered years from the *Annuaire Statistique;* David J. Saposs, *The Labor Movement in Postwar France* (New York: Columbia University Press, 1931), pp. 137–38, 171; Henry W. Ehrmann, *French Labor from Popular Front to Liberation* (New York: Oxford University Press, 1947), pp. 124, 129, 166; Val Lorwin, *The French Labor Movement* (Cambridge: Harvard University Press, 1954), pp. 40, 50, 70, 74, 101, 177, 324–5; and U. S. Department of Labor, *Summary of the Labor Situation in France* (Washington: May 1956), pp. 1–7. These estimates differ in the extent to which the claims of the various unions and federations are accepted at face value. For some years (for example, 1947) the figures represent the unadjusted sum of union claims, and for other years (for example, 1953) scholars have attempted to deflate these claims. The combination of adjusted and unadjusted figures in the same table has the effect of exaggerating the fluctuations in membership, but does not change the trends.

Linear interpolations have been used to estimate membership in years for which no other figures are available. These years include 1927–29, 1931, 1933–35, 1948, 1950–52, and 1954.

Italy. Italian membership figures present the same problems as the French, and similar expedients were used. Data for 1948 and 1956 are the membership claims of the federations, as reported by Maurice F. Neufeld, "The Italian Labor Movement in 1956: The Structure of Crisis," *Annals of the American Academy of Political and Social Science* (March 1957), pp. 75–77. The 1950 membership claim is from J. C. Adams, "Italy," in Walter Galenson (editor), *Comparative Labor Movements* (Englewood Cliffs, N. J.: Prentice-Hall, 1952), p. 447. The 1955 figure is reported by the U. S. Department of Labor, *Directory of Labor*

Organizations, Europe, Vol. I, pp. 17.5–17.35. The figures for 1949 and 1951–54 are linear interpolations of claimed membership.

All writers on the Italian labor movement concur that the membership claims are inflated, but they disagree as to the extent of inflation. In the case of France, scholarly estimates were used along with government reports in the same table because the trend of membership change was not affected, although the extent of change was exaggerated. In Italy, however, use of the deflated estimates together with union membership claims would distort the trend. Therefore the unadjusted claims were used in the absence of a consistent series of reliable estimates.

Japan. Total union membership figures for the postwar years are published in the *Japan Statistical Yearbook* (Tokyo: Bureau of Statistics, Office of the Prime Minister), various issues. Data for the prewar years have been presented in Solomon B. Levine, *Industrial Relations in Postwar Japan* (Urbana: University of Illinois Press, 1958), p. 67.

India. Total membership of unions reporting to the government is published in the *Statistical Abstract, India* (Delhi: Central Statistical Organisation) and (for the preindependence years) *Statistical Abstract, British India,* various issues. Unlike the French and Italian membership data, the Indian figures are too low. Students of Indian labor all point out that many of the unions are very small and do not register. Ornati estimated, for example, that as many as 1,000,000 members may have been unreported in 1950.[4] No adjustment for underreporting was attempted.

Australia. Total union membership figures are published in the *Official Yearbook of the Commonwealth of Australia,* various issues.

Finland. Membership of only the central labor federation is reported in the Finnish statistical abstract, *Suomen Tilastollinen Vuosikirja,* various issues. Since most Finnish unionists are affiliated with the central federation, the inaccuracy is not considered very significant.

South Africa. Aggregate union membership is reported in the *Official Yearbook of the Union of South Africa,* annual issues.

Canada. Total membership (including the Canadian membership of international unions with central offices in the United States) is published in the *Canada Yearbook,* annual issues.

United States. For the years prior to 1934, estimates are presented in Leo Wolman, *Ebb and Flow in Trade Unionism* (New York: National Bureau of Economic Research, 1936), pp. 192–193. For 1935–48 Wolman supplied estimates to Irving Bernstein, who published them in

"The Growth of American Unions," *American Economic Review,* 64 (June 1954), pp. 303–304. The 1949–53 estimates are Bernstein's extrapolation of Wolman's series. Canadian membership in United States unions, as reported by the Dominion government, has been deducted from the Wolman and Bernstein estimates for each year since 1911 to obtain a net figure representing membership within the United States. Membership since 1953 is reported by the U. S. Department of Labor, *Directory of National and International Labor Unions in the United States,* various issues, excluding Canadian members.

Non-agricultural Wage and Salary Earners (Table 5)

These estimates are also imprecise. Actual figures showing the average number of wage and salary earners employed in each year were used wherever they were readily available. In general, the series were deemed acceptable if they excluded proprietors and self-employed, agricultural workers, and unemployed persons. In some cases, time series were available only in the form of index numbers. A variety of methods were used to convert these index numbers into absolute figures. It is fair to state that although some rather arbitrary decisions had to be made, differentials in comparative strike activity are so great as to outweigh any errors which we may have imported into the employment estimates. For example, the number of workers involved in disputes averaged 0.3 per cent of non-agricultural employment in Denmark during the 1948–56 period, as contrasted with 2.7 per cent in the United States and 28.0 per cent in Italy. Differences of this magnitude make it practical to employ estimates that would be altogether too rough if the argument had rested on finer distinctions.

Denmark. We began with annual index numbers of manufacturing employment published by the International Labor Office. These index numbers were converted to numerical estimates of manufacturing employment, using the 1951 census figure as a base. This series was converted into estimates of the number of non-agricultural wage and salary earners in the following manner: (*a*) Total non-agricultural employment as a factor of manufacturing employment was computed for each census year. (*b*) The same factor was estimated for intercensal years by simple linear interpolation. (*c*) These factors were used to expand the manufacturing employment estimates to estimates of total non-agricultural employment.

Netherlands. Index numbers relating to non-agricultural wage and salary earners in mining, manufacturing, construction, commerce, transportation, and service industries, as published in the ILO *Yearbooks,* were used. The published base-year figures were not suitable for conversion purposes because they represented "the number of man-years insured" rather than actual employment. Accordingly, the number of wage and salary earners in 1947 (the latest year for which census figures were available) was used as a base.

United Kingdom. The ILO indexes for the non-agricultural wage and salary earners for the six basic industrial classifications—mining, manufacturing, construction, commerce, transportation, and service—were used. There are two non-overlapping series of index numbers for the United Kingdom. Since 1947 substantially all workers in these industry groups have been covered. Published base-year figures were used to convert the index numbers. The index numbers for 1947 and earlier years were based upon insured workers only. In an effort to make the two series comparable, the 1931 census total for non-agricultural wage and salary earners was used to convert the earlier series to absolute figures. Thus there is a break in our series between 1947 and 1948, but the two parts are approximately comparable.

Germany. The German estimates of non-agricultural employment are based on labor registration statistics and republished in the ILO *Yearbook.*

Norway. Figures on the number of wage and salary earners covered by the compulsory national health plan are available beginning with 1948. Agricultural employment was subtracted from these figures, leaving non-agricultural employment as the remainder. An estimate for 1947 was made by extrapolating the 1948–50 trend. This 1947 estimate was used to convert index numbers of total insured employment for the earlier years.

Sweden. Index numbers of wage earners employed in mining and manufacturing, published in the ILO *Yearbooks,* were used. Absolute figures for mining and manufacturing were computed, using as a base the number of wage and salary earners in those industries reported in the 1950 census. The ratio between manufacturing employment and total non-agricultural employment in each census year was then computed. Similar ratios for intercensal years were estimated by straight-line interpolation. These ratios were used to expand mining and manufacturing employment to total non-agricultural employment.

France. Figures on non-agricultural employment, excluding public and domestic service (published in the ILO *Yearbooks* and the *Annuaire Statistique*) were used for 1950–56. Index numbers published by the

ILO, going back to 1937, were converted on the basis of the 1950 figure. The index numbers for the years before 1937 are not comparable with those for later years. Therefore, a new base—the number of non-agricultural wage and salary earners in the 1936 census—was used to convert the earlier indexes to absolute figures.

Italy. The indexes of wage earners employed in mining and in manufacturing were converted to absolute numbers, using published base-year figures. The ratio between the sum of these two industrial employments and total non-agricultural wage and salary employment in the 1951 census was used to construct estimates of total non-agricultural employment, 1949–56.

Japan. Employment in agriculture and forestry (given only as an aggregate) was subtracted from the figures on total wage and salary employment (published in the *Japan Statistical Yearbook,* annual issues) to yield estimates of non-agricultural wage and salary employment, 1947–56. Estimates for the prewar years were computed from the indexes of mining, manufacturing, construction, transport, and service employment, published by the ILO. The number of non-agricultural wage and salary earners reported in the 1931 census was taken as the base.

India. Separate series showing the number of wage earners employed in mining and in manufacturing have been published in the *Statistical Abstract, India* since 1946. These were added together. The ratio between the number of wage earners in mining and manufacturing in 1951 and the total number of non-agricultural wage and salary earners reported in the 1951 census was used to construct estimates of total non-agricultural employment.

Union of South Africa. Index numbers of wage and salary employment in mining, manufacturing, construction, and transportation are included in the ILO *Yearbooks.* An unusual difficulty is encountered in estimating the number of wage and salary earners in all non-agricultural industries. Separate racial censuses are taken, and information concerning non-whites is less detailed than for whites. The number of non-white wage and salary earners is estimated in the following fashion: First we computed the ratio between wage and salary earners (available as the published base for the ILO indexes) and total employment (from the census) in mining, manufacturing, construction, and transportation, all data relating to 1951. Then we applied this proportion to the total number of gainfully employed non-whites outside of agriculture. This yielded an estimate of non-white wage and salary earners outside of agriculture. It was added to the corresponding 1951 census figure for whites. We then used the combined estimate as a base to convert the indexes to absolute numbers.

Australia. Data on civilian wage and salary earners, excluding rural workers and female domestics, are published in the *Official Yearbook of the Commonwealth of Australia,* annual issues, for 1933 and for all years since 1938. The published figure for 1933 was used as a base to convert and expand the series of manufacturing-employment index numbers for 1938 and earlier years.

Finland. Index numbers of wage earners in manufacturing, published in the ILO *Yearbooks,* were converted to absolute figures, using as a base the number of manufacturing wage earners reported in the 1930, 1940, and 1950 censuses. The proportion of all non-agricultural wage and salary earners represented by manufacturing wage earners was computed for each of these census years. Similar proportions were estimated by linear interpolation for the intercensal years. These proportions were used to expand the manufacturing wage earner series to a total non-agricultural wage and salary earner series.

Canada. Annual estimates of civilian non-agricultural employees are available in the *Canada Year Book,* annual issues.

United States. Annual averages of employed civilian non-agricultural wage and salary earners (estimated by the U. S. Bureau of Labor Statistics and published in the *Handbook of Labor Statistics,* various issues, and *Employment and Earnings,* annual supplement issues) were used.

NOTES TO APPENDIX

1. Most "purely political" strikes are excluded or reported separately by the national governments. In many cases there is a mixture of economic and political motives in varying proportions. It would not be practical to segregate disputes of this type.

2. Knowles' discussion of statistical problems, although concerned with the United Kingdom, is applicable to most of the countries in our study. See K. G. J. C. Knowles, *Strikes* (Oxford: Basil Blackwell, 1952), pp. 301–05.

3. Problems which arise in making international strike comparisons are discussed in Robert Morse Woodbury, "The Incidence of Industrial Disputes: Rates of Time-Loss, 1927–1947," *International Labour Review,* 60 (November 1949), pp. 454–58.

4. Oscar Ornati, *Jobs and Workers in India* (Ithaca: Institute of International Industrial and Labor Relations, Cornell University, 1955), pp. 113, 194–202.

TABLE A-1

Number of Industrial Disputes, Fifteen Countries, 1900–1956

Year	Denmark	Netherlands	United Kingdom	Germany	Norway	Sweden	France	Italy	Japan	India	United States	Canada	Australia	Finland	South Africa
1900	82			852		—	902				1839	—			—
1901	56			727		—	523				3012	104			—
1902	68			861		—	512				3240	121			—
1903	61			1282		142	567				3648	146			—
1904	86			1625		215	1026				2419	99			—
1905	75			2323		189	830				2186	89			—
1906	90			3488		290	1309					141			1
1907	105			2792		312	1275					149		176	1
1908	122			2052		302	1073					68		128	
1909	65			2045		138	1025					69		51	
1910	71	—	—	3194		76	1502		—			84	—	54	5
1911	51	—	872	2914		98	1471		—			99	—	51	4
1912	60	—	834	2825		116	1116		—			150	208	59	1
1913	76	427	1459	2600		119	1073		50			113	337	70	5
1914	44	271	972	1223		115	672		64		1204	44	358	37	12
1915	43	269	672	141		80	98		108		1593	43	508	—	2
1916	66	377	532	240		227	314		398		3789	75	444	483	10
1917	215	344	730	562		475	696		417		4450	148	298	6	22
1918	253	325	1165	532		708	499		497		3353	196	460	39	23
1919	472	649	1352	3719		440	2026				3630	298			47
1920	243	481	1607	3807	—	486	1832		282	—	3411	285	554	146	66
1921	110	299	763	4455	89	347	475		246	396	2385	145	624	76	25
1922	31	325	576	4785	26	392	665		250	278	1112	85	445	53	12
1923	58	289	628	2046	57	206	1068		270	213	1553	91	274	50	2
1924	71	239	710	1973	1	261	1083		333	133	1249	73	504	31	7
1925	48	262	603	1740	84	239	931		816	134	1301	83	499	38	—
1926	32	212	322	356	113	206	1660		1260	128	1035	77	360	72	3
1927	17	230	308	853	96	189	404		383	129	707	74	441	79	12
1928	11	205	302	743	63	201	823		397	203	604	98	287	71	10
1929	22	226	431	441	73	180	1217		576	141	921	90	259	26	10

Year															
1930	37	212	422	366	94	261	1097		906	148	637	67	183	11	12
1931	16	215	420	504	82	193	288		998	166	810	88	134	1	19
1932	17	216	389	642	91	182	362		893	118	841	116	127	3	12
1933	26	184	357	—	93	140	343		610	146	1695	125	90	4	10
1934	38	152	471	—	85	103	385		626	159	1856	191	155	46	12
1935	14	152	553	—	103	98	376		589	145	2014	120	183	23	17
1936	12	96	818	—	175	60	17091		547	157	2172	156	235	29	20
1937	22	95	1129	—	195	67	2616		553	379	4740	278	342	37	34
1938	22	141	875	—	248	85	1220		227	399	2772	147	376	31	19
1939	19	90	940	—	81	45	—		294	406	2613	122	416	29	20
1940	9	23	922		—	38	—		240	322	2508	168	350	4	24
1941	2	—	1251		—	34	—		—	359	4288	231	567	12	35
1942	7	—	1303		—	139	—		—	694	2968	354	602	—	58
1943	17	—	1785		—	167	—		—	716	3752	402	785	—	52
1944	34	—	2194		—	214	—		—	658	4956	199	941	—	53
1945	35	118	2293		16	163	—		—	820	4750	197	945	102	62
1946	59	270	2205		39	137	528		702	1629	4985	228	869	42	54
1947	29	272	1721		47	81	2285		464	1811	3693	236	982	228	80
1948	24	183	1759		58	47	1425		744	1259	3419	154	1141	84	45
1949	17	116	1426		47	31	1426		554	920	3606	137	849	48	37
1950	18	79	1339		30	21	2586	1250	571	814	4843	161	1276	78	33
1951	12	85	1719		28	28	2514	1178	576	1071	4737	259	1344	67	40
1952	9	40	1714		40	32	1749	1558	590	963	5117	222	1627	43	55
1953	8	58	1746		55	20	1761	1412	611	772	5091	174	1459	104	32
1954	20	91	1989		27	45	1479	1990	647	840	3468	174	1490	36	60
1955	13	63	2419		22	18	2672	1981	659	1166	4320	159	1532	72	102
1956	96	80	2648		27	12	2440	1904	646	1263	3825	229	1306	43	105

See pp. 184–87 for sources and discussion of data.

TABLE A-2

Workers Involved in Industrial Disputes, Fifteen Countries, 1900–1956 (in thousands)

Year	Denmark	Nether-lands	United Kingdom	Germany	Norway	Sweden	France	Italy	Japan	India	United States	Canada	Australia	Finland	South Africa
1900	7.6	—		115.8	—	—	222.7				567.7				
1901	4.1	—		48.5	—	—	111.4				563.8	28.1			
1902	2.4			55.7	—	—	212.7				691.5	12.3			
1903	1.1			121.6	3.0	24.6	123.2				787.8	50.0			
1904	2.6			136.0	1.2	12.2	271.1				573.8	16.5			
1905	5.7			508.0	2.0	32.9	177.7				302.4	16.2			
1906	3.9			316.0	3.0	18.7	438.5					26.1			0.05
1907	8.1			281.0	10.0	23.5	198.0					36.3		20.7	6.4
1908	7.6			126.9	12.0	40.4	99.0					25.3		11.4	
1909	2.4			131.2	3.8	302.7	167.5					17.3		3.9	
1910	2.5	—	—	369.0	4.1	3.7	281.4		—			21.3	—	4.4	0.4
1911	28.8	—	952.0	325.3	44.0	20.6	230.6		—			30.1	—	5.8	0.9
1912	4.1	—	1462.0	479.6	14.3	10.0	267.6		—			40.5	—	11.3	0.9
1913	9.7	30.2	664.0	249.0	4.9	9.6	220.4		—			39.5	50.3	5.6	19.8
1914	3.4	15.7	447.0	95.2	5.3	14.4	160.6		7.9			8.7	71.0	6.2	21.9
1915	1.9	15.2	448.0	12.9	9.7	5.1	9.4		7.8			9.1	81.3	—	—
1916	14.3	18.1	276.0	124.2	24.5	20.7	41.4		8.4		1599.9	21.2	170.7	—	1.3
1917	10.1	31.3	872.0	656.5	5.4	46.7	293.8		57.3		1227.3	48.3	174.0	139.8	3.5
1918	9.8	39.7	1116.0	379.1	7.4	61.2	176.2		66.5		1240.0	68.5	56.4	0.3	2.6
1919	35.6	61.7	2591.0	1938.4	25.1	81.0	1150.7		63.1		4160.3	139.0	157.6	4.0	23.8
1920	22.0	66.4	1932.0	1429.1	31.8	139.0	1316.6		36.4	—	1463.1	52.2	155.6	21.0	105.7
1921	48.1	47.7	1801.0	1489.5	154.4	49.7	402.4		58.2	600.4	1099.2	22.9	165.1	6.3	9.9
1922	48.9	44.0	552.0	1823.9	2.2	75.7	290.3		41.5	435.4	1612.6	41.0	116.3	9.8	29.0
1923	1.9	56.4	405.0	1606.5	25.0	102.9	331.0		36.3	301.0	756.6	32.9	76.3	7.6	0.05
1924	9.8	27.7	613.0	1618.0	63.1	24.0	274.9		54.5	312.5	654.6	32.5	152.4	3.1	1.9
1925	102.3	33.6	441.0	756.7	13.8	145.8	249.2		89.4	270.4	428.4	25.8	176.7	2.9	—
1926	1.0	9.9	1154.0	90.4	51.5	52.9	349.3		127.3	—	329.6	24.1	113.0	10.2	0.8
1927	2.9	13.5	108.0	503.2	22.5	9.5	112.6		46.7	131.7	329.9	22.3	200.8	13.4	5.2
1928	0.5	16.9	124.0	780.4	8.0	71.5	210.5		46.3	506.9	314.2	17.6	96.4	27.2	5.7
1929	1.0	21.3	533.0	234.5	4.8	12.7	241.0		77.4	532.0	288.6	12.9	104.6	2.4	2.9

Year															
1930	5.3	11.0	307.0	225.0	4.7	20.8	584.6		81.4	196.3	183.0	13.8	54.2	1.7	5.0
1931	3.7	28.2	490.0	178.2	59.5	40.9	54.2		64.5	203.0	341.8	10.7	37.7	0.1	6.3
1932	5.8	32.0	379.0	127.6	6.4	50.1	71.6		54.8	128.1	324.0	23.4	32.9	0.3	4.0
1933	0.5	14.8	136.0	—	6.3	32.0	87.1		49.4	164.9	1168.3	26.6	30.1	1.3	1.6
1934	11.5	6.2	134.0	—	6.4	13.6	100.6		49.5	220.8	1466.7	45.8	50.9	5.9	2.4
1935	0.8	12.9	271.0	—	3.5	17.2	108.9		37.7	114.2	1117.2	33.3	47.3	2.3	2.4
1936	96.9	10.4	316.0	—	15.3	3.5	2422.8		30.9	169.0	788.6	34.8	60.6	3.0	2.2
1937	1.4	4.6	597.0	—	28.8	30.9	323.8		56.0	647.8	1860.6	71.9	96.2	6.2	6.8
1938	3.7	6.4	274.0	—	24.0	29.0	1133.5		13.3	401.1	688.4	20.4	144.0	4.1	2.6
1939	0.5	5.3	337.0	—	16.0	2.2	—		20.8	409.2	1171.0	41.0	152.8	6.1	4.8
1940	0.3	3.0	299.0	—	—	3.9	—	—	24.2	452.5	577.0	60.6	192.6	0.5	1.8
1941	0.1	—	360.0	—	—	1.9	—	—	—	291.1	2363.0	87.1	248.1	2.2	5.4
1942	3.2	—	456.0	—	—	1.3	—	—	—	772.7	840.0	113.9	169.3	—	14.0
1943	6.3	—	557.0	—	—	6.9	—	—	—	525.1	1981.0	218.4	296.1	—	8.4
1944	7.7	36.5	821.0	—	4.1	7.0	—	—	—	550.0	2116.0	75.3	276.4	—	9.2
1945	8.5	72.1	531.0	—	4.7	133.2	—	—	—	747.5	3467.0	96.1	315.9	37.1	14.2
1946	54.2	59.9	526.0	—	8.2	1.3	180.1	—	517.4	1961.9	4600.0	139.5	348.5	18.9	95.7
1947	7.5	17.7	620.0	—	5.9	56.9	2997.6	—	218.8	1840.8	2170.0	104.1	327.1	114.7	20.0
1948	2.7	14.3	425.0	—	9.0	6.1	6561.2	—	2304.5	1059.1	1960.0	42.8	317.1	16.2	3.9
1949	2.7	—	433.0	58.1	9.0	1.0	4330.0	2894.2	1122.1	685.5	3030.0	51.4	264.6	59.0	7.1
1950	2.8	17.6	302.0	79.3	4.4	2.4	1527.3	3537.1	681.4	719.6	2410.0	192.2	431.7	118.0	3.3
1951	1.7	14.2	379.0	174.3	4.3	15.1	1754.0	2134.7	1162.6	691.3	2220.0	102.9	408.6	11.4	8.3
1952	2.4	3.8	415.0	84.1	6.4	2.1	1155.2	1471.9	1623.6	809.2	3540.0	120.8	505.7	9.4	6.5
1953	0.4	10.8	1374.0	50.6	4.9	26.2	1783.7	4679.1	1341.2	466.6	2400.0	56.0	496.0	15.5	2.7
1954	7.7	18.7	450.0	115.9	2.9	7.7	1318.9	2045.3	927.8	477.1	1530.0	62.3	370.1	19.2	5.8
1955	6.3	21.2	671.0	597.4	10.0	3.9	1060.6	1383.4	1033.3	527.8	2650.0	60.1	444.6	42.4	9.9
1956	65.6	37.0	508.0	25.3	56.2	1.6	981.7	2048.1	1098.3	734.2	1900.0	88.7	428.0	451.3	10.0

See pp. 184–87 for sources and discussion of data.

TABLE A-3

Working Days Lost in Industrial Disputes, Fifteen Countries, 1900–1956 (in thousands)

Year	Den-mark	Nether-lands	United Kingdom	Ger-many	Nor-way	Sweden	France	Italy	Japan	India	United States	Canada	Aus-tralia	Finland	South Africa
1900	236.0	—	—	1234.0	—	—	3760.6					—		—	—
1901	57.0			1194.6	—	—	1862.1					632.3		—	—
1902	133.0			964.3	—	—	4675.1					120.9		—	—
1903	19.0			2622.2	130.0	642.0	2441.9					1226.5		—	—
1904	69.0			2120.2	45.0	386.0	3934.9					265.0		—	—
1905	499.0			7362.8	30.0	2390.0	2746.7					217.2		—	—
1906	68.0			6317.7	95.0	479.0	9438.6					359.8		—	2.6
1907	255.0			5122.5	340.0	514.0	3562.2					622.0		595.9	288.0
1908	85.0			2045.6	380.0	1842.0	1752.0					708.3		436.0	—
1909	58.0			2247.5	185.0	11800.0	3559.9					871.8		252.0	—
1910	61.0	—	—	9037.6	179.0	39.0	4830.0					718.6	—	171.0	10.2
1911	648.0	—	10155.0	6846.2	1115.0	570.0	4096.4					2046.7	—	290.6	16.8
1912	50.0		40890.0	4776.8	446.0	292.0	2318.5					1099.2		529.3	—
1913	382.0	787.8	9804.0	5672.0	122.0	303.0	2223.8					1287.7	624.0	74.4	89.9
1914	56.0	361.4	9878.0		156.0	621.0	2187.3					430.1	1090.0	376.3	160.1
1915	32.0	165.2	2953.0	45.5	315.0	83.0	55.3					106.1	583.0		—
1916	241.0	249.5	2446.0	245.4	720.0	475.0	235.9					208.3	1678.0		1.4
1917	214.0	526.5	5647.0	1862.3	109.0	1109.0	1481.6					1135.0	4599.0	1494.5	18.4
1918	194.0	607.3	5875.0	1452.8	187.0	1436.0	979.6					763.3	580.0	1.7	31.8
1919	916.0	1051.8	34969.0	33082.8	623.0	2296.0	15478.3					3942.2	5652.0	160.1	537.1
1920	1306.0	2288.5	26568.0	16755.6	1199.0	8943.0	23112.0		—		—	886.8	1872.0	455.6	839.4
1921	1321.0	1370.4	85872.0	25874.5	3583.7	2663.0	7027.1		—	6984.4	—	956.5	956.0	119.9	112.4
1922	2272.0	1057.5	19850.0	27732.8	91.4	2675.0	3935.5		—	3972.7	—	1975.3	859.0	252.4	1339.5
1923	20.0	3945.5	10672.0	12477.7	796.3	6907.0	4172.4		—	5051.7	—	768.5	1146.0	261.5	0.7
1924	175.0	3414.1	8424.0	36197.9	5152.4	1205.0	3863.2		—	8730.9	—	1770.8	918.0	51.0	10.1
1925	4130.0	789.9	7952.0	17104.9	666.7	2560.0	2046.0		—	12578.1	—	1744.0	1128.0	113.0	—
1926	23.0	281.3	147233.0	1399.2	224.4	1711.0	4072.2		—	1097.5	—	296.8	1310.0	386.4	0.9
1927	119.0	220.5	1170.0	6043.7	1374.1	400.0	1046.0		1177.4	2020.0	26218.6	152.6	1713.6	1528.2	9.1
1928	11.0	647.7	1390.0	20288.2	363.8	4835.0	6376.1		583.6	31647.4	12631.9	224.2	777.3	502.2	10.5
1929	41.0	990.8	8290.0	4489.9	196.7	667.0	2764.6		571.9	12165.7	5351.5	152.1	4461.5	74.9	—

Year															
1930	144.0	273.0	4400.0	3936.0	240.5	1021.0	7209.3	—	1085.1	2261.7	3316.8	91.8	1511.2	12.1	2.6
1931	246.0	856.1	6980.0	2002.0	7585.8	2627.0	949.6	—	980.1	2408.1	6893.2	204.2	246.0	0.1	54.6
1932	87.0	1772.6	6490.0	1112.1	394.0	3095.0	2244.3	—	618.6	1922.4	10502.0	255.0	212.3	2.3	26.0
1933	18.0	533.8	1070.0	—	364.2	3434.0	1199.3	—	384.6	2169.0	16872.1	317.5	112.0	9.5	16.1
1934	146.0	114.2	960.0	—	235.1	760.2	2393.5	—	446.2	4775.6	19591.9	574.5	370.4	89.7	52.1
1935	14.0	262.4	1960.0	—	168.3	788.0	1182.2	—	301.3	973.5	15456.3	284.0	495.1	60.8	19.6
1936	2946.0	94.8	1830.0	—	396.5	438.0	—	—	162.6	2358.1	13902.0	277.0	497.2	35.4	5.0
1937	21.0	38.8	3413.0	—	1013.5	861.0	—	—	353.4	8982.6	28424.9	886.4	557.1	183.4	27.5
1938	90.0	136.2	1334.0	—	567.3	1284.0	—	—	40.6	9198.7	9148.3	148.7	1338.0	110.5	2.9
1939	16.0	96.6	1356.0	—	859.7	159.0	—	—	35.0	4992.8	17812.0	224.6	459.2	256.6	4.2
1940	5.0	43.7	940.0	—	—	78.0	—	—	54.1	7577.3	6701.0	266.3	1507.3	5.4	—
1941	3.0	—	1079.0	—	—	94.0	—	—	—	3330.5	23048.0	433.9	984.2	27.1	—
1942	11.0	—	1527.0	—	—	53.0	—	—	—	5780.0	4183.0	450.2	378.2	—	49.0
1943	24.0	—	1810.0	—	—	94.0	—	—	—	2342.3	13501.0	1041.2	990.2	—	58.3
1944	88.0	—	3710.0	—	—	228.0	—	—	—	3447.3	8721.0	490.1	912.8	—	20.0
1945	66.0	101.2	2835.0	—	65.1	11321.0	—	—	6266.3	4054.5	38025.0	1457.4	2119.6	357.7	53.0
1946	1389.0	681.6	2158.0	—	79.0	27.0	386.5	—	5035.8	12717.8	116000.0	4516.4	1947.8	116.0	209.3
1947	467.0	203.4	2433.0	—	41.3	125.0	22673.3	—	6995.3	16562.7	34600.0	2397.3	1338.7	479.5	1372.8
1948	8.0	131.4	1944.0	—	92.3	151.0	13133.3	—	4320.7	7837.2	34100.0	885.8	1662.7	243.5	24.6
1949	10.4	289.4	1807.0	270.7	104.8	21.0	7129.2	13262.5	—	6600.6	50500.0	1063.7	1334.0	1195.4	36.0
1950	3.7	162.2	1389.0	380.1	42.3	40.0	11728.8	7760.8	5437.2	12797.9	38800.0	1389.0	2062.9	4644.4	5.8
1951	3.7	66.7	1694.0	1592.9	35.7	530.7	3495.5	4514.5	6014.5	3818.9	22900.0	901.7	873.0	324.0	13.0
1952	3.6	31.2	1792.0	442.9	124.1	78.5	1732.6	3530.6	15075.3	3337.0	59100.0	2880.0	1163.5	54.4	22.2
1953	2.3	28.3	2184.0	1488.2	40.5	581.7	9722.1	5827.6	4279.2	3382.6	28300.0	1324.7	1050.8	63.9	2.8
1954	22.7	59.3	2457.0	1586.5	104.5	24.5	1440.1	5376.7	3836.3	3372.6	22600.0	1475.2	901.6	115.8	13.3
1955	9.9	133.0	3781.0	846.6	108.1	158.8	3078.7	5622.3	3467.0	5697.8	28200.0	1875.4	1010.9	344.2	16.8
1956	1061.9	212.8	2083.0	263.9	964.4	4.0	1422.5	4136.7	4561.9	7136.5	33100.0	1246.0	1121.4	6970.5	12.6

See pp. 184–87 for sources and discussion of data.

TABLE A-4

Union Membership, Fifteen Countries, 1900-1956 (in thousands)

Year	Denmark	Nether-lands	United Kingdom	Germany	Nor-way	Sweden	France	Italy	Japan	India	United States	Canada	Aus-tralia	Finland	South Africa
1900	96.4	—	—	—	4.8	65.8	492.6	—	—	—	868.5	—	—	—	3.8
1901	95.0	—	—	—	7.6	67.3	588.8	—	—	—	1124.7	—	97.2	—	—
1902	88.0	—	—	—	7.5	66.5	614.2	—	—	—	1375.9	—	—	—	—
1903	86.0	—	—	1089.3	7.9	78.1	645.4	—	—	—	1913.9	—	—	—	—
1904	88.0	—	—	1271.6	9.0	97.9	715.6	—	—	—	2072.7	—	—	—	—
1905	88.0	—	—	1650.0	15.6	104.1	780.0	—	—	—	2022.3	—	—	—	6.3
1906	99.0	—	—	2042.6	25.3	179.6	836.1	150.0	—	—	1907.3	—	175.5	—	—
1907	112.0	—	—	2248.7	39.0	230.7	896.0	190.4	—	—	2080.4	—	194.6	—	—
1908	117.0	—	—	2201.8	47.2	212.9	957.1	258.5	—	—	2130.6	—	240.4	—	—
1909	120.0	—	—	2211.5	43.2	147.9	944.8	292.9	—	—	2005.6	—	273.5	—	—
1910	122.9	—	—	2435.0	45.9	118.0	977.4	302.4	—	—	2140.5	—	302.1	15.3	9.2
1911	128.0	196.5	3139.0	2788.4	53.1	113.9	1029.2	387.8	—	—	2225.0	133.1	364.7	19.6	—
1912	139.0	212.8	3416.0	3007.1	60.8	121.5	1064.0	309.7	—	—	2316.0	160.1	433.2	20.1	—
1913	153.0	233.8	4135.0	3023.1	63.8	134.4	1027.1	327.3	—	—	2566.7	175.8	497.9	27.1	—
1914	159.0	266.0	4145.0	2436.2	67.6	140.5	1026.3	320.9	—	—	2546.5	166.2	523.3	30.4	11.9
1915	173.0	273.4	4359.0	1396.7	78.0	150.8	—	233.9	—	—	2468.0	143.3	528.0	30.1	10.5
1916	192.0	298.9	4644.0	1198.8	78.9	188.6	—	201.3	—	—	2643.6	160.4	546.6	41.0	15.4
1917	224.0	352.3	5499.0	1429.5	93.9	244.1	—	237.6	—	—	2896.5	204.6	564.2	160.7	39.2
1918	302.0	420.5	6533.0	2183.5	107.5	302.6	—	249.0	—	—	3262.8	248.9	581.8	—	77.8
1919	359.0	514.6	7926.0	6527.1	143.9	368.5	—	1159.1	—	—	3823.9	378.0	627.7	41.2	113.8
1920	362.4	683.5	8348.0	9192.9	142.6	402.9	1581.0	2200.1	—	—	4775.6	373.8	684.5	59.5	135.1
1921	323.0	651.2	6632.0	8778.9	96.0	389.8	600.0	1128.9	103.4	—	4553.0	313.3	703.0	48.6	108.2
1922	305.0	640.0	5625.0	—	83.6	360.0	1800.0	401.1	137.4	—	3821.0	276.6	702.9	48.2	81.9
1923	303.0	573.6	5429.0	8001.1	85.7	400.3	1800.0	212.0	125.6	—	3418.1	278.1	699.7	48.1	86.9
1924	306.0	517.9	5544.0	5371.1	92.8	416.9	1800.0	201.0	228.3	—	3334.2	260.6	729.2	47.3	87.1
1925	310.5	497.5	5506.0	4920.4	95.9	384.6	1800.0	—	254.3	—	3319.5	271.1	795.7	50.5	93.6
1926	313.0	493.5	5219.0	4739.9	93.1	414.9	1180.0	—	284.7	—	3299.8	274.6	851.5	62.1	116.2
1927	—	504.2	4919.0	4929.0	94.2	438.0	1300.0	—	309.5	—	3341.5	290.3	911.7	75.8	213.6
1928	319.1	520.1	4806.0	5469.0	106.9	469.4	1400.0	—	308.9	100.6	3268.7	300.6	911.5	90.2	114.5
1929	327.7	552.1	4858.0	5748.0	127.0	508.1	1500.0	—	331.0	181.1	3212.0	319.5	901.2	70.4	116.0

Year															
1930	339.2	624.5	4842.0	5644.0	139.6	553.5	1600.0		354.3	242.4	3162.1	322.4	855.8	15.0	118.3
1931	353.7	674.8	4624.0	5177.0	144.6	589.2	1400.0		369.0	219.1	3142.1	310.5	769.0	19.6	101.9
1932	369.7	779.6	4444.0	—	153.4	638.6	1200.0		377.6	235.7	2968.4	283.1	740.8	18.9	106.9
1933	404.1	828.9	4392.0	—	157.5	633.4	1200.0		384.6	237.4	2805.8	285.7	739.4	19.8	106.4
1934	421.7	795.8	4590.0	—	172.5	653.3	1300.0		388.0	208.1	3451.1	281.3	762.6	27.2	126.4
1935	436.9	752.0	4867.0	—	214.6	701.2	1400.0		408.7	284.9	3513.4	280.6	790.8	33.8	150.5
1936	460.3	728.2	5295.0	—	268.3	757.4	1400.0		420.6	268.3	3900.0	322.7	814.8	44.5	189.0
1937	489.9	723.6	5842.0	—	316.0	840.2	5500.0		395.3	257.3	6117.6	383.5	856.3	64.4	223.5
1938	508.1	743.0	6053.0	—	340.0	897.9	4500.0		375.2	390.1	7114.8	381.6	885.2	70.3	253.7
1939	536.5	769.4	6244.0	—	352.5	961.2	3500.0		365.8	399.2	7518.3	359.0	915.5	68.5	264.4
1940	542.6	798.3	6558.0	—	306.5	971.1	1300.0		6.5	511.1	7877.3	362.2	955.9	66.4	272.5
1941	553.0	—	7165.0	—	293.8	991.3	—		0.9	513.8	8310.1	461.7	1075.7	81.4	289.1
1942	569.4	—	7867.0	—	289.0	1023.1	—		—	573.5	9091.0	578.4	1182.4	79.7	307.1
1943	587.8	—	8174.0	—	280.5	1038.8	—		—	685.3	10818.5	664.5	1204.9	86.1	344.9
1944	603.9		8087.0		—	1069.3			—	781.0	12018.9	724.2	1218.8	106.0	403.1
1945	630.7	805.1	7875.0	—	339.9	1106.9	6200.0		380.7	889.4	12210.8	711.1	1200.4	299.6	411.2
1946	630.3	960.6	8803.0	—	407.0	1147.0	6600.0	—	4925.6	864.0	12356.9	831.7	1262.7	311.8	410.1
1947	639.6	1052.9	9145.0	4661.0	442.4	1194.0	7000.0	—	5692.2	1332.0	13438.6	912.1	1339.5	341.6	403.1
1948	677.7	1106.1	9320.0	4845.0	456.3	1238.6	5700.0	9000.0	6677.4	1651.8	13453.0	977.6	1423.2	306.4	390.4
1949	690.9	1160.3	9274.0	4962.0	473.7	1255.9	4400.0	8000.0	6655.5	1951.8	13553.6	1005.6	1520.9	248.4	407.4
1950	713.7	—	9243.0	5513.3	488.4	1278.4	4000.0	7200.0	5773.9	1821.1	13430.0	1028.5	1605.3	268.8	408.6
1951	721.3	1258.3	9482.0	6255.6	503.4	1313.2	3600.0	7200.0	5686.8	1883.9	14730.1	1146.1	1690.3	260.6	420.1
1952	700.0	1137.8	9526.0	6364.9	515.6	1338.8	3200.0	7200.0	5719.6	1996.3	15138.0	1219.7	1637.5	242.4	423.0
1953	715.0	1184.6	9461.0	6435.6	526.0	1350.9	2900.0	7200.0	5842.7	2099.9	16179.8	1267.9	1679.8	240.1	—
1954	714.9	1274.6	9490.0	6509.8	538.6	1354.7	2500.0	7200.0	5986.2	2113.9	16624.0	1268.2	—	248.9	—
1955	715.6		9662.0	6535.4	542.1	1384.5	2200.0	7360.0	—	—	—	—	—	269.4	—
1956	733.3			—	—	1404.3	—	6000.0	—	—	17339.0		—		

See pp. 187–90 for sources and discussion of data.

TABLE A-5

Estimated Number of Non-agricultural Employees, Fifteen Countries, 1927–1956 (in thousands)

Year	Denmark	Netherlands	United Kingdom	Germany	Norway	Sweden	France	Italy	Japan	India	United States	Canada	Australia	Finland	South Africa
1927	—	—	—			—			11389		29691	2119	—	416	1305
1928		—	—			—			10863		29710	2266	—	431	1337
1929		1845	16606			1574			10952		31041	2405	1625	418	1361
1930	—	1772	15895		657	1579	9057		10621		29143	2273	1512	370	1351
1931	849	1771	15295		—	1488	8380		10620		26383	2006	1219	329	1294
1932	779	1573	15164		—	1382	7326		10621		23377	1828	1203	358	1206
1933	874	1568	15726		—	1347	7191		11296		23466	1698	1333	399	1290
1934	986	1597	16456		657	1497	6963		12647		25699	1910	1463	434	1471
1935	1069	1553	16849		677	1602	6657		13323		26792	1920	1625	488	1660
1936	1117	1570	17710		723	1690	6714		13567		28802	1972	1772	510	1848
1937	1173	1688	18721		723	1808	7786		14372		30718	2085	1869	575	1964
1938	1176	1761	18403		762	1823	7996		15091		28902	2053	—	607	2060
1939	1269	1837	19302		—	1883	8105		—		30311	2056	1730	567	2078
1940	1193	1811	19040	—	724	1838	—	—	—		32058	2173	—	608	2186
1941	1177	1995	19302	—	775	1801	7140	—	—		36220	2538	1961	531	2310
1942	1209	1934	19601	—	793	1881	7257	—	—		39779	2770	1913	523	2363
1943	1219	1850	18984	—	782	1917	7552	—	—		42106	2906	1914	541	2278
1944	1187	—	18347	—	756	1915	7171	—	—		41534	2950	1910	527	2300
1945	1069	—	17561	—	663	2002	7303	—	—		40037	2914	1916	647	2380
1946	1146	1991	18441	—	743	2097	7727	—	—		41287	2986	2103	706	2470
1947	1174	2245	19770	—	811	2127	8172	9207	11320	11132	43462	3139	2269	783	2519
1948	1212	2492	19109	11923	831	2172	8390	9043	12230	11437	44448	3225	2375	854	2552
1949	1224	2594	19281	12218	855	2174	8533	8926	11880	11846	43315	3326	3430	890	2662
1950	1280	2716	19549	12705	874	2196	8574	8879	12090	12242	44738	3429	2547	953	2685
1951	1288	2784	19797	13603	884	2241	8775	8974	13180	12543	47347	3625	2630	987	2784
1952	1226	2759	19777	14042	894	2191	8814	8948	13730	12707	48303	3786	2588	945	2832
1953	1242	2841	19946	14684	907	2136	8729	8969	14220	12666	49681	3837	2561	899	2832
1954	1226	2989	20305	15405	934	2153	8826	9086	14620	12824	48431	3776	2656	917	2906
1955	1271	3102	20664	16209	948	2219	8945	9181	15440	13327	50056	3935	2739	951	2979
1956	—	—	20844	17177	951	2238	9042	9361	16740	—	51878	—	2785	977	3027

See pp. 190–93 for sources and discussion of data.

TABLE A-6. Intensity of Organization

Union Membership as a Percentage of Non-agricultural Employment, Fifteen Countries, 1927–1956

Year	Denmark	Netherlands	United Kingdom	Germany	Norway	Sweden	France	Italy	Japan	India	United States	Canada	Australia	Finland	South Africa
1927	—	—	—	—	—	—	17.7	—	2.7	—	11.3	13.7	—	18.2	16.4
1928	—	—	—	—	—	—	16.7	—	2.8	—	11.0	13.3	—	20.9	8.6
1929	—	29.9	29.3	—	—	32.3	16.4	—	3.0	—	10.3	13.3	55.5	16.8	8.5
1930	—	35.2	30.5	—	21.2	35.1	16.7	—	3.3	—	10.8	14.2	56.6	4.1	8.8
1931	41.7	38.1	30.2	—	—	39.6	18.7	—	3.5	—	11.9	15.5	63.1	6.0	7.9
1932	47.5	49.6	29.3	—	—	46.2	21.0	—	3.6	—	12.7	15.5	61.6	5.3	8.9
1933	46.2	52.9	27.9	—	—	47.0	20.9	—	3.4	—	12.0	16.8	55.5	5.0	8.2
1934	42.8	49.8	27.9	—	32.7	43.6	—	—	3.1	—	13.4	14.7	52.1	6.3	8.6
1935	40.9	48.4	28.9	—	39.6	43.8	—	—	3.1	—	13.1	14.6	48.7	7.0	9.1
1936	41.2	46.4	29.9	—	43.7	44.8	70.6	—	3.1	—	13.5	16.4	46.0	8.7	10.2
1937	41.8	42.9	31.2	—	47.0	46.5	56.3	—	2.8	—	19.9	18.4	45.8	11.2	11.4
1938	43.2	42.2	32.9	—	46.3	49.3	43.2	—	2.5	—	24.6	18.6	—	11.6	12.3
1939	42.3	41.9	32.3	—	—	51.0	—	—	—	—	24.8	17.5	52.9	12.1	12.7
1940	—	44.1	34.4	—	42.3	52.8	—	—	—	—	24.6	16.7	—	10.9	12.5
1941	45.5	—	37.1	—	37.9	55.0	—	—	—	—	22.9	18.2	54.9	15.3	12.5
1942	47.0	—	40.1	—	36.4	54.4	—	—	—	—	22.9	20.9	61.8	15.2	13.0
1943	47.1	—	43.1	—	35.9	54.2	—	—	—	—	25.7	22.9	63.0	15.9	15.1
1944	48.2	—	44.1	—	—	55.8	—	—	—	—	28.9	24.5	63.8	20.1	17.5
1945	50.9	—	44.8	—	51.3	55.3	84.9	—	—	—	30.5	24.4	62.7	46.3	17.3
1946	55.0	40.4	47.7	—	54.8	54.7	85.4	—	—	—	29.9	27.9	60.0	44.2	16.6
1947	54.5	42.8	46.3	—	54.5	56.1	85.7	99.5	50.3	12.0	30.9	29.1	59.0	43.6	16.0
1948	55.9	42.3	48.8	40.6	54.9	57.0	67.9	89.6	54.6	14.4	30.3	30.3	59.9	35.9	15.3
1949	56.4	42.6	48.1	40.6	55.4	57.8	51.6	—	56.0	16.5	31.3	30.2	62.6	27.9	15.3
1950	55.8	42.7	47.3	43.4	55.9	58.2	46.7	81.1	47.8	14.9	30.0	—	63.0	28.2	15.2
1951	56.0	—	47.9	46.0	56.9	58.6	41.0	80.2	43.1	15.0	31.1	28.4	64.3	26.4	15.1
1952	57.1	45.6	48.2	45.3	57.7	61.1	36.3	80.5	41.7	15.7	31.3	30.3	63.3	25.7	14.9
1953	57.6	40.0	47.4	43.8	58.0	63.2	33.2	80.3	41.1	16.6	32.6	31.8	65.6	26.7	—
1954	58.3	39.6	46.7	42.3	57.7	62.9	28.3	79.2	40.9	16.5	34.3	33.6	—	27.1	—
1955	56.3	41.1	46.8	40.3	57.2	62.4	24.6	80.2	—	—	—	32.2	—	28.3	—
1956	—	—	—	—	—	62.8	—	64.1	—	—	33.4	—	—	—	—

Source: Computed from Tables A-4 and A-5.

TABLE A-7. Membership Involvement Ratio

Workers Involved in Industrial Disputes as a Percentage of Union Membership, Fifteen Countries, 1900–1956

Year	Denmark	Netherlands	United Kingdom	Germany	Norway	Sweden	France	Italy	Japan	India	United States	Canada	Australia	Finland	South Africa
1900	7.9			17.0			45.2				65.4				
1901	4.3			7.2			18.9				50.1				
1902	2.7			7.6			34.6				50.3				
1903	1.3			11.2	38.0	31.5	19.1				41.2				
1904	3.0			10.7	13.3	12.5	37.9				27.7				
1905	6.5			30.8	12.8	31.6	22.8				15.0				
1906	3.9			15.5	11.9	10.4	52.4								
1907	7.2			12.5	25.6	10.2	22.1								
1908	6.5			5.8	25.4	19.0	10.3								
1909	2.0			5.9	8.8	204.7	17.7								
1910	2.0	—	—	15.2	8.9	3.1	28.8					—		28.8	4.3
1911	22.5	—	30.3	11.7	82.9	18.1	22.4					22.6	—	29.6	—
1912	2.9	12.9	42.8	15.9	23.5	8.2	25.2					25.3	—	56.2	—
1913	6.3	5.9	16.1	8.2	7.7	7.1	21.5					22.5	10.1	20.7	184.0
1914	2.1	5.6	10.8	3.9	7.8	10.2	15.6					5.2	13.6	20.4	—
1915	1.1	6.1	10.3	0.9	12.4	3.4	—			—	—	6.4	15.4	—	—
1916	7.4	8.9	5.9	10.4	31.1	11.0	—				60.5	13.2	31.2	—	8.4
1917	4.5	9.4	15.9	45.9	5.8	19.1	—				42.4	23.6	30.8	87.0	8.9
1918	3.2	12.0	17.1	17.4	6.9	20.2	—				38.0	27.5	9.7	—	3.3
1919	9.9		32.7	29.7	17.4	22.0	—				108.8	36.8	25.1	9.7	20.9
1920	6.1	9.7	23.1	15.5	22.3	34.5	83.3		—		30.6	14.0	22.7	35.3	78.2
1921	14.9	7.3	27.2	17.0	160.8	12.8	67.1		56.3	—	24.1	7.3	23.5	13.0	9.1
1922	16.0	6.9	9.8	—	2.6	21.0	16.1		30.2	—	42.2	14.8	16.5	20.3	35.4
1923	0.6	9.8	7.5	20.1	29.2	25.7	18.4		28.9	—	22.1	11.8	10.9	15.8	0.06
1924	3.2	5.3	11.1	30.1	68.0	5.8	15.3		23.9	—	19.6	12.5	20.9	6.6	2.2
1925	32.9	6.8	8.0	15.4	14.4	37.9	13.8		35.2	—	12.9	9.5	22.2	5.7	—
1926	0.3	2.0	22.1	1.9	55.3	12.8	29.6		44.7	—	10.0	8.8	13.3	16.4	0.7
1927	0.9	2.7	2.2	10.2	23.9	2.2	8.7		15.1	—	9.9	7.7	22.0	17.7	2.4
1928	0.2	3.2	2.6	14.3	7.5	15.2	15.0		15.0	503.9	9.6	5.9	10.6	30.2	5.0
1929	0.3	3.9	11.0	4.1	3.8	2.5	16.1		23.4	293.8	9.0	4.0	11.6	3.4	2.5

Year															
1930	1.6	1.8	6.3	4.0	3.4	3.8	36.5	—	23.0	81.0	5.8	4.3	6.3	11.3	4.2
1931	1.0	4.2	10.6	3.4	41.1	6.9	3.9	—	17.5	92.7	10.9	3.4	4.9	0.5	6.2
1932	1.6	4.1	8.5	—	4.2	7.8	6.0	—	14.5	54.3	10.9	8.3	4.4	1.6	3.7
1933	0.1	1.8	3.1	—	4.0	5.1	7.3	—	12.8	69.5	41.6	9.3	4.1	6.6	1.5
1934	2.7	0.8	2.9	—	3.7	2.1	7.7	—	12.8	106.1	42.5	16.3	6.7	21.7	1.9
1935	0.2	1.7	5.6	—	1.6	2.5	7.8	—	9.2	40.1	31.8	11.9	6.0	6.8	1.6
1936	21.1	1.4	6.0	—	5.7	0.5	173.1	—	7.3	63.0	20.2	10.8	7.4	6.7	1.2
1937	0.3	0.6	10.2	—	9.1	3.7	5.9	—	14.2	251.8	30.4	18.7	11.2	9.6	3.0
1938	0.7	0.9	4.5	—	7.1	3.2	25.2	—	3.5	102.8	9.7	5.3	16.3	5.8	1.0
1939	0.1	0.7	5.4	—	4.5	0.2	—	—	5.7	102.5	15.6	11.4	16.7	8.9	1.8
1940	0.1	0.4	4.6	—	—	0.4	—	—	—	88.5	7.3	16.7	20.1	0.8	0.7
1941	0.02	—	5.0	—	—	0.2	—	—	—	56.7	28.4	18.9	23.1	2.7	1.9
1942	0.6	—	5.8	—	—	0.1	—	—	—	134.7	9.2	19.7	14.3	—	4.6
1943	1.1	—	6.8	—	—	0.7	—	—	—	76.6	18.3	32.9	24.6	—	2.4
1944	1.3	—	10.2	—	—	0.7	—	—	—	70.4	17.6	10.4	22.7	—	2.3
1945	1.3	—	6.7	—	1.2	12.0	—	—	—	84.0	28.4	13.5	26.3	12.4	3.5
1946	8.6	9.0	6.0	—	1.2	0.1	2.7	—	10.5	227.1	37.2	16.8	27.6	6.1	23.3
1947	1.2	6.2	6.8	—	1.9	4.8	42.8	—	3.8	138.2	16.1	11.4	24.4	33.6	5.0
1948	0.4	1.7	4.6	—	1.3	0.5	115.1	—	34.5	64.1	14.6	4.4	22.3	5.3	1.0
1949	0.4	1.3	4.7	1.2	1.9	0.1	98.4	36.2	16.9	35.1	22.4	5.1	17.4	23.8	1.7
1950	0.4	1.5	3.3	1.4	0.9	0.2	38.2	49.1	11.8	39.5	17.9	—	26.9	43.9	0.8
1951	0.2	—	4.0	2.8	0.9	1.1	48.7	29.6	20.4	36.7	15.1	10.0	24.2	4.4	2.0
1952	0.3	0.3	4.4	1.3	1.2	0.2	36.1	20.4	28.4	40.5	23.4	10.5	30.9	3.9	1.5
1953	0.1	0.9	14.5	0.8	0.9	1.9	61.5	65.0	23.0	22.2	14.8	4.6	29.5	6.5	—
1954	1.1	1.6	4.7	1.8	0.5	0.6	52.8	28.4	15.5	22.6	9.2	4.9	—	7.7	—
1955	0.9	1.7	6.9	9.1	1.8	0.3	48.2	18.8	—	—	—	4.7	—	15.7	—
1956	8.9	—	—	—	—	0.1	—	34.1	—	—	11.0	—	—	167.0	—

Source: Computed from Tables A-2 and A-4.

TABLE A-8. Employee Involvement Ratio

Workers Involved in Industrial Disputes as a Percentage of Non-agricultural Employment, Fifteen Countries, 1927–1956

Year	Den-mark	Nether-lands	United Kingdom	Ger-many	Nor-way	Sweden	France	Italy	Japan	India	United States	Canada	Aus-tralia	Finland	South Africa
1927		—	—		0.7	—			0.4		1.1	1.1	—	3.2	0.4
1928		—	—			—			0.4		1.1	0.8	—	6.3	0.4
1929		1.2	3.2			0.8			0.7		0.9	0.5	6.4	0.6	0.2
1930	0.4	0.6	1.9			1.3	6.5		0.8		0.6	0.6	3.6	0.5	0.4
1931	0.7	1.6	3.2			2.7	0.6		0.6		1.3	0.5	3.1	—*	0.5
1932	0.1	2.0	2.5			3.6	1.0		0.5		1.4	1.3	2.7	0.1	0.3
1933	1.2	0.9	0.9			2.4	1.2		0.4		5.0	1.6	2.3	0.3	0.1
1934	0.1	0.4	0.8			0.9	1.4		0.4		5.7	2.4	3.5	1.4	0.2
1935	8.7	0.8	1.6		0.5	1.1	1.6		0.3		4.2	1.7	2.9	0.5	0.1
1936	0.1	0.7	1.8		2.3	0.2	36.1		0.2		2.7	1.8	3.4	0.6	0.1
1937	0.3	0.3	3.2		4.0	1.7	4.2		0.4		6.1	3.4	5.1	1.1	0.3
1938	—*	0.4	1.5		3.3	1.6	14.2		0.1		2.4	1.0	—	0.7	0.1
1939	—*	0.3	1.7		2.1	0.1	—		—		3.9	2.0	8.8	1.1	0.2
1940	—*	0.2	1.6	—		0.2	—	—	—	—	1.8	2.8	—	0.1	0.1
1941	—*	—	1.9	—		0.1	—	—	—	—	6.5	3.4	12.7	0.4	0.2
1942	0.3	—	2.3	—		0.1	—	—	—	—	2.1	4.1	8.8	—	0.6
1943	0.5	—	2.9	—		0.4	—	—	—	—	4.7	7.5	15.5	—	0.4
1944	0.6	—	4.5	—		0.4	—	—	—	—	5.1	2.6	14.5	—	0.4
1945	0.8	3.6	3.0	—	0.6	6.7	—	—	—	—	8.7	3.3	16.5	5.7	0.6
1946	4.7	2.7	2.9	—	0.6	0.1	2.3	—	—	—	11.1	4.7	16.6	2.7	3.9
1947	0.6	0.7	3.1	—	1.0	2.7	36.7	—	1.9	16.5	5.0	3.3	14.4	14.6	0.8
1948	0.2	0.6	2.2	—	0.7	0.3	78.2	—	18.8	9.3	4.4	1.3	13.4	1.9	0.2
1949	0.2	0.6	2.2	0.5	1.1	—*	50.7	32.4	9.4	5.8	7.0	1.5	10.9	6.6	0.3
1950	0.2	0.6	1.5	0.6	0.5	0.1	17.8	39.8	5.6	5.9	5.4	5.6	16.9	12.4	0.1
1951	0.1	0.5	1.9	1.3	0.5	0.7	20.0	23.8	8.8	5.5	4.7	2.8	15.5	1.2	0.3
1952	0.2	0.1	2.1	0.6	0.7	0.1	13.1	16.4	11.8	6.4	7.3	3.2	19.5	1.0	0.2
1953	—*	0.4	6.9	0.3	0.5	1.2	20.4	52.2	9.4	3.7	4.8	1.5	19.4	1.7	0.1
1954	0.6	0.6	2.2	0.8	0.3	0.4	14.9	22.5	6.3	3.7	3.2	1.6	13.9	2.1	0.2
1955	0.5	0.7	3.2	3.7	1.1	0.2	11.9	15.1	6.7	4.0	5.3	1.5	16.2	4.5	0.3
1956	—	—	2.4	0.1	5.9	0.1	10.9	21.9	6.6	—	3.7	—	15.4	46.2	0.3

* Less than 0.1 per cent.

Source: Computed from Tables A-2 and A-5.

TABLE A-9. Employee-Loss Ratio

Working Days Lost per Hundred Non-agricultural Wage and Salary Earners, Fifteen Countries, 1927–1956

Year	Denmark	Nether-lands	United Kingdom	Ger-many	Nor-way	Sweden	France	Italy	Japan	India	United States	Canada	Aus-tralia	Finland	South Africa
1927	—	—	—			—	79.6		10.3		88.3	7.2	—	367.4	0.7
1928	29.0	—	—			—	11.3		5.4		42.5	9.9	—	116.5	0.8
1929	11.2	53.7	49.9		36.6	42.4	30.6		5.2		17.2	6.3	274.6	17.9	—
1930	2.1	15.4	27.7			64.7	16.7		10.2		11.4	4.0	99.9	3.3	0.2
1931	14.8	48.3	45.6			176.5	34.4		9.2		26.1	10.2	20.2	0.03	4.2
1932	1.3	112.7	42.8			224.0	17.8		5.8		44.9	13.9	17.6	0.6	2.2
1933	263.7	34.0	6.8			254.9	—		3.4		71.9	18.7	8.4	2.4	1.2
1934	1.8	7.2	5.8			50.8			3.5		76.2	30.1	25.3	20.7	3.5
1935	7.7	16.9	11.6		25.6	49.2			2.3		57.7	14.8	30.5	12.5	1.2
1936	1.3	6.0	10.3		58.6	25.9			1.2		48.3	14.0	28.1	6.9	0.3
1937		2.3	18.2		140.2	47.6			2.5		92.5	42.5	29.8	31.9	1.4
1938		7.7	7.2		78.5	70.4			0.3		31.7	7.2	—	18.2	0.1
1939		5.3	7.0		112.8	8.4			—		58.8	10.9	26.5	45.3	0.2
1940	0.4	2.4	4.9			4.2		—		—	20.9	1.3	—	0.9	—
1941	0.3	—	5.6			5.2		—		—	63.6	17.1	50.2	5.1	
1942	0.9	—	7.8			2.8		—		—	10.5	16.3	19.8	—	2.1
1943	2.0	—	9.5			4.9		—		—	32.1	35.8	51.7	—	2.6
1944	7.4	—	20.2		9.8	11.9		—		—	21.0	16.6	47.8	55.3	0.9
1945	6.2	34.2	16.1		10.6	565.5		—		—	95.0	50.0	110.6	16.4	2.2
1946	121.2	9.1	11.7		5.1	1.3	5.0	—		—	281.0	151.3	92.6	61.2	8.5
1947	39.8	5.3	12.3		11.1	5.9	277.5	—	44.5	148.8	79.6	76.4	59.0	28.5	54.5
1948	0.7	11.2	10.2		12.3	7.0	156.5	—	57.2	68.5	76.7	27.5	70.0	134.3	1.0
1949	0.8		9.4	2.2		1.0	83.5	148.6	36.4	55.7	116.6	32.0	54.9		1.4
1950	0.3	6.0	7.1	3.0	4.8	1.8	136.8	87.4	45.0	104.5	86.7	40.5	81.0	487.3	0.2
1951	0.3	2.4	8.6	11.7	4.0	23.7	39.8	50.3	45.6	30.4	48.4	24.9	33.2	32.8	0.5
1952	0.3	1.1	9.1	3.2	13.9	3.6	19.7	39.5	109.8	26.3	122.4	76.1	45.0	5.8	0.8
1953	0.2	1.0	10.9	10.1	4.5	27.2	111.4	65.0	30.1	26.7	57.0	34.5	41.0	7.1	0.1
1954	1.9	2.0	12.1	10.3	11.2	1.1	16.3	59.2	26.2	2.3	46.7	39.1	33.9	12.6	0.5
1955	0.8	4.3	18.3	5.2	11.4	7.2	34.4	61.2	22.5	42.8	57.3	47.7	36.9	36.2	0.6
1956	—		10.0	1.5	101.4	0.2	15.7	44.2	27.3	—	63.8	—	40.3	713.5	0.4

Source: Computed from Tables A-3 and A-5.

TABLE A-10. Duration of Strikes

Working Days Lost per Striker, Fifteen Countries, 1900–1956

Year	Den-mark	Nether-lands	United Kingdom	Ger-many	Nor-way	Sweden	France	Italy	Japan	India	United States	Canada	Aus-tralia	Finland	South Africa
1900	31.1			10.7	—	—	16.9					—			—
1901	13.9			24.6	—	—	16.7					22.5			—
1902	55.4			17.3	—	—	22.0					9.8			
1903	17.3			21.6	4.3	26.1	19.8					24.5			
1904	26.5			15.6	37.5	31.6	14.5					16.1			
1905	87.5			14.5	15.0	72.6	15.5					13.4			
1906	17.4			20.0	31.7	25.6	21.5					13.8			52.0
1907	31.5			18.2	34.0	21.9	18.0					17.1		28.8	45.0
1908	11.2			16.1	31.7	45.6	17.7					28.0		38.2	
1909	24.2			17.1	48.7	39.0	21.3					50.4		64.6	—
1910	24.4	—	—	24.5	43.7	10.5	17.2					33.7	—	38.9	25.5
1911	22.5	—	10.7	21.0	25.3	27.7	17.8					68.0	—	50.1	18.7
1912	12.2	—	28.0	10.0	31.2	29.2	8.7					27.1	—	46.8	
1913	39.4	26.1	14.8	22.8	24.9	31.6	10.1					32.6	12.4	13.3	4.5
1914	16.5	23.0	22.1	—	29.4	43.1	13.6					49.4	15.4	60.7	7.3
1915	16.8	10.9	6.6	3.5	32.5	16.3	5.9					11.7	7.2	—	—
1916	16.9	13.8	8.9	2.0	29.4	22.9	5.7					9.8	9.8	10.7	1.1
1917	21.2	16.8	6.5	2.8	20.2	23.7	5.0					23.5	26.4	5.7	5.3
1918	19.8	15.3	5.3	3.8	25.3	23.5	5.6					11.1	10.3	40.0	12.0
1919	25.7	17.0	13.5	17.1	24.8	28.3	13.5					28.4	35.9		22.6
1920	59.4	34.5	13.8	11.7	37.7	64.3	17.6		—	—	—	17.0	12.0	21.7	7.9
1921	27.5	28.7	47.7	17.4	23.2	53.6	17.5		—	11.6	—	41.8	5.8	19.0	11.4
1922	46.5	24.0	36.0	15.2	41.5	35.3	13.6		—	9.1	—	48.2	7.4	25.8	46.2
1923	10.5	70.0	26.4	7.8	31.9	67.1	12.6		—	16.8	—	23.4	15.0	34.4	14.0
1924	17.9	123.3	13.7	22.4	81.7	50.2	14.1		—	27.9	—	54.5	6.0	16.4	5.3
1925	40.4	23.5	18.0	22.6	48.3	17.6	8.2		—	46.5	—	67.6	6.4	39.0	—
1926	23.0	28.4	127.6	15.5	4.4	32.3	11.7		—	—	—	12.3	11.6	37.9	1.1
1927	41.0	16.3	10.8	12.0	61.1	42.1	9.3		25.2	15.3	79.5	6.8	8.5	114.0	1.7
1928	22.0	38.3	11.2	26.0	45.5	67.6	30.3		12.6	62.4	40.2	12.7	8.1	18.5	1.8
1929	41.0	46.5	15.6	19.0	41.0	52.5	11.5		7.4	22.9	18.5	11.8	42.7	31.2	—

Year															
1930	27.2	24.8	14.3	17.5	51.2	49.1	12.3		13.3	11.5	18.1	6.7	27.9	7.1	0.5
1931	66.5	30.4	14.2	11.2	127.5	64.2	17.5		15.2	11.9	20.2	19.1	6.5	1.0	8.7
1932	15.0	55.4	17.1	8.7	61.6	61.8	31.3		11.3	15.0	32.4	10.9	6.5	7.7	6.5
1933	36.0	36.1	7.9	—	57.8	107.3	13.8		7.8	13.2	14.4	11.9	3.7	7.3	10.1
1934	12.7	18.4	7.2	—	36.7	55.9	23.8		9.0	21.6	13.4	12.5	7.3	15.2	21.7
1935	17.5	20.3	7.2	—	48.1	45.8	10.9		8.0	8.5	13.8	8.5	10.5	26.4	8.2
1936	30.4	9.1	5.8	—	25.9	125.1			5.3	14.0	17.6	8.0	8.2	11.8	2.3
1937	15.0	8.4	5.7	—	35.2	27.9			6.3	13.9	15.3	12.3	5.8	29.6	4.0
1938	24.3	21.3	4.9	—	23.6	44.3			3.1	22.9	13.3	7.3	9.3	27.0	1.1
1939	32.0	18.2	4.0	—	53.7	72.3			1.7	12.2	15.2	5.5	3.0	42.1	0.9
1940	16.7	14.6	3.1	—	—	20.0	—	—	2.2	16.7	11.6	4.4	7.8	10.8	—
1941	30.0	—	3.0	—	—	49.5	—	—	—	11.4	9.8	5.0	4.0	12.3	—
1942	3.4	—	3.3	—	—	40.8	—	—	—	7.5	5.0	4.0	2.2	—	3.5
1943	3.8	—	3.2	—	—	13.6	—	—	—	4.5	6.8	4.8	3.3	—	6.9
1944	11.4	—	4.5	—	15.9	32.6	—	—	—	6.3	4.1	6.5	3.3	—	2.2
1945	7.8	2.8	5.3	—	16.8	85.0	—	—	—	5.4	11.0	15.2	6.7	9.6	3.7
1946	25.6	9.5	4.1	—	5.0	20.8	2.1	—	12.1	6.5	25.2	32.4	5.6	6.1	2.2
1947	62.3	3.4	3.9	—	15.6	2.2	7.6	—	23.0	9.0	15.9	23.0	4.1	4.2	68.6
1948	3.0	7.4	4.6	—	11.6	24.8	2.0	—	3.0	7.4	17.4	20.7	5.2	15.0	6.3
1949	3.9	20.2	4.2	4.7	—	21.0	1.6	4.6	3.9	9.6	16.7	20.7	5.0	20.3	5.1
1950	1.3	9.2	4.6	4.8	9.6	16.7	7.8	2.2	8.0	17.8	16.1	7.2	4.8	39.4	1.8
1951	2.2	4.7	4.4	9.1	8.3	35.1	2.0	2.1	5.2	5.5	10.3	8.8	2.1	28.4	1.6
1952	1.5	8.2	4.3	5.3	19.4	37.4	1.5	2.4	9.3	4.1	16.7	23.8	2.3	5.8	3.4
1953	5.7	2.6	1.6	29.4	8.3	22.2	5.5	1.2	3.2	7.2	11.8	23.7	2.1	4.1	1.9
1954	2.9	3.2	5.5	13.7	36.0	3.2	1.1	2.6	4.1	7.1	14.8	23.7	2.4	6.0	2.3
1955	1.6	6.3	5.6	1.4	10.8	40.7	2.9	4.1	3.4	10.8	10.6	31.2	2.3	8.1	1.7
1956	16.2	5.8	4.1	10.4	17.2	2.5	1.4	2.0	4.2	9.7	17.4	14.0	2.6	15.4	1.3

Source: Computed from Tables A-2 and A-3.

TABLE A-11. Membership-Loss Ratio

Working Days Lost per Hundred Union Members, Fifteen Countries, 1900–1956

Year	Den-mark	Nether-lands	United Kingdom	Ger-many	Nor-way	Sweden	France	Italy	Japan	India	United States	Canada	Aus-tralia	Finland	South Africa
1900	244.8				—	—	763.4								
1901	60.0				—	—	316.3								
1902	151.1				—	—	761.2								
1903	22.1			240.7	1645.6	822.0	378.4								
1904	78.4			166.7	500.0	394.3	549.9								
1905	567.0			446.2	19.2	2295.9	352.1								
1906	68.7			309.3	375.5	266.7	1128.9								
1907	227.7			227.8	871.8	222.8	397.6								
1908	72.6			92.9	805.1	865.2	183.1								
1909	48.3			101.6	428.2	7978.4	376.8								
1910	49.6	—		371.2	390.0	33.1	494.2					—	—	1117.6	110.9
1911	506.3	—	323.5	245.5	2099.8	500.4	398.0					1537.7	—	1482.7	—
1912	36.0	—	1197.0	158.9	733.6	240.3	217.9					686.6	125.3	2633.3	—
1913	249.7	337.0	237.1	187.6	191.2	225.4	216.5					732.5	208.3	274.5	1345.4
1914	35.2	135.9	238.3	—	230.8	442.0	213.1					258.8	110.4	1237.8	
1915	18.5	60.4	67.7	3.3	403.8	55.0						74.0	307.0	—	
1916	125.5	83.5	52.7	20.5	912.5	251.9						129.9	815.1	—	9.1
1917	95.5	149.4	102.7	130.3	116.1	454.3						554.7	99.7	930.0	46.9
1918	64.2	144.4	89.9	66.5	174.0	474.6						306.7	900.4	—	40.9
1919	255.2	204.4	441.2	506.9	432.9	623.1						1042.9	—	388.6	472.0
1920	360.4	—	318.3	182.3	840.8	2219.7	1461.9		—	—	—	237.2	273.5	765.7	621.3
1921	409.0	210.4	1294.8	294.7	3733.0	683.2	1171.2		—	—	—	305.3	136.0	246.7	103.9
1922	744.9	165.2	352.9	—	109.3	743.1	218.6		—	—	—	714.1	122.2	523.7	1635.5
1923	6.6	687.8	196.6	155.9	929.2	1725.5	231.8		—	—	—	276.3	163.8	543.7	0.8
1924	57.2	659.2	151.9	673.9	5552.2	289.0	214.6		—	—	—	679.5	125.9	107.8	11.6
1925	1330.1	158.8	144.4	347.6	1738.0	665.6	113.7		—	—	—	643.3	141.8	223.8	—
1926	7.3	57.0	2821.1	29.5	241.0	412.4	345.1		—	—	—	108.1	153.8	622.2	0.8
1927	—	43.7	23.8	122.6	1458.7	91.3	80.5		380.4	—	784.6	52.6	188.0	2016.1	4.3
1928	3.4	124.5	28.9	371.0	340.3	1030.0	455.5		188.9	31458.6	386.4	74.6	85.3	556.8	9.2
1929	12.5	179.5	170.6	78.1	154.9	131.3	184.3		172.8	6717.7	166.6	47.6	495.1	106.4	—

Year															
1930	42.5	43.7	90.9	69.7	172.3	184.5	450.6	—	306.3	933.0	104.9	28.5	176.6	80.7	2.2
1931	69.6	126.9	151.0	38.7	5246.1	445.9	67.8	—	265.6	1099.1	219.4	65.8	32.0	0.5	53.6
1932	23.5	227.4	146.0	—	256.8	484.7	187.0	—	163.8	815.6	353.8	90.1	28.7	12.2	24.3
1933	4.5	64.4	24.4	—	231.2	542.2	99.9	—	100.0	913.6	601.3	111.1	15.1	48.0	15.1
1934	34.6	14.4	20.9	—	136.3	116.4	184.1	—	115.0	2294.9	567.7	204.2	48.6	329.8	41.2
1935	3.2	34.9	40.3	—	78.4	112.4	84.4	—	73.7	341.7	439.9	101.2	62.6	179.9	13.0
1936	640.0	13.0	34.6	—	147.8	57.8	—	—	38.7	878.9	356.5	85.8	61.0	79.6	2.6
1937	4.3	5.4	58.4	—	320.7	102.5	—	—	89.4	3491.1	464.6	231.1	65.1	284.8	12.3
1938	17.7	18.3	22.0	—	166.9	143.0	—	—	10.8	2358.0	128.6	39.0	151.2	157.2	1.1
1939	3.0	12.6	21.7	—	243.9	16.5	—	—	9.6	1250.7	236.9	62.6	50.2	374.6	1.6
1940	0.9	5.5	14.3	—	—	8.0	—	—	—	1482.5	85.1	73.5	157.7	8.1	—
1941	0.5	—	15.1	—	—	9.5	—	—	—	648.2	277.3	94.0	91.5	33.3	16.0
1942	1.9	—	19.4	—	—	5.2	—	—	—	1007.8	46.0	77.8	32.0	—	16.9
1943	4.1	—	22.1	—	—	9.0	—	—	—	341.8	124.8	156.7	82.2	—	5.0
1944	14.6	—	45.9	—	—	21.3	—	—	—	441.4	72.6	67.7	74.9	—	12.9
1945	10.5	84.7	36.0	—	19.2	1022.8	—	—	—	455.9	311.4	205.0	176.6	119.4	51.0
1946	220.4	21.2	24.5	—	19.4	2.4	5.9	—	127.2	1472.0	938.7	543.0	154.3	37.2	340.6
1947	73.0	12.5	26.6	—	9.3	10.5	323.9	—	88.5	1243.4	257.5	262.8	99.9	140.4	6.3
1948	1.2	26.2	20.9	—	20.2	12.2	230.4	—	104.8	474.5	253.5	90.6	116.8	79.5	8.8
1949	1.5	—	19.5	5.5	22.1	1.7	162.0	165.8	64.9	338.2	372.6	105.8	87.7	481.2	—
1950	0.5	14.0	15.0	6.9	8.7	3.1	293.2	107.8	94.2	702.8	288.9	—	128.5	1727.8	1.4
1951	0.5	—	17.9	25.5	7.1	40.4	97.1	62.7	105.8	202.7	155.5	87.7	51.6	124.3	3.1
1952	0.5	2.5	18.8	7.0	24.1	5.9	54.1	49.0	263.6	167.2	390.4	251.3	71.1	22.4	5.2
1953	0.3	2.5	23.1	23.1	7.7	43.1	335.2	80.9	73.2	161.2	174.9	108.6	62.6	26.6	—
1954	3.2	5.0	25.9	24.4	19.4	1.8	57.6	74.7	64.1	159.5	135.9	116.3	—	46.5	—
1955	1.4	10.4	39.1	13.0	19.9	11.5	139.9	76.4	—	—	—	147.9	—	127.8	—
1956	144.8	—	—	—	—	0.3	—	68.9	—	—	190.9	—	—	2581.7	—

Source: Computed from Tables A-3 and A-4.

Index

Abstention from strikes, 54–59
Accommodation, employer and union, 47–49, 176, 179
Adams, John Clarke, 124, 139, 188
Agrarian Party, Finland, 154–155
  Sweden, 112
All-India Trade Union Congress, 134
American Federation of Labor–Congress of Industrial Organization (AFL–CIO), 164, 166, 168, 178
American Occupation of Japan, and growth of unionism, 127
"Americanization" of Canada, 162
Apartheid, South Africa, 158
Arbitration, compulsory, in general, 52–53
  Australia, 54, 148–149
  India, 137
  United Kingdom, 93
Australia, duration of strikes, 4–5, 24, 26–27, 142, 208–209
  employee involvement, 22–23, 141, 206
  intensity of organization, 143–144, 203
  membership involvement, 18–21, 141, 204–205

Australia, time lost in strikes, 15, 16, 30–32, 145, 186, 207, 210–211
  union membership, 16–17, 189, 200–201
Australian Council of Trade Unions (ACTU), 144, 146, 147, 148, 150
Australian Workers' Union, 147

Barbash, Jack, 7
Bendix, Reinhard, 176, 182
Board of Mediators, Netherlands, 74, 86
"Boulwareism," 48
Brown, Douglas V., 47, 60
Bull, Edvard, 104, 113

Canada, duration of strikes, 24, 26–27, 162–163, 208–209
  employee involvement, 22–23, 206
  membership involvement, 18–21, 161, 162, 204–205
  time lost in strikes, 15, 30–32, 186, 207, 210–211
  union membership, 16–17, 189, 200–201

213

Canada, white-collar workers, 46
Canadian Brotherhood of Railway Employees, 164
Canadian Congress of Labour, 168
Catholic Party, Netherlands, 88, 101
Catholic unions, Canada, 164
Chamberlain, Neil W., 7, 167, 170, 171
Christelijk Nationaal Vakverbond (CNV), 101
Christian Democratic Party, Italy, 122, 126
Civic reintegration of the industrial work force, 176
Clegg, H. A., 101
Coal and maritime industries, Australia, 145–146, 160
Codetermination, Germany, 100
Cole, G. D. H., 59
Collective bargaining structure, Australia, 146–147
    Denmark, 83, 84
    Finland, 153
    France, 118
    Germany, 98–99
    India, 134–135
    Italy, 124–125
    Japan, 129
    Netherlands, 86
    Norway, 106
    Sweden, 110–111
    United Kingdom, 91–92
    United States, 79, 166–167, 178–179
Commons, John R., 59
Communists and the labor movement, Denmark, 83–84
    India, 134
    Japan, 128
    Netherlands, 87–88, 101
    Norway, 103, 105
    Sweden, 109
    United Kingdom, 90–91
    United States, 164
Communists, as a factor in industrial conflict, general, 66–67
    Australia, 147–148
    Finland, 152–153, 154–155
    France, 117–118, 120
    Italy, 123–124

Conciliation, compulsory, Canada, 52, 170
Confédération Française des Travailleurs Chrétiens (CFTC), 117
Confédération Générale du Travail (CGT), 117, 118
Confédération Générale du Travail —Force Ouvrière (FO), 117, 120
Confederazione Generale Italiana del Lavoro (CGIL), 122–126, 139
Confederazione Italiana Sindicati Nazionali dei Lavoratori (CISL), 122–123, 125–126, 139
Configuration, variables involved in industrial conflict, 174–175
Confindustria (Italian Employers' Federation), 125
Congress Party, India, 132, 134, 137
Cooperative Commonwealth Federation (CCF), 168
Crisp, L. F., 150, 159, 160
Crutchfield, Richard S., 59

Dansk Arbejdsgiverforening (Danish Employers' Association), 84
Davie, Maurice R., 7
De Samvirkende Fagforbund i Danmark (The Danish Federation of Labor), 83
Degree of organization; see Intensity of organization; Union membership
Denmark, duration of strikes, 24, 26–27, 82, 208–209
    employee involvement, 22–23, 82, 206
    membership involvement, 18–21, 204–205
    time lost in strikes, 29, 30–31, 32, 185, 207, 210–211
    union membership, 83, 187, 200–201
    white-collar workers, 45
Deutsche Angestellten Gewerkschaft, 101
Deutsche Gewerkschaftsbund (German Federation of Labor), 97
Douglas, Paul H., 60
Drucker, Peter F., 182

Dubin, Robert, 6, 7, 170
Due process in employment relation-
    ship, 49
Dunlop, John T., 7, 41, 60, 181
Duration of strikes, 4, 12, 13, 15, 24,
    26–27, 208–209

Economic development and industrial
    conflict, 34, 36–38
Economic Development Pattern, 36, 173
Economic loss from strikes, 29, 33, 55
Egypt, development of, 5
    strike activity, 36
    union membership, 36
Ehrmann, Henry W., 188
Elfvengren, Elizabeth, 160
Employee involvement ratio, 12, 13,
    22–23, 206
Employee loss ratio, 12, 13, 32, 207
Employer associations (collective bar-
    gaining structure), Germany, 98
    Netherlands, 88
    Sweden, 111
    see also Multi-employer bargaining
Employer policies toward unions, gen-
    eral, 47–50, 67–68
    Canada, 165–166, 167
    France, 119
    Italy, 125–126
    United States, 165–166, 167, 180
Employment, non-agricultural, 9, 190–
    193, 202
"Enterprise" unions, Japan, 129
Ericson, Anna-Stina, 160
"Extension" of collective agreements,
    52–53, 98

Farley, Miriam S., 139
Federalism and economic policies, Aus-
    tralia, 150
Finland, duration of strikes, 24, 26–27,
    151, 208–209
    economic environment, 153
    employee involvement, 22–23, 206
    membership involvement, 18–21, 151,
    204–205
    time lost in strikes, 4, 29–32, 151,
    186, 207, 210–211

Finland, union membership, 16–17,
    152, 189, 200–201
    white-collar workers, 46
Fisher, Lloyd H., 60
Fisher, T. R., 60
Fitch, John A., 14
Flanders, Allan, 101
Forchheimer, K., 8, 13, 55, 60
Foundation of Labor, Netherlands, 86
France, duration of strikes, 24, 26–27,
    116, 208–209
    employee involvement, 22–23, 116,
    206
    membership involvement, 18–21, 116,
    204–205
    outcome of strikes, 55
    time lost in strikes, 30–32, 116, 207,
    210–211
    union membership, 16–17, 116–117,
    138, 188, 200–201
    white-collar workers, 46
Friedman, Milton, 60
Future trend of strike activity, 38–39,
    181

Galbraith, J. Kenneth, 59
Galenson, Walter, 83, 84, 100, 101, 105,
    106, 107, 113
Garbarino, Joseph W., 60
General strike, disappearance of, 48–49
General strike of 1909, Sweden, 57, 110
General strike of 1926, United King-
    dom, 57, 185
Germany, duration of strikes, 24, 26–27,
    95, 208–209
    employee involvement, 95, 206
    membership involvement, 18–21, 95,
    204–205
    outcome of strikes, 55
    time lost in strikes, 29, 30–31, 32, 95,
    207, 210–211
    union membership, 16–17, 96–97,
    187, 200–201
    white-collar workers, 46, 97, 101
Gillen, J. F. J., 102
Goldner, William, 60
Gotoh, Hiroshi, 139
Government employment and strikes,
    South Africa, 158

Government intervention in labor market and industrial disputes, 51–54
  Denmark, 85
  Finland, 153–154
  France, 119–120
  India, 53, 136
  Italy, 125
  South Africa, 157–158
  United States, 169
  see also Arbitration, compulsory; Conciliation, compulsory
Government ownership and strikes, 50
Government planning, and strikes, 50
  Norway, 107
Goyol, Ramesh C., 140
Great Britain, see United Kingdom
Griffin, John I., 170

Hansson, Sigfrid, 113, 188
Harbison, Frederick H., 7, 41
Hirsch-Dunker unions, 96
Horrell, Muriel, 160
Hoxie, Robert F., 49
Human relations, 47

Income, national, in various countries, 173–174
Income redistribution, by union action, 58
India, duration of strikes, 24, 26–27, 131–132, 208–209
  employment involvement, 22–23, 206
  intensity of organization, 132–133, 203
  membership involvement, 18–21, 131, 204–205
  time lost in strikes, 4, 29–32, 131–132, 207, 210–211
  union membership, 133, 140, 189, 200–201
  white-collar workers, 46
Indian Labour Association, 134
Indian National Trade Union Congress, 134
Industrial conflict, see Strikes
Industrialization, see Economic development and industrial conflict
Industry, effect on strikes, 64
Intensity of organization, 11, 13, 16–17, 203

International Labor Office, 9
Iron Workers' Association, 147, 159–160
Irwin, Donald, 8, 14, 33, 81
Isaac, J. E., 149
Israel, development, 5
  strike activity, 36
  union membership, 36
Issues involved in strikes, Australia, 41
  India, 40–41
  Italy, 124
Italy, duration of strikes, 24, 26–27, 121, 208–209
  economic and social conditions conducive to industrial unrest, 124
  employee involvement, 22–23, 120–121, 206
  membership involvement, 18–21, 121, 204–205
  time lost in strikes, 30–32, 207, 210–211
  union membership, 16–17, 121–122, 139, 188–189, 200–201

Jackson, J. Hampton, 160
Jamieson, Stuart, 60, 162, 165, 170
Japan, duration of strikes, 24, 26–27, 127, 208–209
  employee involvement, 22–23, 206
  membership involvement, 18–21, 126, 204–205
  time lost in strikes, 30–32, 207, 210–211
  union membership, 16–17, 127, 189, 200–201
  white-collar workers, 46, 130
Jensen, Orla, 100
Job evaluation, 49
Joint Industrial Councils, United Kingdom, 92
Jung, C. G., 35, 41
Jurisdictional disputes, see Rivalry among unions

Kennedy, Van Dusen, 133, 135, 140
Kerr, Clark, 5, 7, 8, 14, 37, 41, 58, 60, 61, 72, 81, 96, 97, 99, 100, 102
Knowles, K. G. J. C., 54, 57, 59, 60, 93, 94, 95, 101, 102, 147, 193

Kornhauser, Arthur, 6, 170
Krech, David, 59
Kuhn, James W., 159

Labor Market Board, Sweden, 110
Labor movement, age of, as a factor in industrial conflict, 63, 65
  centralization, as a factor in eliminating industrial conflict, 66
Labor parties and strike activity, 58–59, 68–69
Labor Party, Netherlands, 88–89, 101
  Norway, 103–105, 106–107
Laborers' Union, Denmark, 83, 84, 101
Labour Party, Australia, 141, 145, 147, 150, 160
  South Africa, 157
  United Kingdom, 93
Landrum-Griffin Act, United States, 178
Landsorganisationen i Sverige (LO), 108–109
La Palombara, Joseph, 122, 123, 125, 139
Legislation, railway labor, United States, 53–54, 169
  social, and industrial conflict, 50–51
  France, 119
Leiserson, Mark, 13, 113
Lester, Richard A., 5, 7, 37, 41, 44, 47, 59, 60
Levine, Solomon B., 139
Liberal Democratic Party, Japan, 130
Liberal Party, Canada, 168
Lindbom, Tage, 110, 113, 114
Logan, H. A., 170
Lorwin, Lewis L., 170
Lorwin, Val R., 119, 138, 188

Mannio, Niilo, 160
McPherson, W. H., 102
Measures of strike activity, 10–13
Mediterranean-Asian pattern, 25, 75–77, 115–116, 161, 173
Membership involvement ratio, 11, 13, 18–22, 204–205
Membership loss ratio, 4, 12, 13, 29–32, 210–211
Metal Workers' Union, Denmark, 84, 101
  Sweden, 109–113

Millis, Harry A., 165, 170
Miners' Federation, Australia, 147
"Mond-Turner conferences," 92
Montgomery, Royal E., 165, 170
Morton, Walter A., 60
Multi-employer bargaining, and industrial conflict, 49–50, 67–68
  see also Collective bargaining structure
Multi-employer bargaining, United States, 49, 166–167, 178–179
Municipal Workers' Union, Denmark, 83
Myers, Charles A., 7, 41, 47, 60, 109, 113, 114, 133, 140

National Association of Manufacturers, 48, 166
National Wage Stabilization Board, United States, 53
National War Labor Board, United States, 53
Nationalism, 38
Nederlands Verbond van Vakverenigingen (NVV), 101
Nederlandse Katholieke Arbeidsbeweging (KAB), 101
Netherlands, duration of strikes, 24, 26–27, 85–86, 208–209
  employee involvement, 22–23, 85, 206
  membership involvement, 18–21, 85, 204–205
  time lost in strikes, 29, 30–31, 32, 207, 210–211
  union membership, 87, 187, 200–201
  white-collar workers, 45
Neufeld, Maurice, 125, 139, 188
"No-contract" era, Japan, 130
Norgren, Paul, 110, 111, 113, 114
North American pattern, 25, 77–81, 161, 163
North European pattern—first variant, 25, 70–74, 161, 173
North European pattern—second variant, 25, 74–75, 103, 161, 173
Norway, duration of strikes, 24, 26–27, 103, 208–209
  employee involvement, 22–23, 103, 206

Norway, membership involvement, 18–21, 204–205
strikes and lockouts, 1920–1931, 105–106
time lost in strikes, 29, 30–31, 32, 103, 207, 210–211
union membership, 16–17, 105, 187, 200–201
white-collar workers, 45
Nossiter, Bernard D., 179, 181

O'Brien, Sir Tom, 160
Ornati, Oscar A., 60, 134, 135, 137, 140, 193
"Outside leaders," in India's unions, 137
Oxnam, P. W., 159

Participation in strikes, see Employee involvement ratio; Membership involvement ratio; Union membership, and strike activity
Passivity, of union members, 44
"Pattern bargaining," United States, 166–167
Patterns of industrial conflict, 4, 25, 28, 70–81, 172–173
Australia, 28–29, 141–143
Finland, 28–29
South Africa, 28–29, 156–157
see also Mediterranean-Asian pattern; North American pattern; North European pattern—first variant; North European pattern—second variant
Pels, P. S., 101
Perlman, Mark, 148, 159
Peterson, Florence, 56, 60, 186
Political action, by labor, 58–59
Canada, 168
Denmark, 84–85
Finland, 154–155
France, 118
Japan, 130–131
Netherlands, 88–89
Norway, 104, 107
United Kingdom, 93
United States, 168, 178
see also Labor parties and strike activity; Labor Party; Labour Party; Social Democratic Party

Political strikes, 184, 193
Popular Front, France, 118, 119
Poverty, general decline, 44
and strikes, 173–174
Powell, Webster, 138
Praja Socialists, India, 134
Progressive Conservative Party, Canada, 168
Propensity to strike, psychological, 43–45
Protest strike, see Strikes, demonstrations or protests
Punekar, S. D., 140

Rees, Albert, 41
Reynolds, Lloyd G., 61
Rivalry among unions, as a factor in strike activity, 63, 65–67
Japan, 127–128
Sweden, 109
United Kingdom, 90
United States, 164, 177–178
see also Communists; Labor movement, centralization
Roberts, B. C., 101
Robie, E. A., 60
Roll, Erich, 102
Ross, Arthur M., 6, 8, 14, 33, 41, 60, 81, 170, 171

Salaried employees, see White-collar workers
"Saltsjöbaden Agreement," 110
Sanbetsu, 128
Sanseverino, Luisa Riva, 139
Saposs, David J., 188
Saragat Socialists, 126
Seltzer, George, 171
"September Agreement," 83
Siegel, Abraham, 8, 14, 81
Social barriers to collective bargaining, India, 135
Social Democratic Party, Denmark, 84–85
Finland, 151, 152, 154, 155
Germany, 95, 96, 99
Japan, 130
Sweden, 112
"Social minimum" wage, Netherlands, 87

Sodomei, 128
Sohyo, 128, 129
South Africa, duration of strikes, 24,
    26–27, 208–209
  employee involvement, 22–23, 206
  intensity of organization, 157, 203
  membership involvement, 18–21,
    204–205
  racial composition of the labor force,
    156
  time lost in strikes, 29–32, 186, 207,
    210–211
  union membership, 157, 189, 200–
    201
Sowden, Lewis, 160
State ownership, planning, etc., see
    Government . . .
Steel dispute of 1959, 179
Steelworkers' union, see United Steel-
    workers of America
Stettner, Leonora L., 101
Strike, definition, 3, 6
"Strike Experience in Five Countries,"
    8–9, 14, 19, 33, 62–63, 173
Strikes, conventional view, 1–2, 5–6
  decline, 4, 24–25, 42
    significance of trend, 38–39
  demonstrations or protests, 40, 94,
    124, 131, 146
  distinction between ability and need
    to, 19
  evolution, 6, 36–38
  number, by country and year, 194–
    195
  outcome of, 55–57
  statistics, 39–40, 184–187, 194–199
Sturmthal, Adolf, 60, 117, 119, 120,
    138, 139, 173, 181
Sumner, William Graham, 3
Suppression of Communism Act, South
    Africa, 158, 159
Svenska Arbetsgivare Föreningen (SAF;
    Swedish Employers' Confedera-
    tion), 110, 111, 113
Sweden, duration of strikes, 24, 26–27,
    108, 208–209
  employee involvement, 22–23, 206
  membership involvement, 18–21,
    107–108, 204–205
  outcome of strikes, 55–56

Sweden, time lost in strikes, 15, 29, 30–
    31, 32, 108, 207, 210–211
  union membership, 16–17, 108, 188,
    200–201
  white-collar workers, 45, 109, 113–
    114
Syndicalism, decline, 57–58

Taft, Philip, 98, 101, 170
Taft-Hartley Act, 169, 175, 179
Taylor, Dr. George W., 2, 7
Temperament, national, as a factor in
    strikes, 36, 174
Tracey, Herbert, 101
Trade Union Congress, United King-
    dom, 90, 91
Trades and Labour Congress, Canada,
    168

Ulman, Lloyd, 61, 170
Umbach, John P., 101
Underdeveloped countries, 36
Union federations, France, 117, 138
  Germany, 96–97
  India, 133–134, 140
  Italy, 122, 139
  Japan, 128
  Netherlands, 87, 101
  Norway, 104
Union income, India, 133
Union membership, 9, 10, 187–190,
    200–201
  effect of strike waves on, 57
  and strike activity, 11, 19–20, 63, 65
Unione Italiana del Lavoro (UIL), 122,
    126, 139
United Kingdom, duration of strikes,
    24, 26–27, 89, 208–209
  employee involvement, 22–23, 206
  membership involvement, 18–21, 89,
    204–205
  outcome of strikes, 55, 57
  time lost in strikes, 15, 29, 30–31,
    32, 207, 210–211
  union membership, 90, 187, 200–201
  white-collar workers, 46
United States, duration of strikes, 40,
    162–163, 169, 177, 208–209
  employee involvement, 22–23, 206

United States, intensity of organization, 177, 203
    membership involvement, 18–21, 161, 162, 177, 204–205
    outcome of strikes, 56–57
    time lost in strikes, 4, 15, 29–32, 186, 207, 210–211
    union membership, 16–17, 163, 189, 200–201
    white-collar workers, 46, 177
United Steelworkers of America, 43
Unofficial strike, United Kingdom, 89–90, 94

Vannutelli, Cesare, 139
Varma, Madhurendra Kishore, 140
Vidalenc, Georges, 138

Wages Councils, United Kingdom, 92
Walker, Kenneth F., 54, 60, 142, 145, 147, 149, 159, 160

Waterside Workers' Federation, Australia, 146, 147
Webb, Beatrice and Sidney, 90
Westinghouse strike of 1955, 167
White-collar workers, effects on strikes, 45–46
Whitley Councils, 92
Windmuller, John P., 101
Woodbury, Robert Morse, 8, 13, 193
Work rules and work practices, 180–181
Workers involved in industrial disputes, by country and year, 196–197
Working days lost in industrial disputes, by country and year, 198–199
Working days lost in strikes, measure of economic loss, 33
    see also Employee loss ratio; Membership loss ratio
Works councils, Germany, 98

Zenro Kaigi, 128